Saint-Just

Saint-Just

NORMAN HAMPSON

Upon a starlit night Prince Lucifer uprose . . .
He reached a middle height, and at the stars,
Which are the brains of heaven, he looked, and sank.
Around the ancient track marched, rank on rank,
The army of unalterable law.

George Meredith

Basil Blackwell

First published 1991

Basil Blackwell Ltd
108 Cowley Road, Oxford, OX4 1JF, UK

Basil Blackwell Inc.
3 Cambridge Center
Cambridge, Massachusetts 02142, USA

British Library Cataloguing in Publication Data

A CIP catalogue record for this book is available from the British Library.

Library of Congress Cataloging in Publication Data

Hampson, Norman.
Saint-Just/Norman Hampson.
p.   cm.
Includes bibliographical references and index.
ISBN 0–631–16233–x
1. Saint-Just, 1767–1794.   2. Revolutionaries—France—Biography.
3. France—History—Revolution. 1789–1794.   I. Title.
DC146.S135H36   1991
944,04′092—dc20
[B]   90-39891
CIP

Typeset in 11/13pt Bembo
by Hope Services (Abingdon) Ltd.
Printed in Great Britain by
Billing and Sons Ltd, Worcester

Contents

To the other five pillars

O dulces comitum valete coetus,
Longe quos simul a domo profectos
Diversae variae viae reportant.

Preface

It is impossible to write a conventional biography of any of the leaders of the French Revolution, such as Robespierre and Danton. Most of them were quite young men who had not made much of an impression before 1789, and we know very little about their private lives. After 1789 they tended not to have any. The Revolution was no time for expansive friendships and epistolary confidences. In all probability not much that might have proved to be incriminating was put on paper, and certainly very little has survived. All that remains are the postures of the public man, what he wanted people to think of him rather than what he was or believed himself to be. This problem is especially acute in the case of Saint-Just who was not yet twenty-two when the Bastille fell. The reader who is hoping for a rounded picture of the man, with all his likings and aversions, his foibles and idiosyncrasies – the things that define a personality and make it fully human – will be disappointed. We know a fair amount about his political activities, but virtually all the evidence of what he thought has to be inferred from what he said or wrote in the hope of persuading people to see things his way and to do what he wanted. Its purpose was to influence others rather than to explore or reveal himself.

Perhaps this does not matter very much. If their followers during their lifetime and their more ecstatic biographers tended to present people like Robespierre and Saint-Just as colossi, immune from the trivialities that common flesh is heir to, there is perhaps a better case for seeing them as infra- rather than as super-human. From 1789 onwards their lives *were* politics. They lived on whatever cultural capital they had accumulated before the Revolution; they had allies rather than friends and they mused in manifestos. Their whole lives were spent as actors on the political stage and they became the parts they played. This made for desiccation at best – one is tempted to think that they must have dreamed in political clichés – and could easily degenerate into fanaticism. Cut off from normal people and their many-sided practical preoccupations, they lived like political monks, in the company of other zealots, in a world of abstraction where people were transmuted into principles.

This book is therefore about Saint-Just as a revolutionary politician, since he scarcely existed in any other capacity; a man of great talents and even greater ambition who, despite his youth, aspired to direct the extraordinary events of his brief lifetime. It is drawn almost entirely from his writings, his speeches and his activities as a military commissar. I have tried to show how his ideas evolved with the changing course of the Revolution and how he tried to make political circumstances correspond to his conception of what ought to be.

I am not so naïve as to be unaware how quaint this approach must appear to anyone brought up on a modern diet of symbolism and semiotics. To suggest that, on the whole, the revolutionary orators said what they meant and that their audiences generally understood what they said in the sense in which they meant it, is to confess oneself a very dull dog indeed. I remain impenitent. Of course people sometimes reveal aspects of themselves that they had not intended and of which they may have been unaware. How things are presented is not without importance, although it usually matters less than *what* is being presented. Of course a symbol, when it is not invented by those in authority for purposes of manipulation, may sum up a mood or define a situation. Major political events, especially revolutionary ones, generate symbols as a fire throws off sparks, but the sparks are not responsible for the fire. The capture of the Bastille was the perfect symbol of the overthrow of both royal absolutism and a 'feudal' past by the all-conquering people, but that was not why they attacked it. The crowd, which had collected muskets from the Invalides, was looking for powder, and if it could have obtained it with less danger and cost it would very happily have done so.

To treat symbols as causes and to imagine that the course of the French Revolution can be explained in terms of an interlocking sequence of symbols is to subscribe to a form of determinism and to assume that its development was inherent in its beginnings. This is not how we interpret the events of our own times, which we tend to regard as the product of purposive action and political choice. To exaggerate the importance of semiotics and symbols risks taking the mind out of history. This is a dangerous business when the survival of life on an over-active planet may depend on people's ability to make rational choices. If I am right about this, I wish humanity luck. It is certainly going to need it as it gropes its symbolic way through the twenty-first century.

I can at least comfort myself with the thought that the French revolutionaries themselves believed in the power of ideas. Of course they exploited the emotive force of symbols, some of which they manufactured in order to reinforce the point of view that they were trying to impose, but, so far as they were concerned, the medium was not the message. To understand what Saint-Just was trying to do, and why he ultimately failed to do it, one has to listen to what he said. The reader does not have to accept his ideas, or to share my own view that their inhuman logic transformed him from a utopian dreamer into a satanic monster. Each of us has to decide whether his conception of politics was a revelation or a mirage. The question is as relevant now as it was then and the answer has lost none of its importance.

I

Shades of the Prison-house

Much of the evidence for what happened to Saint-Just between his birth on 25 August 1767 and the outbreak of the French Revolution twenty-two years later is a matter of births, marriages and deaths. We know when and where his parents married and when his two sisters were born, in 1768 and 1769, but there is very little hard information indeed about the kind of boy and adolescent that he was. To a limited extent we can try to compensate for this by falling back on oral traditions preserved in the tiny market-town of Blérancourt, in north-east France, where he grew up. These have to be treated with caution since they consist of the reminiscences of people who were looking back on what he had been from the perspective of what he became, and the evidence becomes increasingly suspect as the decades lengthened into generations and both the witnesses and their interrogators were more concerned to explain what occurred afterwards than to recall the distant years. Two hundred years later the historian finds himself in front of a locked door to which there is no key. He has no alternative but to speculate about what happened on the other side, but his guesses are almost bound to involve constructing plausible patterns on the flimsy foundation of memory and gossip, or projecting Saint-Just's future back into his past. Imagination can create a legend, or rather a choice of legends, whose interlocking inferences and assumptions build up a kind of internal credibility, though they may be as insubstantial as rainbows; scepticism is liable to miss the grains of ore in its determination to be rid of the fool's gold.

On 30 May 1766, in the village of Verneuil, near Decize in central France, Louis Jean Saint-Just married Marie Anne Robinot, in the presence of only three witnesses, two of them illiterate.[1] The simplicity of the occasion contrasted with the social status of the main participants. Louis Jean, who called himself for the occasion *de* Saint-Just de Richebourg, *écuyer* (Esquire), was a captain in a cavalry regiment whose war service had earned him the Cross of Saint Louis, and his wife was the daughter of a prosperous notary who held a minor royal office in Decize. He was fifty and she was thirty-six. The reason for the lack of ceremony and the celebration of the marriage in a country village was her father's refusal to agree to the match. Since his daughter was of age she had been able, and prepared, to overcome this by a formal legal action. The whole business was rather unusual. The Robinots were a wealthy bourgeois family, already well advanced along the kind of road that could lead to eventual noble status. One of Marie Anne's brothers was a barrister and the other a notary like his father. Louis Jean Saint-Just had less money, though he did own some land in Picardy and he could look forward to a modest pension, but what he lacked in cash was compensated by the prestige of his commission and his decoration, which had raised him to the ambiguous no man's land that divided nobles from commoners. When he retired to the Aisne his family was exempt from some of the taxation that was paid only by commoners. Whatever the nature of Robinot's objection to the marriage, he seems to have overcome it. His grandson was probably born in his house. Louis Jean retired from the army soon after his marriage and went back to Picardy, but he returned to

---

[1] The best account of Saint-Just's early life is to be found in Bernard Viot, *Saint-Just* (Paris, 1985), chs. 1–6.

Decize about 1773 and lived with his father-in-law until the latter's death in 1776, when the Saint-Justs finally settled in the north.

Louis-Antoine, or Antoine as he was generally known, was born in Decize on 25 August 1767. As was customary in bourgeois families, he was handed over to a wet-nurse, with whom he remained when his parents left for Picardy. During the first six years of his life he lived in Decize and saw very little of them. When he was nine the family moved to Blérancourt where Louis Jean paid over 6,000 livres (about £300 in eighteenth-century currency) for one of the most substantial houses in the little town.

In view of the attempts made by some historians to link the mature Saint-Just's views on agrarian problems with the experiences of his youth, it is worth trying to locate the position of the family within Blérancourt society. In this small pool they were relatively big fish. Louis Jean owned one of the best houses, besides enjoying the prestige of his military service: the two other members of the Order of Saint Louis in the district were both nobles. To his pension of 600 livres a year he added the rents from 50 acres of land, and for a time he seems to have collected the dues owed to one of the local seigneurs. It did not add up to very much, even though the Saint-Justs were one of the few Blérancourt families to keep a servant, and surviving contracts suggest that Louis Jean and, after his death, Marie Anne, drove hard bargains with their tenants. It still situated him firmly, if modestly, within the local elite, as a *bourgeois vivant noblement* rather than a farmer. The young Antoine, from the circumscribed perspective of childhood, must have felt that he was a person of some consequence. He was perhaps more attuned to the realities of rural society than most of his future colleagues in the Convention who had been brought up in real towns – Blérancourt's population was only about 1,000 – but he saw it from above, from the vantage-point of those who collected dues and rents rather than those who paid them. His family had emerged from farming, and the next step on the usual eighteenth-century road would have been for Antoine to cut his links with the land altogether and become a lawyer in some local town. This does not necessarily imply that he accepted the legitimacy of the kind of society in which he grew up, but nothing in his family circumstances would have predisposed him to see it as a source of personal injustice or to take much interest in the actual business of farming.

Louis Jean died in 1777 leaving his widow in charge of a young family and financial resources barely adequate for the maintenance of her social status. She presumably saw her only son as her sole hope of recovering and perhaps even improving on the kind of situation that she had known in her father's home. That would mean investing precious resources in giving him a good education and then launching him on a legal career.

In 1779, when he was twelve, he was sent to the Oratorian college at Soissons, about a dozen miles from home. This was a place of considerable merit, thanks to the presence of a team of young and able teachers. By contemporary standards it offered its students a good deal of variety and relaxation. It also treated them as little gentlemen; they were allowed to curl and powder their hair, and on feast-days a professional hairdresser did it for them. They also put on theatrical performances. Where the school differed most from a nineteenth-century British public school was in its monastic flavour and the heavy emphasis on religion. There was mass every day, prayers in class, conversation was frowned on as a source of idle dissipation and close friendships treated as morally suspect. Everywhere the emphasis was on salvation rather than learning as an end in itself. The historian Fleury, who published a biography of Saint-Just in 1851, said that he had been told by one of Antoine's old fellow-students that he was a reserved and solitary boy who acquired a reputation as the writer of burlesque verse. That sounds likely enough. The story that he once led a student revolt and tried to set the college on fire is rather more improbable since the fathers allowed him to complete his studies there. He won the odd prize, but nothing that he wrote afterwards suggests that he looked back on his schooldays with any nostalgia, and he probably rejected the whole atmosphere of the place and was glad to see the back of it. There would have been nothing exceptional about that.

The earliest surviving manuscript of Saint-Just's is a 126-page history of the neighbouring château of Coucy, that probably dates

4

from his schooldays. Some of his biographers have seized on this as a basis for speculation about his adolescent interests, his taste for historical research and even his sentimental exploration of the ruins of the château in company with his sweetheart, Thérèse Gellé.[2] Unfortunately the entire work consisted of an edited version of the *Histoire de la ville et des seigneurs de Coucy*, published by Dom Toussaint du Plessis fifty years earlier. The manuscript contains no reference to the original author, which could imply that Saint-Just hoped to pass it off as his own work. It is certainly a tribute to his industry, and perhaps to his interest in local history, but it does not tell us much more about him.

In 1786 he made his entrance on to the historical stage with the kind of melodramatic gesture that was to become part of his style. On 25 July Thérèse Gellé was married to the son of a local notary, Emmanuel Thorin. Antoine and Thérèse had grown up in the same small town and they had been joint godparents at a christening in 1785. Daubigny, a local man who was living in Paris but maintained contact with Blérancourt, was to write after Saint-Just's death that he had offered to marry her. She moved to Paris in 1793, when he was a member of the Committee of Public Safety and she divorced her husband a few days before Saint-Just's death. He may have hoped to marry her before the Revolution and even offered to do so, but it could not have been in the near future since he had neither job nor prospects and it would be several years before he could hope to keep her in any sort of comfort. Oral tradition credits them with being lovers, both before and after Thérèse's marriage, but oral tradition is rather prone to that sort of thing and memories of ancient village gossip are not the most convincing sort of historical evidence. Thérèse and her husband certainly married young – he was twenty and she nineteen – and it has been suggested that the ceremony was rushed through while Saint-Just was away from Blérancourt, with his mother concealing news of the preparations from him. She was certainly unlikely to have favoured a love-match between her son and Thérèse, which would have left her with another mouth to

---

[2] See, for example, Claude Manceron, *La Révolution qui lève* (Paris, 1979), pp. 341–5.

feed. Gellé was a powerful and autocratic man and Thérèse would have needed his consent.

In other words, it seems likely enough that Thérèse and Antoine enjoyed each other's company, but it has certainly not been proved that she was married off against her will, in his absence, as a result of a kind of conspiracy to which his mother was a party. What makes this of more than sentimental interest is its possible contribution to what happened next. During the night of 14–15 September, almost two months after the wedding, Antoine disappeared from home, taking with him a fair quantity of miscellaneous silverware, a pair of pistols with gold inlays and various other pieces of jewellery. It is customary to interpret this as an outraged – if rather belated – protest against the falsity of women, both Thérèse and his mother. It may have been something very different: the gamble of an impulsive and ambitious provincial, not inclined to underestimate his claim on the world's attention, who had decided, like a fair number of his contemporaries, to risk his luck in Paris.[3] Thérèse's marriage may have been the last straw, but it is unlikely to be the entire explanation of Saint-Just's escapade.

The sequel is well documented and, if it suggests that Antoine's mother was rather a Tartar, one has to put things in their contemporary context. It was not rare for the young men of the time to break away from their families and establish themselves in Paris, where they could hope to find moneylenders who would help them to run heavily into debt. Marie Anne, grimly hanging on to a social situation almost beyond her means, with a son whose unfinished education had already cost her a good deal, and dowries to find for two daughters, could not afford to be indulgent. There was a recognized way, in eighteenth-century France, for dealing with situations of this kind, and she took it.

From the start she seems to have realized where her son had gone, which could suggest that she had diagnosed something other than a broken heart. On 17 September she wrote to the

---

[3] Saint-Just's absconding with the silver has been denied by some of his biographers, but the evidence of the police archives is beyond any doubt. See the documents cited in *Annales historiques de la révolution française*, 168 (1962), pp. 218–20.

6

comte d'Evry, a local seigneur who was in Paris at the time, asking him to report the affair to the *lieutenant de police* and get him to restore her missing property and lock up her son, 'so that he will no longer be exposed to this sort of misdeed and will be given time to repent of his fault'. D'Evry did nothing, presumably because there was no proof that Saint-Just was actually in Paris and no way of discovering his address if he was. Things might have remained like that for a long time if Marie Anne had not received a letter, written on the 20th, purporting to come from a Dr Richardet, to the effect that her son had sold some of the silver to pay him for treating 'a very dangerous disease of the temple, unlike anything that my colleagues have ever seen'. When the good doctor discovered what was going on, he tried to buy back the property but was too late to save more than a goblet. Antoine had told him that he had attempted to join the Oratorian order but had been rejected. He was therefore about to leave for Calais – although not for two or three weeks – in order to emigrate. 'Your son is dying, Madame . . . if he goes on working he has no more than a year to live'. Although Antoine had forbidden the doctor to communicate his address, the anxious Richardet – who did not supply his own – hastened to tell her that her son was staying at the Hôtel Saint Louis in the rue Fromenteau.[4]

Marie Anne remained unmoved by this harrowing prospect, and one can understand why she refused to take the letter at its face value. She could not have mistaken her son's peculiar punctuation and idiosyncratic use of capitals, even though he had tried to disguise his handwriting. She may not have known the unsavoury reputation of the rue Fromenteau but she perhaps knew enough about Paris to realize that it was close to the actresses, brothels and gaming-houses of the Palais Royal. Her son's choice of address probably confirmed her suspicions, and she immediately passed it on to d'Evry. The count seems to have gone round to the hotel and checked the presence of both Antoine and the silver. He made no attempt to see him and persuade him to return home but wrote to the *lieutenant de police*, asking him to comply with Marie Anne's

---

[4] Quoted in Manceron, *La Révolution*, pp. 322–5.

request and telling him that he had already made contact with the local *commissaire*, who was ready to make the arrest as soon as he received his orders. There was not much doubt about where d'Evry's sympathies lay. He may have had strong views about property and parental authority. On the other hand he presumably knew both Antoine and his mother.

Neither the *commissaire* nor his superior, the *lieutenant de police* de Crosne, was in any hurry. The latter began by writing to d'Evry to ask him to provide some evidence for his allegations. He received in reply Marie Anne's letter and that from the elusive Dr Richardet. Even then de Crosne, who was probably used to this sort of case, merely ordered one of his inspectors to have Saint-Just examined and to release him if that seemed appropriate. He left it to the *commissaire* to act in accordance with his discretion. If he thought that imprisonment was necessary, this should be in a house at Picpus that the police used for this purpose. On 2 October d'Evry returned to the attack, asking for Saint-Just to be locked up in the prison of Saint-Lazare 'since his mother is not well-to-do'. De Crosne noted in the margin, perhaps a little wearily, that this was why he had chosen the house at Picpus, which was cheaper. The whole incident throws an interesting light on the policing of Paris in the years before the Revolution. It may have been arbitrary but it was a good deal less ferocious than what was to happen when Saint-Just was a member of the Committee of Public Safety.

The interrogation took place on 6 October. Saint-Just admitted all the charges, claimed, not very plausibly, that he had been on the point of being received into the bodyguard of the king's brother, the comte d'Artois – and refused to sign the transcript. There was nothing for it but to lock him up, and he remained in Paris under arrest for the next six months. His mother wrote to d'Evry to express her 'gratitude and satisfaction', saying that she was 'much relieved' to learn of Antoine's arrest.

> it is with renewed concern that I see from your letter, and from the one of his that you enclosed, that he regards the action he has brought upon himself with indifference, but we

must hope that his detention will incline him to better ways and that, acknowledging his misdeeds, he will try to use his reason to bring himself to give me more satisfaction and provide himself with a sound situation.[5]

This could reasonably be interpreted as implying that Antoine's misbehaviour referred to something rather more long-term than a sudden reaction to disappointed love.

His mother may even have been right in thinking that detention was the kind of lesson he needed. When he returned home in the spring of 1787 he remained there for the next five years, which suggests that family relations were at least tolerable. It looked for a time as though he had sowed his wild oats, however briefly, and that he was going to settle down. He is thought to have worked as clerk to a Soissons solicitor and he enrolled as a law student at Reims, a university notorious for its laxity and venality. As Dr Johnson said of a similar establishment at St Andrews, it 'got rich by degrees'. It does not look as though Saint-Just took one. Perhaps he could not afford the fees. This did not prevent him, later on, from referring to himself as a lawyer and even a barrister. He seems to have left the solicitor's office at Soissons and returned to Blérancourt without any occupation. To a man whose imperious temperament and eager ambition were soon to become very obvious, the penny-pinching in Blérancourt must have been bitterly humiliating. His mother too must have wondered whether he was ever going to do anything.

For the provincial intellectual in eighteenth-century France the magic instrument that might just conceivably transmute one's obscurity into fame was the pen.[6] The more earnest, like Robespierre, competed for the essay prizes awarded by local academies. It was a couple of these that had launched Rousseau. This was something that not very busy lawyers could do in their spare time, and a little modest success might be good for their

[5] Manceron, *La Révolution*, p. 351.

[6] See R. Darnton, 'The High Enlightenment and the Low Life of Literature in Pre-revolutionary France', *Past and Present*, 51 (1971), and 'The Grub Street Style of Revolution: J.-P. Brissot Police Spy', *Journal of Modern History*, 40 (1968).

careers. There was another way. The more frivolous, or perhaps the more impatient and ambitious, were tempted by belles-lettres. Saint-Just was a man who went for the top. In France, as in England, the quickest way to fame was through the theatre.

It was at this time that he wrote a one-act verse play, *Arlequin-Diogène*. It does not sound a particularly interesting one. In order to overcome the resistance of Pérette, Arlequin puts on the airs of Diogenes, an affected indifference to the conventional delights of this world. More or less *en passant* this involves him in rejecting a throne and allows him to throw a financier into goal. Suitably impressed, Pérette changes tack and begins to pursue him. After enjoying this situation for some time, Arlequin eventually admits his real feelings for her, at which point she reverts to her initial indifference. As light entertainment, the plot has possibilities, but even Saint-Just's more earnest admirers have not pretended to see it as the vehicle for profound social comment. He re-worked it at different periods but there is no evidence that he ever tried to have it produced. By now he was after bigger fish. In the spring of 1789 he published *Organt*, a mock-heroic epic in 20 books that, in Vellay's edition of his collected works, runs to over 200 pages. It was to be the longest thing that he ever wrote.

Critics of *Organt* may be divided into two schools, the maximalists and the minimalists. The former argue that since Saint-Just was, within a couple of years, to reveal himself as a political theorist of some depth and originality, he could not have produced so substantial a piece or work, even if it was burlesque, without giving away indications of profundity beneath the slapstick. *Organt* should therefore be read as a kind of treasure hunt with concealed clues. The minimalists reply that if Saint-Just had not gone on to become a celebrated revolutionary statesman, no one would now give a second thought to this laboured specimen of adolescent cynicism. There is no treasure to be found and the crazed prospector must beware of mistaking pebbles for diamonds. There is something to be said for each point of view. The two are not entirely contradictory and each provides a useful warning against the danger of going too far in the opposite direction. One school of maximalists sees the poem as straightforward autobiography, with the hero's description of his mistress's charms and their effect on him as a direct reference to Antoine's feelings about Thérèse.[7] This is wholly gratuitous and can be sustained only by resolutely ignoring the passages that do not fit. 'Je relirai les lignes que je trace / Dans le transport d'un amour fortuné' scarcely reads like a referencee to Thérèse and her marriage. Others see the poem as essentially political and are rather inclined to enthuse over the profundity of what are, in fact, fairly conventional exercises along the lines of 'If I were king . . .' or even, on one occasion, 'If I were God . . .'[8]

Organt purports to describe an episode in the wars of Charlemagne against the Saxons. The entire Frankish kingdom has fallen under the dominion of Folly, who has turned all men's brains, while a succession of magicians and enchanters deal with their bodies. This could have provided a basis for social and political satire in which the accepted values of Charlemagne's – or Saint Just's own – society are treated as moral or logical absurdities. Occasionally it does, as in the description of the city of Asinomaïe, which has its church assemblies, *parlements*, theatre and academy, all staffed by braying asses. Saint-Just goes much further than that. He mocks, not , merely chivalric values and the failure of individuals, especially monks, to live up to the standards they profess, but Christianity itself and any suggestion that men are more than sensual animals, activated mainly by lust and alcohol. There are occasional hints that the pagan Saxons in their forests constitute a rather better breed, but when it comes to raping nuns they are in the same class as Charlemagne's paladins. If Saint-Just had intended to write a social satire he soon lost control of it. The poem develops into a chaotic sequence of battles between Franks and Saxons, saints and Olympian gods, with innumerable digressions, a descent into hell, Organt's pursuit of his mistress, men transformed into donkeys, magicians and guardian angels. Its

---

[7] See, for example, M.-A. Charmelot, *Saint-Just ou le chevalier Organt* (Paris, 1957), and Manceron, *La Révolution*, pp. 343–6.

[8] Albert Ollivier, in his *Saint-Just et la force des choses* (Paris, 1954), p. 40, writes of the 'profound theme that underlies the poem from beginning to end'.

dominant themes are a peculiarly strident blasphemy and an obsession with sex, which usually takes the form of rape. In a couple of pages of notes Saint-Just indicated that some of his characters represented contemporaries, such as Madame Dubarry and her lover, Cossé-Brissac, and their adventures sometimes referred to events of his own times. There were probably more of those than can be identified at this distance in time. Whenever they occur they relate to social rather than political events: duels or sexual scandals, such as the deflowering of the daughter of the comtesse de Polignac by a page. It is difficult to see all this as any kind of profound meditation on the human condition.

If one is to make anything of *Organt* it is not by looking for any central theme. It is not a poem with a message. It still remains a very ambitious undertaking – even if not a very successful one – for a man of twenty-one. Much of it may have been written when its author was in detention in Paris with plenty of time on his hands. It has been suggested that the imprisonment of lunatics in the house at Picpus may have given Saint-Just the idea of a reign of Folly, but his point was not that there were madmen at large, but that all the conventions and beliefs of Christian society were absurd. What is most striking about the poem is its rejection of all ideal values. At a time when the cult of sensibility, eloquently championed by Rousseau, had conquered the majority of Saint-Just's generation, including future revolutionaries like Robespierre, Brissot and Madame Roland, one might have expected a young author to have assaulted the false values of chivalry and honour in the name of natural virtue. There are occasional faint hints of this, but the man whom Saint-Just invokes as his mentor is not Rousseau but Voltaire, and the Voltaire of the *Pucelle* rather than of *Brutus*. Buried in Blérancourt he may not have realized how old-fashioned he was in his mockery of feeling as well as convention. If one compares *Organt* with the poetical effusions of Robespierre in praise of one or two of the young ladies of Arras, one is struck by the totality of the contrast. Where Robespierre aspires to soulful earnestness Saint-Just is all cynicism. He is also much more ambitious and technically proficient. His genre is *libertinage*, wit, impiety and literature as entertainment. Where

Robespierre hoped to impress a recipient, Saint-Just was out to conquer a public.

This is probably the real explanation of *Organt*. It was not intended as any sort of confession, creed or exploration of the human predicament. Its purpose was to establish Saint-Just's reputation as a wit, and it would be a mistake to look for expressions of personal conviction in what was essentially an exercise in a genre. He was always to be a professional, whether as writer, orator or commissar. The most acute comment on the poem was made by Michelet:

> He thought he was imitating Voltaire since he did not know that the *Pucelle* is more of a political satire than a libertine tract, enhanced by its audacity and by the risk involved . . .
> In general *Organt* is neither a libertine nor an obscene poem; there are only three or four passages of brutal obscenity. What there is everywhere, what bores and wearies is the laboured imitation of some of the liveliest spirits who have ever lived, Voltaire and Ariosto. The author seems to aim at the lightness of touch of the nobility and no doubt he was counting on his book to secure admission to it. His piece of calculated cynicism is perhaps evidence not so much of libertinage as of ambition.[9]

To accept this is not to exclude the possibility that, here and there, Saint-Just's personal opinions may have more or less coloured what had been intended as literary artifice. An obvious example of this is his portrait of Charlemagne and his consort. 'Charlot' is described on several occasions and always in the same tone of condescending indulgence as a well-intentioned but weak-willed and easily influenced ruler, the ineffectual tool of tyrannical agents, prone to take refuge in sensual pleasures from the consciousness of his inadequacy, while he allowed the country to be misgoverned in his name. This may well have been intended as a character study of Louis XVI, as they saw him at Blérancourt. If

[9] *Histoire de la révolution française* (Paris, 1847), Book IX, ch. 5.

so, it is again in striking contrast with Robespierre who, at the time, regarded the king as a providential ruler who saw his mission as the moral regeneration of his realm. Saint-Just was equally wide of the mark, if he was indeed thinking of Louis, when he wrote of Charlemagne,

> Il essayait de rompre enfin sa chaîne,
> Mais les plaisirs revenaient sur ses pas,
> La volupte le berçait dans ses bras
> Et le bon Sire oubliait l'entreprise.[10]

He kept insisting that 'Charlemagne' was 'bon par lui-même / Et ne devint méchant que par autrui'. His favourite word for him was *benoît*, which could imply either real or affected goodness.

The queen came in for much harsher treatment. To begin with, he gave her the name of the shop-soiled heroine of Voltaire's *Candide*, Cunégonde.

> Reine, autrefois les délices du monde,
> Elle devint sans remords, sans pitié,
> Immola tout à sa rage lubrique,
> Vit les forfaits avec un oeil stoïque.

It was her insatiable greed for money to squander that had turned her husband into a tyrant and impoverished the entire country. 'Et les sueurs et les pleurs des Provinces / Moussent dans l'or à la table des Princes.' All this may well have been aimed at Louis and Marie Antoinette but it tells us rather less than might appear at first sight. In 1791 Saint-Just was to publish an essay on the Revolution that contains no criticism of the king or queen. He was not likely to have changed his mind about them because of what they had done in the intervening years. If one takes both the poem and the essay as serious comment, then one of them involves the suppression of his real opinion. If he did believe what he wrote about 'Charlot'

---

[10] Translations of these lines and other extracts from *Organt* which follow are given in the appendix to chapter 1.

and Cunégonde, he was merely echoing the comment of the Grub Street press, in language whose audacity was more a matter of calculation than conviction. If his intention had been to write serious political satire there were plenty of obvious targets in the arrogant servility of courtiers and the venality of ministers, which he scarcely mentioned.

His comments on the origins of the universe and the nature of man have also to be understood within the conventions of the literary genre that he had adopted. They were at variance with his later ideas and read like the literary exercises of a clever undergraduate. The universe was the product of a cosmic accident. Once created, matter behaved in accordance with its own laws and properties: 'l'ordre naît de leur fougue liée.' Life emerged much later and in a succession of stages. Eventually the arrival of man spoiled it all.

> Que l'homme enfin, vil Roi de l'Univers,
> Leur dit: Tremblez, je suis le Roi du monde;
> Car, avant lui, ces êtres fortunés
> Ne connaissaient aucune dépendance,
> Et les forfaits n'étaient point encore nés;
> Mais avec lui, tous ils prirent naissance.

If it were true, as others affirmed, that the universe was a divine creation, the Almighty ought to have made a better job of it. Whenever man is described, it is in totally dismissive terms.

> Homme est un mot qui ne caractérise
> Qu'un animal, ainsi qu'ours et lion;
> Son naturel est erreur et sottise,
> Malignité, superbe, ambition.

This, of course, rather contradicts his argument that things had not been going too badly until Folly took over. It is also at variance with the occasional hints that life had been better in 'la vertueuse et simple antiquité'.

15

'C'est grand' pitié qu'on ait ainsi chassé',
Disait Organt, 'ces Dieux du temps passé!
Valaient-ils pas ce que valent les nôtres? . . .
Oh si jamais j'en avais le pouvoir,
J'aurais bientôt l'antiquité vengé
Et balayé le divin Apogée
D'anges, de Saints à froc ou blanc ou noir.'

For this opinion 'peu catholique' our hero at present 'grille à jamais au fin fond de Tartare'.

All this is routine stuff, imposed by the requirements of the libertine genre. He would probably have been the first to ridicule anyone who saw it as proof of his cosmic despair. To this general conclusion there are one or two exceptions. In a rather more serious vein, he repeatedly denounced *Intérêt* or self-interest as the source of most injustice and oppression. There is one passage in particular, in a relatively sober section of the poem, that startlingly anticipated views he was later to express in an essay on nature, which provided the theoretical basis for his political activity.[11]

Dans ces beaux jours écoulés à jamais,
Et dont nos coeurs conservent la chimère,
Jours fortunés de candeur et de paix,
Où Dieu sans doute habitait sur la terre,
L'Indépendance avec l'Egalité
Gouvernaient l'homme, enfant de la Nature,
Et destiné, par son essence pure,
A la vertu comme à la liberté.
L'autorité de criminelles lois
De ses penchants n'étouffaient point la voix.
Les coeurs égaux, d'un accord unanime,
Brûlaient sans honte et se damnaient sans crime.
Mais dans le monde arrive l'Intérêt;
L'Egalité tout à coup disparaît,

[11] For a discussion of *On Nature* see below, ch. 4.

16

L'Ambition dresse sa tête immonde,
L'Amour en pleurs abandonne le monde;
La tyrannie invente les serments;
Le Désespoir égare les amants;
L'or fait des lois, et l'Intérêt amène
Le déshonneur, les forfaits et la haine.
Ah fallait-il, o Ciel, dans ta rigueur,
Captiver l'homme et lui laisser un coeur.

This is not just another example of Saint-Just's self-contradictory mockery of human folly. The tone is quite different and the ideas were ones that he took in deadly earnest. Man had originally lived in a state of grace whose natural harmony was founded on equality and independence. Free love flourished in this happy natural anarchy that had no need of laws. Self-interest and ambition had replaced it with a society founded on contracts and repressive laws which were both the symbols of human corruption and the means of its perpetuation. This was a vision that was to haunt him for the rest of his life, and he had arrived at it before he was twenty-two. There *is* ore to be mined in *Organt* but it is not where most people have looked for it.

When the poem was published in the spring of 1789 the reading public had other things to think about. Grimm's *Correspondance littéraire* dismissed it as 'the work of a young man who has read too much of the *Pucelle* – or not enough'. Otherwise hardly anyone seems to have been aware of it. Someone who was, was the censor, who took understandable objection to it. De Crosne, the man who had rather reluctantly given the order for Saint-Just's imprisonment a couple of years earlier, tried to confiscate the copies on sale in Paris. His policemen reported that the booksellers had all heard of it but those who had been invited to sell it had declined in view of its price of 7 livres 10 sous. If Saint-Just had ever hoped that *Organt* would bring him fame, fortune, or a single ticket from Blérancourt to Paris, he had missed his mark.

His early life therefore remains essentially unknown. The scraps of evidence accumulated by revolutionary historians and local antiquarians, even when reinforced by *Organt*, do not add up to very much, and there is an obvious danger in combining a fact here, an inference there and a morsel of ancient gossip in order to build up a picture of the frustrated visionary, the disappointed lover or the would-be rake. Although everything must be tentative, it looks as though he had angered – but not finally estranged – his mother by rejecting the safe and steady legal career that could have restored the family's fortunes, in favour of the kind of mirage that had peopled the streets of Paris with so many literary hacks, driven to support themselves by writing anything for which someone would pay. Saint-Just had ambition, willpower, some talent for self-expression, and *Organt* suggested that he was not over-scrupulous about the means to his literary ends. If he had been born ten years earlier he might have become another Mercier or Brissot. He launched the poem on which his literary hopes were founded into a world where that kind of thing had suddenly become irrelevant. That was the end of his literary aspirations, apart from a couple of pages, apparently from a projected novel, that were found amongst his papers. He was still ambitious and probably as determined as ever to get away from Blérancourt and appear on the national stage in one guise or another. The events of 1789 suggested that the most promising opening was not through literature but through politics.

APPENDIX TO CHAPTER I: EXTRACTS FROM *ORGANT*

He tried at last to break free from his bonds
But pleasures dogged him still at every step,
Voluptuousness still took him in her arms
And the good king forgot his enterprise. *(Book XIII)*

            . . . good of himself,
His wickedness came all from other men. *(Book XIII)*

A queen who once delighted all the world
Became remorseless and compassionless,
Sacrificed all to her lubricious rage
And turned a stoic eye on all her crimes. *(Book IV)*

18

And all the provinces' hard toil and tears
Foams in gold cups at royal banqueting. *(Book XVI)*

And man at last, Creation's abject king,
Cried to them, 'Tremble, I am the world's king!'
Until he came, these happy creatures lived
Free from subordination and dependency,
And sins of any kind were yet unborn;
It was through him that all were brought to birth.
(Book XIII)

Man is a word whose definition is
Merely an animal, like bear or lion.
Error and folly are his natural gifts,
Malignity, ambition, arrogance. *(Book XVI)*

'It's a great shame that we have driven out',
Said Organt, 'all those Gods of former times!
Were they not worth as much as these of ours . . .
If only I could have the power I'd need,
I'd be the avenger of antiquity
And sweep the holy sky entirely clean
Of angels and of Saints in black and white.' *(Book XVII)*

In those most happy days, forever gone,
Whose phantom lingers on within our hearts,
Most blessed days of innocence and peace,
Who can deny that God lived on this earth,
That men were Nature's sons, equality
And independence governed all their lives?
Their spotless essence had predestined them
For virtue and to live in liberty.
Their natural instincts were not stifled yet
By the authority of guilty laws;
Equal at heart, united, all as one,
Shameless in passion, damned but innocent.
Into this world Self-interest found its way.
Equality was banished at a stroke,
Ambition raised its foul disgusting head

And love, in tears, took flight out of the world
Where tyranny invents compelling oaths
And lovers lose their way in their despair.
Gold makes the laws, Self-interest in its train
Brings hatred, crimes, all things dishonourable.
O Heaven, in your implacability,
When you enslaved men, must you leave them hearts?

(Book IX)

2

Achieving Lift-off

It would be misleading to suggest that there had been no politics in Blérancourt before 1789. There were no formal elections, but there were local officials who were supposed to represent the community and a power structure that was recognized by all the inhabitants. Things had gone a little further than that in 1788. The newly created provincial assembly took its job seriously, and its investigation into the local government of the Blérancourt area had allowed the humbler members of a population, who were beginning to think of themselves as citizens, to protest and even to achieve the redress of one of their grievances.[1]

The little town was firmly under the control of a group of its wealthier landowners, whose leader was Gellé, the father of Thérèse. Gellé's power was derived partly from his own wealth and influence, as notary, landowner, timber-merchant and manager of his wife's clothing business, and partly from his position as agent and collector of manorial dues for the absentee seigneur,

---

[1] Anyone trying to understand Saint-Just's life at Blérancourt between 1789 and 1792 is deeply indebted to Bernard Viot's *Saint-Just* (Paris, 1985). Chs. 6–10 of Viot's biography supersede all that has been previously written on the subject.

Grenet, which made him a kind of surrogate lord of the manor. His poorer neighbours were always liable to find themselves dependent on him for a loan, the deferment of some payment, or employment on the seigneurial estate. Gellé was pursuing a typical bourgeois career that had already taken his family out of farming and into estate-management and the lower reaches of the law. Such social advancement in eighteenth-century France did not usually involve challenging what the urban intellectuals referred to as 'feudalism'. It was much easier and more profitable to exploit its possibilities. Gellé was typical of the ambitious commoners who welcomed the Revolution as something that gave political recognition to the economic status they had won for themselves. Since their wealth rested in part on the seigneurial rights and privileges that they exploited on behalf of others, they tended, like the seigneurs themselves, to see these dues as legitimate property rights. Those who resented the domination of men who could be hard-hearted as well as hard-headed were consequently led to challenge the legitimacy of the manorial system that under pinned their power.

Gellé does not seem to have had any male heirs. The marriage of his daughter to the only other notary in Blérancourt was therefore a kind of dynastic alliance, with Gellé undertaking to transfer his notarial office to his son-in-law. If Saint-Just had indeed hoped to marry Thérèse himself, and had been rejected by her father, he may have had personal reasons for disliking the old notary. In that case, his rejection by the Gellé clan would have meant that any political ambitions he might entertain could be realized only in opposition to them. Not being able to join them, he had no alternative but to try to beat them. It is interesting, if pointless, to wonder what would have happened to him if Gellé had accepted the match.

Gellé's assertion of his authority had not made him popular. During the food riots that had broken out in parts of France in 1775, the so-called *guerre des farines*, he had defied a stone-throwing crowd at Blérancourt and stopped them from imposing price controls on grain offered for sale in the market. He was denounced to the standing committee of the provincial assembly in 1788 for packing the town council with his own supporters, and in August he and Thorin – Thérèse's father-in-law – were expelled from it by the assembly.

When the revolutionary crisis broke in 1789, Gellé was challenged by a reformist party, led by the *curé* and Decaisne, to whom Thorin transferred his notarial office when Decaisne married his daughter. She died soon afterwards and Decaisne then married Saint-Just's sister, Louise, in February 1790. It was Decaisne who drafted Blérancourt's relatively radical *cahier*, or list of grievances, in the spring of 1789. This complained of the appropriation of common lands by seigneurs, expressed the hope that no farmer might be allowed to cultivate more than about 150 hectares and invited the king, 'who understands charity', to take over the property of the local monastery. This was not a programme that was likely to appeal to Gellé, but if he was defeated over the *cahier* he still got himself elected as one of Blérancourt's representatives to the meeting that elected the deputies to the Estates General.

During 1789 a more radical group emerged, consisting of young men and older inhabitants with grievances. Honnoré was a grazier with a personal interest in the protection of the communal grazing rights on which the seigneur was said to have encroached. Thuillier had been dismissed as gamekeeper at the château and reduced to keeping an unpretentious inn. His son, who was a friend of Saint-Just, had once worked as a clerk for Gellé. There was a nice incestuous quality to Blérancourt politics: almost everything revolved around Gellé or the château, which came to much the same thing. On 6 December 1789 some of the young people who had been celebrating the feast of Saint Nicholas, perhaps with rather more than evangelical fervour, set off a food riot. When Gellé tried to repeat his success of 1775 he was told that times had changed and seigneurial justice had been abolished. The revellers then persuaded the *syndic*, or village representative, to impose price controls. Their headquarters was Thuillier's inn and the *syndic*'s sister was the mother-in-law of Thuillier *fils*. They had overplayed their hand; Thorin, Thérèse's father-in-law, asked for troops from the nearest town, and when Blérancourt soon afterwards raised its own National Guard Gellé became its first commanding officer.

The first genuine municipal elections ever held in Blérancourt, at the beginning of 1790, allowed the radicals to take control. Honnoré was chosen as mayor and Thuillier *fils* replaced the gamekeeper of the château as secretary. Decaisne took over from Gellé as head of the National Guard. There is no evidence to suggest that Saint-Just was involved in any of these activities, but the leading radicals were his personal friends. His own sights may have been set on more ambitious targets. Two awkward obstacles seemed to exclude him from a political career: the minimum age for holding any elected office was twenty-five, and a tax qualification was required for anyone who wished to become an elector or to represent the new department of the Aisne in the next national assembly. Living at home, without property or employ-ment, Saint-Just would not be liable for direct taxation. This difficulty could be surmounted with a little goodwill: Thuillier, as secretary, recorded his son's friend as paying 100 livres in direct taxation, which would have made him one of the three wealthiest men in Blérancourt. The difficulty about his age was less easily overcome. Fortunately he had been born a long way from his present home and he did whatever he could to prevent anyone discovering his actual date of birth.

The only opportunity that was immediately open to him was in the National Guard, and even that should have involved a fiscal qualification that he could not meet. By the summer of 1790 he had become its commanding officer. Decaisne presumably got out of his way, perhaps with some relief since, unlike Saint-Just, he had other work to do, and Thuillier dignified Antoine with the resounding title of lieutenant-colonel. He seems to have been a severe disciplinarian – his conception of equality always involved rigorous subordination to elected leaders – who gave the maximum publicity to the punishments he imposed 'pour encourager les autres'. This suggests that his behaviour as a military commissar in Alsace in 1793 was a matter of temperament as well as a reaction to a crisis. He represented Blérancourt at the rally of National Guards in Paris to commemmorate the first anniversary of the taking of the Bastille. This may have given him the idea of launching a movement to 'federate' the National Guards in his own locality, to create an alternative power structure to the elected local authorities. As he put it, the object of this initiative was to 'do something to counterbalance the power of the political state if it should lose its popularity'. 'Political state', in his vocabulary, referred to an illegitimate authority resting on force, in contrast to the natural sociability that prevailed within a free society. It was perhaps significant that he already saw the instrument of this sociability in paramilitary terms. The elected local authorities did not share his point of view. His approach to Soissons was politely evaded, and when he began to conclude federal pacts with neighbouring villages the 'political state', in the shape of the department of the Aisne, ordered him to stop. There were no short cuts, and if he was to get anywhere he would have to win an election.

The Blérancourtois of all persuasions were curiously addicted to giving the maximum possible publicity to the washing of their dirty linen. In September 1789 their absent son, Daubigny (yet another of those who had once been dismissed by Gellé; it was almost the equivalent of a union card) wrote to the *Courier de Versailles* to denounce an unnamed man who was trying to stop people from wearing the national cockade. Gellé waited until March 1790 and then complained to the national assembly itself. Recognizing that he was the man in question, he denied the charge and then took the offensive. He accused Daubigny (temporarily resident in Blérancourt), Decaisne and 'a young man of twenty to twenty-two' of packing the National Guard with their supporters, dominating the town council, imposing illegal fines and announcing that all seigneurial dues had been abolished. There was not much doubt about the identity of the young man of twenty to twenty-two; at the time the three men were all living in Saint-Just's home, and Gellé made it his business to be well informed about his real age. If he chose to refer to him by age when he was well aware of his name, it was presumably to concentrate attention on Saint-Just's Achilles' heel.

It was about this time that Saint-Just engaged in a public

relations exercise of his own. Claiming, rather implausibly, that he had been sent thirty copies of a counter-revolutionary pamphlet, with an invitation to campaign against the anti-religious policies of the national assembly, he succeeded in getting an extraordinary meeting of the town council to consider this scandalous business. When it was decided to burn the offending brochure Saint-Just thrust his hand into the flames and took an oath to die for his country in case of need. According to the minutes, this brought tears to everyone's eyes and elicited a suitable comment from the mayor, Honnoré, who may not have heard of Mucius Scaevola but seems to have understood the object of the exercise: 'Young man, I knew your father, your grandfather and your great-grandfather. Carry on as you have begun and we shall see you in the national assembly.' The minutes of this patriotic ceremony were then sent to Paris where they were read to the assembly, which ordered them to be printed. It was not much, but it probably went down well in Blérancourt.

Saint-Just had already mastered one of the politician's arts, that of being, if not exactly all things to all men, at least different things to different men. Blérancourt sent its Mucius Scaevola to a meeting of the representatives of the entire department to decide whether the county town should be Laon or Soissons. Saint-Just himself said privately that he regarded the question as merely one of *amour propre*. His concern was to appear to advantage before a wide audience of influential people whose votes he would need if he was ever to be elected to the assembly, and to ingratiate himself with the supporters of both towns.[2] He got off to a bad start when the ubiquitous Gellé accused him of being under age, but he managed to have Gellé forcibly ejected. Saint-Just then produced a highly effective speech. He began with the modest confession that, had he not already perceived the indulgence of the audience, his youth and his respect for the meeting would have prevented him from speaking at all. He regretted the necessity to take sides when his heart wanted to support both. 'Young as I am, I must

---

[2] Unless otherwise indicated, Saint-Just's speeches and letters are to be found in C. Vellay, *Oeuvres complètes de Saint-Just*, 2 vols (Paris, 1908).

observe and profit from wise examples, and what has touched me most has been the moderation of both parties.' He did allow himself to lash out at one fairly safe target: the iniquity of the pre-revolutionary system of government. The Intendance of Soissons, 'a monument of despotism and cruelty, will henceforth serve a more useful purpose, like those idolatrous temples where human victims were once sacrificed, which were later dedicated by purer hands to the God of peace'. How could anyone not have warmed to him? He insisted on his speech being inserted in the minutes of the meeting and he signed it 'Florelle de Saint-Just'. Viot described this as 'the first of a long series of declarations' all designed to make it difficult for anyone to track down his birth certificate.

As soon as the meeting was over he wrote to Desmoulins, a more or less local man and the editor of one of the most popular Parisian newspapers, to tell him all about it. The tone, as befitted the author of *Organt* and the irreverent recipient, was somewhat less edifying than the speech itself. 'I came away loaded with compliments like the donkey with relics, nevertheless with the confidence that I can join you in the national assembly.' Parliamentary elections would be held as soon as the constitution had been completed, and the prospect dominated Saint-Just's whole life.

His speech to the departmental electors had been a well pitched appeal to moderate opinion. He was simultaneously trying to consolidate his immediate local support by more radical action. On his way back from the departmental meeting he led a crowd of peasants in a demonstration outside the château of Manicamp. 'I behaved like Tarquin. I had a stick with me with which I cut down a shoot of bracken under the windows of the château.' After this symbolic decapitation, 'a Blérancourt mischief-maker called Saint-Just', to quote the seigneur of Manicamp, purged the local council. The district (the intermediate local authority, between the department and the commune) was tempted to send in troops or National Guards to restore order but apprehensive that the intervention of the National Guards from Blérancourt might set off a general insurrection. The department had fewer inhibitions. Despite a letter from 'Saint-Just, barrister [*sic*] at Blérancourt' it put its foot down and ordered an inquiry to discover the ringleaders. This came to nothing when confronted by a conspiracy of silence amongst the locals, but it probably convinced Saint-Just that he had been sailing too near the wind. When the department, a little later, put a stop to his attempt to create a power base by federating the local National Guards he seems to have abandoned direct action for more constitutional tactics.

Viot suggests that it was Blérancourt's reputation for militancy that gave rise to rumours that it was to be deprived of its lucrative market. It would not have done Saint-Just's career any good if its most conspicuous result had been an economic disaster from which the poor had most to lose. It may have been in something of a panic that he wrote to Robespierre, who had made a reputation in the assembly as an extreme democrat and someone who was always ready to fly to arms against what were alleged to be intrigues or conspiracies. Saint-Just's letter is further proof of his ability to attune his language to his audience. Robespierre was inundated with fan mail and similar requests for help from unknown correspondents. This was one of the letters that he kept. Saint-Just hit the right note in his opening sentence. 'You who sustain the tottering nation against the torrent of despotism and intrigue, you whom I know, like God, only through your miracles.' This was laying it on rather thick, but Saint-Just seems to have sensed the kind of flattery that Robespierre could acknowledge as the recognition of his innate moral worth. He explained that he was offering the assembly to surrender his own inheritance to the Treasury in return for the preservation of Blérancourt's market. He had probably not inherited it yet, and there was not much prospect of this bizarre proposal being taken seriously, but it might appear touching, if naïve, to the man who was already being called the Incorruptible. After asking Robespierre for his intercession, Saint-Just concluded in the major key. 'I do not know you, but you are a great man. You are not merely the deputy of one province but of humanity and the Republic.' That must have eased the introduction when they eventually met.

When his more militant plans had failed, Saint-Just settled down to the defence of the poorer inhabitants of Blérancourt against the encroachments of their seigneur on their common lands. In October 1790 he represented them in negotiations with Grenet, their seigneur, and came away under the mistaken impression that he had won his case, protesting his thanks and attachment to Grenet. A year later, when Grenet failed to deliver what Saint-Just believed him to have promised, this gave way to denunciations of deviousness. Saint-Just's friends insisted, even after his death when it was dangerous to defend him, that he did not spare himself in his concern for his poorer neighbours, tramping all over the area to consult them and providing them with legal representation in suits that often involved the seigneur on the other side. There is no reason to doubt his genuine devotion to the less fortunate, even if this concern tended to become a matter of somewhat chilly abstractions when he was a member of the government in Paris. It would be gratuitous cynicism to suppose that he saw his neighbours merely as constituents, but he could not have been unaware that that was what he hoped they were soon to be.

In October 1790 he tried his first electoral contest when Blérancourt and the surrounding villages were called upon to choose their first justice of the peace, which would free them from dependence on seigneurial judges like Thorin. The minimum age for a justice of the peace was thirty, so that there could be no question of Saint-Just offering himself as a candidate. What was at issue was control of the meeting, which would allow the victors to secure the election of one of their own sympathizers. What happened cannot be reconstructed with any precision, but it looks as though the radicals created difficulties and perhaps dragged out the proceedings in the hope that the farmers would eventually lose patience and go back to the autumn sowing, abandoning the meeting to those who had fewer calls on their time. On the first day 427 electors assembled, and when they came to choose a chairman, the *curé*, with 213 votes, was only one short of a majority. On the following day, when he might have been expected to carry all before him, his vote mysteriously dropped to 151. In view of the disorder at the meeting it was then agreed to ask the district to send a commissioner to take charge of proceedings. On the third day Saint-Just presented himself as a candidate for the chairmanship. He defeated the *curé* by 152 votes to 146 and was declared elected. This was the signal for a friend of Gellé's who was employed by the château to raise the question of Saint-Just's age, which gave rise to 'rude comments and even acts of violence'. Realizing that he was not going to get anywhere, Saint-Just then assumed his alternative role as the deferential young moderate. He resigned from the chair but inserted in the minutes a long declaration about the subordination that was appropriate to his youth and the fact that he was not making any complaints against anyone. He did point out that his opponents had failed to establish what his age really was. From his point of view it was probably a tactical retreat, designed to prevent any official investigation into his actual age. Having tasted blood, the Gellé clan then asserted that many of those present did not meet the fiscal requirement for membership of the assembly. A whole week had now gone by and nothing had been done. The commissioner from the district, who could presumably think of better ways of spending his time, denounced the intrigue and electoral fraud, at which some mayors had connived, and adjourned proceedings until December, when the session would be resumed at the centre of the district, ten miles from Blérancourt. This greatly reduced the attendance and transformed the political balance. The *curé* was elected to the chair, Thuillier *fils* ejected on the ground that he did not satisfy the tax requirement, and Thorin *père* elected justice of the peace. This was an ominous result for Saint-Just. When his faction had been getting the better of it by a combination of procrastination and, perhaps, intimidation, the fatal question of his age had enabled the Gellé clan to launch a victorious counter-attack. In alliance with the moderates they had succeeded in enthroning the status quo in the sense that the new justice of the peace was merely the old seigneurial judge in revolutionary dress. This was a discouraging rehearsal for the forthcoming elections to the national assembly on which Saint-Just's hopes depended.

While waiting for the elections he wrote *L'Esprit de la révolution et de la constitution de France*, which he published in June 1791, and perhaps worked on another essay, *De la Nature*, that he never completed.[3] Both of these were attempts to think out for himself the significance of the Revolution, the principles on which the new order ought to rest, and the ways in which these principles should be implemented. The published essay was part history and part political programme, the kind of thing that politicians produce when they have the time, to clear their own minds and publicize their claims to leadership. Saint-Just was certainly not short of time. Like all politicians in free societies, he was something of a chameleon. This does not mean that he did not believe in what he said, but the way he said it, and parts of the message that he chose to emphasize, varied with his audience. His book was written on the moderate tack. He was indulgent towards the king – 'since he aspired to do good he believed that he was achieving it' – and even to the queen – 'deceived rather than deceiving' – and fulsome in his praise of the Constituent Assembly. In a somewhat embarrassed argument he even justified its failure to abolish seigneurial tenure and its respect for *intérêt*, which would have surprised anyone who had seen him on the warpath in the Aisne. The posture he cultivated was that of the mature and responsible statesman, firmly committed to the constitutional monarchy. Three days before the book was published Louis XVI tried to escape from Paris, and his flight discredited all his professions of support for the Revolution, set off a republican movement in Paris and threw the future of the monarchy into question. *Organt* had disappeared from view in the excitement over the convocation of the Estates General, and the *Esprit de la révolution* coincided with the flight to Varennes. Saint-Just was not very good at timing. He had also got the different images that he hoped to present to the local and the national public the wrong way round. In Paris, where the republican movement was being bloodily suppressed and the constitutional monarchists had invoked martial law, his moderation was already out of date. In his own department, where

---

[3] For a discussion of these works see below, chs. 3 and 4.

election depended on his appealing to a predominantly conservative electorate, they knew him as a firebrand.

With the constitution almost finished, the national electoral process had already been set in motion when it was interrupted by the king's flight. Electors had to be chosen, in local assemblies, and only those who cleared this first hurdle were likely to stand any chance when the electors from the department as a whole met to decide which deputies to send to Paris. Feelings were running high: at Blérancourt the size of the electoral register had increased by 50 per cent since the previous year, which could imply some gerrymandering. On the first day Gellé revived the question of Saint-Just's age, but was overruled. Two members of the Gellé clan were then chosen as electors. When the meeting resumed next day the balance had tilted. Saint-Just and two of his followers were elected, although with only 141 votes each, which suggests that his opponents had retired from the field after their success on the first day. He was through the first round, though his local following amounted to only about a quarter of the electorate.

On 4 September the electors from all over the department met at Laon. This was the climax towards which Saint-Just had been working throughout the previous year. He took the precaution of writing to the chairman of the meeting to explain that he had satisfied all doubts about his eligibility. It was perhaps this that drew attention to the fact that he had not. He was required to produce evidence that he was over twenty-five and, on his failure to do so, he was ejected. To add insult to injury, his place was taken by Gellé, who must have been enjoying himself. The national assembly that was being elected was due to sit for two years, which probably felt like eternity to a man of twenty-four. All Saint-Just's hopes had collapsed and he was back where he had started.

It may have been at this time, in a mood of black fury, that he wrote a very strange letter to Daubigny, in Paris.[4] He may never have sent it, since the only known copy was found in his papers after his death. The letter is actually dated 20 July 1792. This is

[4] Reprinted in Vellay, *Oeuvres complètes*, vol. I, pp. 348–9.

almost certainly wrong since Saint-Just asks Daubigny to show something that he had written or published to Lameth and Barnave, important political leaders in 1791, who had disappeared from the scene a year later, when Barnave was no longer in Paris. Most historians have assumed that '1792' was a mistake for 1791 and that Saint-Just was reacting to his failure to get elected to the assembly, but on 20 July things seemed to be going well and it was not until September that his hopes were suddenly destroyed. The main point of the letter was to ask Daubigny to show something that Saint-Just had written to Lameth and Barnave, who were mentioned in it. In Viot's opinion, this means that the text cannot have been the *Esprit de la révolution*, which refers to Lameth but not to Barnave. This is perhaps being rather too precise: the two politicians were closely associated and Saint-Just may well have thought that a reference to one covered the other. A more serious objection is that the letter includes some harsh criticism of Desmoulins, who was praised without qualification in the book. There is no way of telling exactly when the letter was written, or to what it referred. What it does give us is an extraordinary insight into the mentality of its writer.

It is most unfortunate that I cannot stay in Paris. I feel that I have what is needed to come to the top (*surnager*) in my century . . . Go and see Desmoulins, embrace him for me and tell him that I will never see him again, that I respect his *patriotisme* but that I despise him as a man because I have seen into his soul and he is afraid that I may denounce him. Tell him not to desert the good cause and urge this on him, since he has not yet acquired the daring that goes with magnanimous *vertu*. Farewell; I am above misfortune. I will put up with everything but I will speak the truth. You are all cowards who have not appreciated me. And yet my laurels will rise and perhaps overshadow yours. You are a bunch of wretches; I am a rogue and a scoundrel because I have no money to give you. Tear my heart out and eat it; you would then become the opposite of what you are now: great . . .

O God! Must Brutus languish far from Rome! Anyway,

my mind is made up and if Brutus does not kill the others he will kill himself.

'Brutus' was actually going to do both. Whatever the occasion of the letter, all of Saint-Just is in it: the arrogant self-confidence that allows him to read moral lessons to Desmoulins; his total conviction of his own vocation for leadership; the melodramatic gesturing and Roman posturing, together with the conviction that, at bottom, what mattered was character and that he had it. Robespierre shared many of Saint-Just's principles, besides his self-absorption and conviction of his own *vertu*, but he would never have written a letter like that, where the tension and the terseness fuse in a kind of steely authoritarianism that leaves no room for sentiment and offers no concessions to human fallibility. When he wrote it Saint-Just was still a political nobody, but he was already a dangerous man.

For the time being it was back to Blérancourt and the defence of peasants' cases before a justice of the peace who belonged to the opposite faction. Saint-Just had given up direct action and was on the moderate tack all the time. It did not do him much good. By February 1792 he had even been relegated to second in command of the National Guard. What he could do was to make himself legally eligible for election. By August he would at last be twenty-five. He bought sequestrated Church lands to the value of 13,275 livres, which meant that he could hope to satisfy the tax requirement. It was one thing to be eligible, and something quite different to persuade conservative and God-fearing voters to elect him.

What transformed the situation and catapulted him into the seat that he had sought so eagerly was the revolutionary crisis in Paris. On 10 August 1792 a crowd of Parisian National Guards, reinforced by detachments from Brest and Marseille, stormed the royal palace, from which Louis and Marie Antoinette fled for protection to the assembly. The king was suspended, and the assembly voted to disband itself as soon as a convention could be elected by universal male suffrage. Saint-Just would not have to wait until 1793 for his second chance, and the whole political climate had been transformed. The August insurrection was seen as a second revolution, of a democratic and anti-seigneurial stamp. Constitutional monarchists and liberal nobles retired from the field and tried to make themselves as inconspicuous as possible. During the elections a massacre in the Paris prisons, in which over a thousand people were hacked to death, reinforced the message that politics was no longer a matter of manipulating votes but of survival. The slogan 'La Liberté ou la Mort' was not something that referred merely to the foreign 'tyrants' with whom France was now at war, and liberty for some was already coming to mean death for others.

The effects of all this were soon visible in the Aisne. When the citizens of Blérancourt chose their electors, Saint-Just got 164 votes, which was not much of an improvement on his performance of the previous year. What *was* different was the fact that the opposition had melted away. His opponents obviously thought discretion the better part of survival, and there were only 177 voters present, despite the widening of the franchise. Saint-Just's 164 votes could scarcely be called a popular triumph since at least 80 per cent of the electorate had stayed away from the poll, but it was decisive enough for his purposes. This initial victory was confirmed at the actual election of the deputies in Soissons. The two sitting members were returned, followed by two international celebrities, Tom Paine and Condorcet. Saint-Just came fifth, with 349 votes out of 600. He was there at last, and he was not to know that he had rather less than two years left to live.

3

The 'Spirit of the Revolution'

Saint-Just's *Esprit de la révolution et de la constitution de France*, which he published in June 1791 was virtually dedicated to Montesquieu. It began by quoting what was perhaps the most conservative sentence in *De l'esprit des lois*: 'If I could provide everyone with new reasons for loving his duty, his prince, his country, his laws, so that men could be more aware of their good fortune . . . I should think myself the happiest of mortals.' Saint-Just borrowed from Montesquieu both the title and the form of his own essay, which consisted of five books, each divided into very short chapters which rarely exceeded a couple of pages. His treatment of monarchy, aristocracy and democracy, each given a chapter on its 'nature' and another on its 'principle' was also inspired by *De l'esprit des lois*. More fundamentally, Saint-Just began by subscribing to Montesquieu's belief that the individual took precedence over the citizen, and that the object of a good constitution was not to impose some kind of ideal harmony but to regulate and maintain in equilibrium the competing interests within a pluralist society. He saw the French constitution as providing such a balance, in much the same way that Montesquieu had idealized the British system of government.

Saint-Just's style perhaps owed more to Roman historians, with its insistent moralizing, its reduction of all situations to what he took to be their moral essence and his painful search for the resounding aphorism. For the rest of his life his prose was inclined to leap from one epigram to another, which sometimes makes his reasoning difficult to follow. In his search for emphasis he never used 'ne . . . pas' by always 'ne . . . point'. One reason for the occasional obscurity of his message was the fact that he was trying to express in classical prose emotional insights that he had not fully digested. From time to time he said as much himself, wondering if his reader would understand what he felt, but suspected that he had failed to communicate.

His description of the society of the *ancien régime* may serve as a typical example of his style.

I leave to others the history of courtesans and prelates, those Court buffoons; calumny destroyed honour and poison destroyed the life of men of goodwill. Maurepas and Vergennes [Ministers of Louis XVI] died; the latter especially was devoted to the good that he did not know how to achieve; he was a virtuous satrap; after his death the Court offered nothing but the spectacle of a torrent of lewdness, villainy and prodigality that consummated the ruin of principles . . .

Posterity will scarcely be able to imagine the extent to which the people were grasping, miserly and superficial, how the needs engendered by their presumption made them dependent on the great, with the result that the credit of the multitude was mortgaged to the favours of the Court and the knavery of debtors; the links of deception reached up to the sovereign and down from the sovereign into the provinces, making civil society one long chain of iniquity.

There is something both absurd and disquieting in this spectacle of a man of twenty-three affecting the pose of Cato the Censor, especially if one remembers that it was only a couple of years since he had published *Organt*.

I am not aware that anyone, until now, has taken the trouble to seek out, from the bottom of his heart, the extent of his *vertu*, in order to discover how much liberty he deserved. I do not presume to put anyone in the dock. Everyone does well to think what he thinks, but whoever speaks or writes owes the city an account of his *vertu*.

One thing that he did not lack was self-assurance: 'Many have spoken of this revolution and the majority have had nothing to say.' Even his youth, to which he always liked to draw attention, was a source of privileged insights: 'I am very young . . . but since I was young it seemed to me that I was closer to nature.'

He wrote his book from the perspective that the Revolution was an accomplished fact, something that had already changed the nature of French society. The constitution had not yet been completed but its general shape was already clear enough, and he assumed that it would endure indefinitely. He therefore set himself two objectives: to describe how it had come into being and, more particularly, to analyse the structure of the new France. He was not drafting a programme for future change but trying to elucidate the principles that were implicit in the institutions of the regime that had been created.

History as such was of little interest to him, and he made no serious effort to explain how the golden present had emerged from the corrupted past. 'The Bastille was abandoned and taken, and with it perished despotism, which is merely the illusion of slaves.' That left rather a lot of questions unanswered. What he had to say about the king and queen was quite shrewd and not unsympathetic. 'Louis reigned like a private individual, hard and frugal where he himself was concerned, brusque and weak in action. He thought himself to be implementing the goodness of his own intentions.' 'Marie Antoinette was deceived rather than deceiving, superficial rather than perjured.'

This was what a good many people thought, even if most obscure provincials might have hesitated before committing it to print. Where Saint-Just struck out on a line of his own was in his treatment of the crisis of July 1789. Whatever the opinion of the educated men in the national assembly had been at the time, those who approved of the Revolution had subsequently elevated the Parisian insurrection into an assertion of popular sovereignty. Saint-Just's view of the events, which he claimed to have witnessed himself, was less flattering. 'The people had no moral principles but they were lively. Love of liberty was a sudden impulse. Then their weakness bred cruelty.' The mutilation of their enemies and the parading of heads on pikes was the behaviour of rioting slaves.

> Their outburst and their stupid joy at first made the people inhuman; their coup made them proud; their pride made them jealous of their glory. For an instant they were activated by principle; they disowned the murders with which they had polluted their hands and they had the happy idea – either from fright, or following the prompting of cool heads – of giving themselves leaders whom they obeyed.

'Everything would have been lost if some people of intelligence and ambition had not taken charge of a conflagration that did not know how to stop.' That was how a good many moderate revolutionaries felt but few of them would have cared to describe the Parisian revolutionaries as 'riotous slaves'.

Some historians have treated Saint-Just as the spokesman of the peasants and sans-culottes.[1] He certainly believed, in a conventional way, that the cultivation of the soil promoted virtue and that the poor were to be regarded as deserving unless they provided evidence to the contrary, but he never had any doubt that they were incapable of understanding what was good for them, without the guidance of men like himself. 'Anyone who sees things sensibly must realize that the revolutions of those days were a war of reckless slaves who fought with their own chains.' 'The people are eternal children' who alternated between panic and audacity.

[1] For example, C. A. Michalet, who maintained that he defended the rights of small property owners because that was what the sans-culottes wanted. 'Economie et politique chez Saint-Just: l'exemple de l'inflation' in *Actes du Colloque Saint-Just* (Paris, 1968).

He had nothing good to say about any of the Parisians. The electors who had, in fact, provided the kind of leadership that he praised, by taking charge of the insurrection and disciplining it by the creation of the National Guard, were 'reckless men, lost in squalor and luxury'. Some had made money out of the Revolution. The small minority of the well-intentioned withdrew in disgust and the rest retired for other reasons, 'covered with fright and booty'. Tacitus might have approved of that, but it did not bear much relationship to what had actually happened. Bailly, the mayor of Paris, and Lafayette, the commander-in-chief of the National Guard (Saint-Just thought it wiser not to mention either by name since they were still serving in those capacities) would have liked to use the insurrectionary force of Paris as the foundation of their own power but were out-manoeuvred by the assembly. The sixty Paris districts, with their practice of 'direct democracy', would have thrown everything into disorder if they had not fallen foul of their rivals, Bailly and Lafayette. Left to themselves, the Parisians would have made a complete mess of the Revolution. This reads very much like Paris observed through a telescope in Blérancourt.

The collective hero of Saint-Just's story was the national assembly, which he professed to regard as almost infallible. 'Consistent in its policies, constant amidst change, it began by acting with skill, then with firmness, eventually with vigour and always with prudence.' 'It exploited the enlightenment and vanity of those days in the same way that Lycurgus had used the principles of his own times.' That was praise indeed. Its labours had produced 'that prodigious legislation which has only a few minor defects'. He would not have been the man he was if there had been *nothing* that he could not improve, but he did have the modesty to admit that he had eventually come to recognize as strokes of genius some of the assembly's policies that had baffled him at the time. It was 'full of inflexible souls dominated by the love of good, and refined spirits illuminated by the taste for truth . . . The unthinking people curbed themselves beneath a superior reasoning that led them on despite themselves.' As Saint-Just must have known very well, the sessions of the assembly had actually been exceptionally acrimonious. Every major policy decision had been the subject of a pitched battle, and by the time his book appeared, even the former leaders of the Left were being denounced by Robespierre, the man to whom he had written in the most flattering terms. There is scarcely a hint of this in his book. He even had a polite word for the conservative Malouet, that 'estimable orator' who had called for the prosecution of Saint-Just's other correspondent, Desmoulins, for abusing the freedom of the press. This is rather puzzling. It certainly suggests that he was not trying to ingratiate himself with the members of any particular faction, which would have meant espousing their quarrels. Ambitious though he certainly was, he had no intention of jumping on anyone else's band-wagon and he preferred the role of the lofty sage to that of the aspiring politician in quest of allies and protectors. One has to assume that his enthusiasm for the Constituent Assembly was genuine, which helps to explain his determination to get himself elected to its successor. Since the rest of his book was to be devoted to the elucidation of the principles behind the emerging constitution, considered as a kind of Mosaic Law for regenerated France, he perhaps felt that the aesthetics of *histoire à la romaine* required that the antagonisms of the men who had equalled Lycurgus should be veiled in decent obscurity.

Saint-Just's main concern, to which he devoted the remaining four books of his *Esprit de la révolution*, was not history but political theory, the analysis of the constitution and a discussion of its implications for France's civil and political institutions and her relations with other states. Throughout his life he adhered to the argument of the first part of Montesquieu's *De l'esprit des lois*, that every type of state was based on a governing principle, to which all its institutions should conform. This presented him with certain difficulties. Montesquieu had divided all states into three different types: despotisms, monarchies and republics, activated by fear, honour (in the sense of an aristocratic code that imposed limits on the kind of obedience that a king could obtain from his more eminent subjects) and *vertu*, or the total identification of the citizen with the well-being of the society to which he belonged. None of these three types fitted the France of 1791, and Saint-Just did not try to argue that France was, in effect, a republic whose leading magistrate happened for historical reasons to be called a king. He chose instead to follow the message of the latter part of *De l'esprit des lois* that, irrespective of the type of regime, the best solution was moderate government, in which the legislative and executive powers checked each other so that political authority was to some extent neutralized, giving free play to the general spirit of the community which the government existed to preserve rather than to transform.[2] This was to give primacy to the individual as an autonomous entity with his own interests, beliefs and ambitions, rather than to dissolve his identity in that of the citizen. It implied stopping one's ears to the siren song of Greece and Rome and their assumption that the highest objective of political action was the regeneration of a community by infusing it with the kind of civic morality that went by the name of *vertu*.

As he saw it, France was governed by a happy combination of democracy, aristocracy and monarchy. This was quite close to Montesquieu's idealized picture of British government, but the light that had shone like a good deed in a naughty world when *De l'esprit des lois* was published in 1748 looked a good deal dimmer after the blaze of 1789, and Saint-Just understandably ignored the British parallel. Democracy prevailed in civil society, in the sense that everyone was equal in the eyes of the law. The elected legislature constituted a particular kind of aristocracy: Saint-Just never had much use for 'direct democracy' or the idea that deputies were merely mandatories of the sovereign people. He saw them instead as an elective aristocracy whose duty was to give the mass of the population what was good for it, rather than what it believed itself to want. The king provided the executive power with the unity that it needed in order to function efficiently, but his authority was limited to implementing what the assembly had decided.

Following Montesquieu, Saint-Just claimed that a balanced representative constitution of this kind provided a type of

---

[2] For an exposition of this view of Montesquieu's argument, see N. Hampson, *Will and Circumstance: Montesquieu, Rousseau and the French Revolution* (London, 1983), ch. 1.

government in which the individual enjoyed more freedom than he had done in the classical republics. 'The rights of man would have destroyed Athens and Sparta. All that men knew there was their beloved fatherland; they forgot themselves in its behalf. The rights of man strengthen France; here it is the fatherland that forgets itself for its children.' The classical republics had been restless and warlike, but the Constituent Assembly had renounced all wars of aggression. France, in other words, had turned its back on glory and was wholly concerned with the pacific enjoyment of things as they were. Liberty, in the sense of resistance to oppression, was an essentially negative force; once the threat of tyranny had been overcome it implied stability. Equality, in the modern world, did not mean, as it had done in Sparta, a share in collective poverty. Like Montesquieu and unlike Rousseau, Saint-Just welcomed the fact that France was a commercial state in which every man could hope to better himself. In such a society equality could only mean equality of political rights. He justified this apparently conservative argument, much favoured by the deputies of the Right, in a way of his own that would have prompted Montesquieu to raise an interrogative eyebrow: 'The spirit of equality is not that one man should be able to say to another, "I am as powerful as you." Power is never legitimate. Even the laws of God are not questions of power but merely theoretical statements of what is right.' As yet this was still an almost instinctive feeling whose implications he had not explored.

In the best Montesquieu style Saint-Just then described the nature and principles of each of the component parts of the French government. Like his master he criticized the direct democracy of Athens on the ground that it made for impulsive judgements and offered too much scope to those who knew how to manipulate the emotions of a crowd. 'The principle of French democracy is acceptance of the laws and the right to vote.' He even accepted the disfranchisement of those under twenty-five, like himself, and of all those too poor to pay direct taxation. When he turned to consider the aristocratic element in the constitution he was even more conservative. Aristocratic leadership was necessary since 'Natural equality would destroy society. There would be neither power [he seemed to have forgotten that it was never legitimate] nor obedience and the people would run off into the wilderness.' He justified the property qualification for deputies, which prevented the constitution from becoming 'popular and anarchic'. He argued that those who were disfranchised by their poverty or were ineligible for office because they did not own enough property were free to choose between independence and the enterprise that could procure them full political rights. Where ancient aristocracies had been warlike, that of France could only suffer from conquest and upheaval. 'The principle of French aristocracy is repose.'

Where Saint-Just parted company from most of the conservatives was in his attitude to the king and the Church. Soon after his book was published the Constituent Assembly was to declare the king's authority to be a constituent part of the general will by which the French people exercised its sovereignty. Saint-Just would have none of this. The king was merely the executive agent of the legislature and his suspensive veto was not an assertion of will but merely a decision to refer an issue to the arbitration of the electorate. In a digression on the Church he indicated that he shared all the Enlightened misconceptions about the role of religion in eighteenth-century France. He claimed that everyone welcomed the Civil Constitution of the Clergy (a radical reorganization of the Church which had, in fact, split the country from top to bottom). Monks rejoiced at the suppression of monastic vows. When he did recognize the gulf that separated educated legislators from the mass of the population, he dismissed it in the loftiest of terms. 'God himself and all things good are merely prejudices where the weak-minded are concerned. Only the sage is aware of the truth.' The 23-year-old sage did not say what it was.

He summed up this whole argument in terms that would have earned him Montesquieu's approval. 'In a mixed constitution all powers must be repressive [of each other]; apparent incoherence is actual harmony. Every kind of uniformity implies disorder.' He admitted that this was something that he had been slow to appreciate.

At first sight I thought, like a good many other people, that the principles of the French constitution, incoherent by their very nature, would wear themselves out when it came to practice, and not reinforce each other, but when I had fully understood the spirit of the legislator I saw order born from chaos, the different elements separate out and bring the whole thing to life.

The rest of his book consisted of a study of the relationship between the constitution and the institutions that were, or ought to be, its logical consequences. This led him into the consideration of how things should happen in an ideal society, and towards ideas that contradicted the moderation and individualism of the early part of his essay.

Book III dealt with civil society. Taking up an idea that he had already expressed in *Organt*, he claimed that the primary emotions of natural man were filial piety, love and friendship. Society corrupted these into fear, gallantry and familiarity. Any good constitution must therefore lead a people back towards the recovery of its natural principles. This did not imply regeneration by *vertu*, which Saint-Just rejected as a condition of moral conflict between duty and self-interest. In his ideal state men did not have unworthy instincts to suppress. Natural goodness was an unconscious thing and to be truly good was to be unaware of one's goodness. In a community of such beings there would be no need for carefully contrived political checks and balances. There would, in fact, be no need for any government at all, except for the defence of a society against possible foreign enemies. Thanks to the Constituent Assembly, France had already begun to move in the right direction, from corruption to a kind of moral neutrality where the three cardinal principles were now respect, civil marriage and amusement. This was an improvement on the *ancien régime* but no more than a base camp from which to take off for the ascent of the ideal. 'Nature has fled from men's hearts and taken refuge in their imagination.' Instead of being an instinct, common to all, that regulated everyone's behaviour, it was an

45

insight – presumably available only to a minority – into what might and ought to be.

This presented him with a problem that was to obsess him for the rest of his life: how to progress from a tolerable but unsatisfactory present to the ideal state of his dreams. He had to envisage three situations: the promising present, the ideal future and the kind of transitional regime required to conduct France from the former to the latter. Since this would involve reshaping the mass of the population in ways that it could not recognize to be for its own good, one could rely neither on the sovereignty of the individual nor on the spontaneous instincts of a regenerated society. However libertarian the goal, this meant that the only way to attain it was by disciplining the majority and repressing those who refused to conform.

He now affirmed that a good constitution *réprime les moeurs*; in other words, it must make men better by the suppression of their anti-social tendencies. This called for something rather different from the state of repose that he had commended earlier in his essay. French civil law was admirable as a rational construct but it rested on the defence of property instead of the 'social law of nature', or disinterestedness. To his own and his reader's confusion, he claimed to be excluding what ought to be from his vision of what actually existed – 'it is no part of my plan to dream' – and to be merely discussing the kind of laws that would prevent fallen man from making himself more miserable than he need be. This allowed the political theorist to give two cheers for democracy and to defend the merits of a balanced constitution. It was not so easy for the moralist to compromise with sin. If 'natural' sociability was the goal, everything had to be made to point in that direction. The classical republics, whose political arrangements had been rejected in Book II, were now held up as models of virtuous social practice. 'With us, what were virtues for the ancients have become matters of good breeding and we are civilized ingrates.' 'The more dissolute private habits have become, the more important it is that good and humane laws should be firm in their resistance to disorder. Virtue must make no concessions to individuals.' Having rejected the Church as an

independent arbiter of morals, there could be only one source for
these 'good and humane laws' that were to make no concessions to
individuals. What he saw as the moralizing function of law could
be exercised only by the state.

This was followed by some fairly conventional chapters on
women and the protection of their 'faiblesse intéressante', the
impracticability of Spartan naked gymnastics – he could have
invoked Montesquieu's theory of climate here but he was thinking
of the moral corruption of the age – the immorality of divorce and
the equal guilt of male and female adulterers. For those who were
hoping for a sequel to *Organt*, this must have seemed rather tame
stuff.

By now he had gone round in a half-circle and abandoned
Montesquieu for a modified version of Rousseau. Citizenship was
all. 'When men have no fatherland they become villains.'
'Indifference towards one's country and love of self are the source
of all evil; indifference to one's self and love of one's country are
the source of all good.' 'Everything good is derived from the
goodness of the laws, everything evil from their corruption.'
Appropriately enough, in view of his new source of inspiration,
he inserted a short chapter on the theatre, the subject of Rousseau's
famous breach with the philosophes, but merely to dismiss it with
the easy epigram that its effect on public morals in France was
negligible since 'one goes in bored and comes out disgusted'. This
was a throw-back to the adolescent cynicism of *Organt* and may
have owed something to Saint-Just's lack of success as a dramatist.

He included the military establishment in France's civil rather
than her political institutions, which was logical enough since he
saw military service primarily in terms of character-formation. He
proposed to abolish the standing army and return its unwilling
members to the soil, but spoiled the effect by insisting that the
entire male population should do four years' military service
instead of 'wearing themselves out amongst the delights and
vicious idleness of towns'. That was scarcely the life-style of most
French teenagers, and Saint-Just did not stop to investigate the
effects on French agriculture of such an enormous increase in the
army. Where the present army was a source of corruption, his

militia would teach French youth to become more serious and would generate intense patriotism. This sort of thing was to become typical of all his attempts at social engineering: blind confidence regarding ends and a refusal to pay any serious attention to means.

His treatment of religion demonstrated the same airy indifference to what people were actually like, what they believed and how they behaved in real life. He took issue with Rousseau's argument, in the penultimate chapter of *Du Contrat Social*, that Christianity, unlike classical paganism, was not good at moulding warrior-citizens, since its believers were too preoccupied with the next world to identify themselves with the fortunes of their nation in this one. Rousseau, according to Saint-Just, had confused the doctrines of the Church with those of the Gospel, which he proceeded to elucidate. The real message of the New Testament referred only to the private man. Obedience was admittedly due to Caesar, but this alluded to the true sovereign, in other words, to the people. The duty of forgiveness applied only to private wrongs and not to those who violated the social contract. Since the government would, in practice, claim the right to define who these offenders were, Saint-Just's argument implied indulgence towards ordinary offences but the pitiless repression of political dissent. It would take another two years before this became government policy. Divine sovereignty was not represented by the clergy but by the sovereign people – any people. Christianity, in fact, had nothing to do with Christ but was the religion of any people with moral principles who recognized the obligation of charity. This included the ancient Greeks, the Romans and the Egyptians. Most so-called Christians since the days of Constantine had actually been either savages or mad. What he was doing was to champion something rather like Rousseau's civic religion and to pretend – unlike Rousseau – that it constituted 'true' Christianity. This reflected both his tendency to believe that things were what he would like them to be and his promotion of society, or its government, to the role previously claimed by the Church.

The contrast between Books II and III could scarcely be more complete. This was because his admiration for the practical work of the Constituent Assembly was superimposed on a utopian view of society that pointed in a very different direction. Rather curiously, Montesquieu, who provided most of the inspiration for the earlier part, was not specifically mentioned in it but was twice described as a 'great man' in Book III, which rejected his philosophy. Rousseau did not make his appearance until Book III, where he became a target for criticism. This should not mislead us. Whatever his reservations about particular issues, Saint-Just had moved from the assertion that the object of civil society was to protect the rights of the individual, to the Rousseauist conviction that it was for society to make men what they ought to be.

Book IV, on political institutions, was mostly about what would be necessary to restore society to its 'natural' state. This led him to confront the problem that Rousseau had set himself in *Du contrat social*: how men might enjoy in society the freedom that they had known in a state of nature. Saint-Just asserted that this was not so much freedom as independence, which they had forfeited when they opted for societies divorced from moral principle. Since morality was a poor substitute for instinctive goodness, the liberty that men might hope to enjoy in civil society was inferior to their initial independence, unless society itself conducted them back to natural simplicity 'by force of virtue'. Otherwise what was called liberty was merely a form of pride which, Saint-Just claimed, was what Rousseau always meant when he used the term. In a genuine state of nature the concept of human rights was meaningless since to define rights meant defining their limitations and no collection of such rights could be an acceptable substitute for natural independence.

In the meantime, society existed and, with all its limitations and inadequacies, it could be made to function more or less well. It needed some collective force, which it called sovereignty, in order to preserve itself, and laws to regulate the multiple relationships between its members. There were therefore two ways of considering political societies. As a second best, when compared to a state of nature, they had their own rules, constitutions and officials, like those he had described in Book II, which could be

49

more or less efficient and humane. They could therefore be compared, criticized and improved in terms of their proclaimed objectives. At the same time, men should not be content with making the best of a bad job. Every society, irrespective of its satisfactory functioning in terms of conventional morality, should therefore be working to transform itself into something qualitatively different. It should be consciously moving back towards that state of nature in which alone all conflicts were finally resolved. Understandably enough, Saint-Just found these two objectives pulling him in different directions. Freedom was good, even if it was a poor substitute for independence, but to move from freedom to independence involved society as a whole being taken vigorously in hand by those who knew what was wrong with it, a process liable to be resisted by the majority since they were unaware of their own deficiencies. Until people had been taught what was good for them a society in the process of moral regeneration could therefore not be conducted on the liberal principles appropriate to the state of repose that Saint-Just had acclaimed in Book II. It was indeed arguable that it could not be run on any democratic principles at all. As he explored the implications of his theory, Saint-Just was inclined to stray from one dimension to another and to entangle himself in contradictions between what was appropriate to conventional society, a state of nature and a regime that aspired to progress – or rather regress – from the one to the other.

In a natural society he thought that the function of magistrates, clergy and soldiers was purely economic. Their purpose was not to provide any kind of service to a population that had no need of them, 'a wise people has no need of justice or of soldiers', but to consume public money. This could be raised only by heavy taxation, which would make for equality by redistributing wealth and would discourage the rich from regarding themselves as separate from the rest of society. He then modified this argument and went on to say that the object of taxation was not so much to fund public services as to provide the means for rewarding merit and helping the unfortunate. That perhaps applied to the world as it was, since, in a natural society, people would be unaware of the merits that they all possessed instinctively and they could be relied on to act spontaneously in the relief of misfortune. Unlike most of the revolutionaries, Saint-Just wanted as much taxation as possible levied on luxuries, with land taxation reduced to a minimum. With his usual blithe optimism he claimed that the heavy taxation of luxuries would put an end to both poverty and prostitution. He did not explain how. A low rate of land taxation and no conscription (he seemed to forget that he had already proposed four years' compulsory service for everyone) would produce a decline in the drift of peasants into domestic service in the towns and 'you will not see any more poverty.'

Forgetting what he had just written, he then said that all public officials were tyrants and justice should be administered by the people themselves. In terms of his own argument, either statement about justice and administration had something to be said for it, but it was difficult to combine them both.

Political laws should be based on nature, and civil laws were derived from political ones. From this it followed that officials who corrupted the laws were worse than parricides since they were responsible for the spiritual death of an entire community. Where ordinary crimes were concerned, Saint-Just thought that the entire responsibility lay with society. Crime was a product of tyranny and virtually unknown amongst savages. All men must be presumed good, and Rousseau was unpardonable for his justification of the death penalty.

> You say that it is to avoid becoming the victim of an assassin that you agree to die if you become one, but you should not agree to become an assassin; you violate both nature and the inviolability of the contract, and the admission of the possibility of the crime already presupposes that you might be capable of steeling yourself to commit it.

What this meant was that Saint-Just was already postulating the existence of an ideal state of nature while Rousseau was writing about how to achieve it. When he later found himself one of those responsible for guiding France through the transitional stage he was to endorse capital punishment on a scale that would have horrified Rousseau. What needed watching was not crime but the corruption of the laws. The parties to the social contract derived their protection from virtue not from force. Otherwise society was faced with an endless spiral of ever-increasing crime and ever more severe punishment. The ideal solution would be for the guilty to be convicted of weakness and then pardoned, but even Saint-Just admitted that one would have to reform morals before going as far as that. How it would be possible to reform the morality of the majority, in ways that they would not immediately understand, without the massive use of punishments that were inherently self-defeating, was a question that he left unanswered. The eventual goal was a state of innocence in which the pursuit of good and the abhorrence of evil had become so instinctive as to be unconscious reflexes.

After losing himself and, one suspects, most of his readers in these abstract speculations, Saint-Just suddenly returned to practical politics. He used a chapter on the freedom of the press to praise most of the leading radical journalists (although Marat was 'too anxious') and politicians, apparently unaware of their own reservations about each other. Once back on the theme of everyday politics, he resumed his former conservatism. It was necessary for the king to control the executive in order to prevent the assembly from becoming an omnipotent aristocracy. Most of the men he had just been praising would have been less than enthusiastic about that. 'It is wonderful to see how the national assembly closed its ears to the clamour of the multitude, demanding one day that the ministers should render their accounts and another that they should be dismissed.' If it was difficult to follow Saint-Just's ideas as they whisked from one level to another, one thing at least was abundantly clear: whatever his views about popular sovereignty and the virtues of the people, he believed in leadership from above, and he saw his own place as amongst the top people.

His fifth Book, ostensibly on France's relationships with other nations, took up a mere half-dozen pages and contained nothing very substantial. Patriotism had been purified by the assembly's renunciation of wars of conquest. Since France had opted out of the European rat-race she had no need of diplomats. Bits and pieces on the Family Compact with Spain, the army and navy, customs duties, forests and the erection of statues to famous men, suggested that he had not much to say about international relations and was throwing in whatever occurred to him.

In his conclusion he tried to 'moralize' the contents of the rest of the book. The assembly, in 1789, had been the embodiment of the sovereignty of the people. Once liberty had been secured, like some collective Lycurgus, it had voluntarily surrendered its sovereignty and restricted itself to drafting institutions. He conceded that the constitution did not embody the unanimous will of the French people, but said that it would be ridiculous to treat 'the resistance of a handful of villains' as part of the national will. He broke a final lance with Rousseau, who had described the general will as 'incommunicable, imprescriptible and eternal'. Saint-Just insisted that this was not enough: it must also be just and reasonable. 'It is no less criminal that the sovereign [people] should be tyrannized by itself than by someone else, for in that case the laws would flow from an impure source and the people would be enslaved or licentious, with each individual forming a portion of the tyranny and servitude.' Taken at its face value, this looked like a challenge, in the name of absolute values, to Rousseau's relativism, in which there existed no moral values superior to the self-interest of a particular community. In its context, what Saint-Just was actually saying was that those who were identified as wicked – he did not say by whom – could be regarded as having excluded themselves from the community, which was rather a different proposition.

Despite the somewhat apocalyptic passages of Book III, he ended on a note of optimism: 'Wherever I turn my eyes I discover marvels.' Everything was liable to change, even the social contract itself, and the man who appealed to the sanctity of former laws – a reference to the royalists – deserved exile. The man who took up arms against the supreme will of the sovereign people merited death. The death penalty seemed to have its merits after all. His object had been not so much to prove that France actually was free as that it could become so. All that was needed was political tranquility and heavy taxation to redistribute wealth and to force the idle rich to work. 'When men become free they will become equal; when they become equal they will become just.' That made a suitably pithy ending, even if it involved a frightful confusion of the three levels of his argument.

To reiterate that Saint-Just was only twenty-three when he wrote the *Esprit de la révolution* is not to patronize him but to invite the reader to consider his book in perspective. Younger men have produced works of genius, although not, perhaps, in political philosophy. To criticize him for failing to measure up to his two guides would be the real injustice. When *De l'esprit des lois* was published Montesquieu was fifty-nine and Rousseau was fifty when he produced *Du contrat social*. Each of these works reflected a lifetime's experience and reflection and a gradual crystallization of its author's ideas. Saint-Just was exposing thoughts and feelings that he had not had time to develop or relate to each other, and the interest of his essay lies in what it tells us about the nature of a man who was still in the process of coming to terms with the world in which he found himself, a world in rapid and violent change. His ideas were still in a state of flux; how they developed would be determined to some extent by the evolution of the political situation. What the book does reveal is something about the character of the writer, certain leading principles that would shape the ways in which he would assimilate whatever experiences the future had in store for him. Many of the ideas that he was to try to implement during the next two years were already present in embryo in the *Esprit de la révolution*.

There could be little doubt about his ambition. He saw himself as someone capable of extracting the essential meaning from the welter of day-to-day events. He envisaged politics not as a matter of making the best of each situation as it arose, but as harnessing contingency to the service of principle. He was trying, in his own way, to apply to the circumstances of his own times Montesquieu's belief that all the attitudes and institutions of a society were related to its political principles. In the France of 1791 he accepted the kind of constitutional monarchy that seemed to be emerging from the work of the Constituent Assembly. His attitude to the franchise, the powers of the assembly, the monarchy and economic policy, was determined by the nature of a regime of which he approved. If that regime were to change, everything else would have to change too.

At the same time he had absorbed from Rousseau the belief that the *raison d'être* of civil society ought to be the moral improvement of its members. This involved, consciously or not, the assumption that some men were able to discern what was good for others, whether the others recognized this or not. Saint-Just, like Rousseau, had no doubts about whether he himself belonged to the sheep or the goats. The ignorant majority, who were unlikely to welcome what they could not see to be to their ultimate advantage, would require direction. If this involved the coercion of the unregenerate, the end would justify the means. Moralizing society meant the pursuit of unitary goals and an ultimate objective of harmony and unanimity that was at odds with the diversity that had originally seemed to him so valuable.

A possible resolution of this paradox, at all events, the final objective, was a return to that state of nature in which the repressive and moralizing state would have withered away and men would be unaware of their instinctive goodness and in need of neither direction nor control. This was no doubt a distant dream but it was the ultimate standard by which present political action must be judged. Whenever possible the attitudes appropriate to a state of nature must be cultivated within a society that, although corrupted, was in the process of working out its own redemption. There was an obvious contradiction between the Spartan tactics of regeneration and the idyllic independence of a state of nature, which Saint-Just was later to resolve to his own satisfaction by the argument that the repressive action of the state could only legitimately be directed against those in need of regeneration and must never be applied to people whose conduct already embodied the moral norms of natural society.

For the time being, the three strands in Saint-Just's theorizing pointed in different directions and led to different destinations, but they were to remain his guiding principles for the rest of his brief life. How they were to be made to coexist and which parts of them would be sacrificed to the pursuit of others, would be determined by circumstances, but Saint-Just was not the man to be content with merely reacting to circumstances. Whatever the limitations imposed by an existing situation, the ultimate object of all political action, so far as he was concerned, was to edge society in the direction of the distant ideal. His next step was to clarify his ideas about what that ideal implied.

4

'On Nature'

Saint-Just's essay on nature survives in the form of a small notebook that was deposited with the Bibliothèque Nationale in 1947. This gives no indication of its author's identity, but the handwriting is that of Saint-Just and the argument could not have been written by anyone else. The text was first deciphered by the late Albert Soboul, who published it in *Annales historiques de la révolution française* in 1951.[1]

To anyone familiar with the published version of Saint-Just's writings and speeches, the notebook comes as something of a shock. He could not spell, and although his grammar was usually correct he left out most of the punctuation and he had very idiosyncratic ideas about the use of capitals. He usually omitted them from the names of people and places and invariably wrote 'De'. His diminutive handwriting is occasionally indecipherable and his manuscript is full of deletions. This is not because he was

---

[1] No. 124, 'Un manuscrit oublié de Saint-Just'. For a version that reproduces more of the peculiarities of Saint-Just's style and includes more of the passages that he deleted, see A. Liénard, *Saint-Just, théorie politique* (Paris, 1976), pp. 138–80. There is an interesting, if tendentious, critique of *De la Nature* by Miguel Abensour, 'La Philosophie politique de Saint-Just' in *Annales historiques de la révolution française*, 183 and 185 (1966), pp. 1–32, 341–58.

jotting down ideas in a commonplace book written for his personal satisfaction. Various asides to the reader show that the text was intended for publication.

The form of the text poses problems of its own. The first thirty-six pages are similar to the *Esprit de la révolution* in the sense that they are arranged in Books consisting of short chapters, eleven in Book I and sixteen in Book II. Book III contains one such chapter and a deleted sentence or two of a second. This is immediately followed by a table of contents that reproduces fairly faithfully the ground covered in Books I and II and provides the titles of sixteen chapters for Book III, on the nature of the city, and eight for Book IV, on the king. The rest of the notebook is blank, except that Saint-Just turned it over, began again at the end and wrote three new chapters, on nature, the principle of the Divinity and the characteristics of a natural society. There is no obvious reason why, after interrupting his work at the beginning of Book III, he should have followed this with a table of contents and then abandoned Books III and IV. The chapters at the end of the notebook, although basically similar to the rest in their approach, give a new emphasis to the relationship of nature to God and may have been written at a different time. One can speculate about what all this means, but one guess is as good as another.

Various ideas have been advanced about the dating of the manuscript. Soboul himself initially opted for 1791–2, when he drew attention to the existence of the notebook in 1949.[2] In 1951 he amended this to 1792–3. Miguel Abensour preferred the earlier date, mainly on two grounds. Saint-Just wrote, 'If marriages were free few couples would separate', which seemed to antedate the introduction of divorce on 20 September 1792. The projected Book V, on the king, was perhaps overtaken by events, when the monarchy was overthrown. Abensour suggested that this may have been the reason why Saint-Just abandoned a work that had become irrelevant. His date of 1791–2 looks probable but neither of his arguments is entirely conclusive. A deleted passage, 'France,

---

[2] 'Les Institutions républicaines de Saint-Just d'après les manuscrits de la Bibliothèque Nationale', *Annales historiques de la révolution française*, 111 (1948), pp. 198–262.

which has renounced wars of conquest and proscribed laxity, has of necessity re-established the independence of spouses', could be taken as referring to the legalization of divorce. In the second place, Saint-Just did not actually interrupt his book when he reached the section on the king, but at the beginning of Book III. His list of contents suggested – for example, by the inclusion of a chapter on 'the division of the king' – that he was using 'king' as a synonym for 'executive power' and he could easily have retained his argument whilst making the necessary change in wording. It is perhaps more likely that what led him to stop writing was his election to the Convention, which deprived him of his abundant leisure and gave him the opportunity to put his ideas into practice instead of having to communicate them in print.

The precise dating is important only if the text itself implies that Saint-Just was changing his ideas as a result of the impact of events. Liénard, who accepts the date of 1791–2, takes this view, suggesting that the failure of the constitutional monarchy had undermined the premises on which the *Esprit de la révolution* had been based. This has to be viewed with caution since *De la nature* actually develops concepts that had been expressed more tentatively in the earlier book and indeed went back as far as *Organt*.[3] Ideas and passages from *De la nature* were to be reproduced in the jottings on republican institutions that were probably compiled in the last period of Saint-Just's life. In other words, there was a basic continuity about his views on the nature of society, that did not change throughout his life. He continued to develop their implications and to have new thoughts about how they might be implemented, but his fundamental assumptions remained constant. Logically, and probably chronologically, *De la nature*, with its attempt to define natural society and the institutions appropriate to it, comes between the *Esprit de la révolution* and Saint-Just's election to the Convention, when he had to concentrate on the application of his ideology to the solution of concrete political problems.

De la nature was based on the assumption – denied by Rousseau

---

[3] See above, p. 16.

– that man was naturally a social animal. 'Everything that breathes is independent by nature and lives in the society of its own species.' Natural society implied that individuals were at the same time independent and integrated parts of a social whole. True to his eighteenth-century upbringing, Saint-Just assumed that 'nature' was an essentially harmonious unity, an organism whose parts sustained each other by unconscious co-operation, like the members of a healthy human body. Members of the same species lived in amity with each other and resorted to force only against different species. He could not have been expected to anticipate Darwin and 'nature red in tooth and claw' but he might have drawn different conclusions from watching the odd dog-fight. Man, in a natural or 'social' state, regulated his relationships with other men by more or less instinctive social laws that called for neither political organization nor the use of force. 'In social life, which admits of no *magistrat*, man is neither oppressed nor corrupt.' His needs and affections created links of mutual dependence, uniting him with other men, which gave rise to social laws. So long as these were in accord with nature they consisted of spontaneous non-contractual relationships which were self-regulating and self-perpetuating. In natural society there was therefore no hierarchy and no giving of orders. 'No one on earth ought to command. All power is illegitimate.' Saint-Just defended himself against the charge of preaching anarchy, but on the assumption that anarchy implied chaos, which he attributed to reliance on force. What he believed to be a state of nature was certainly anarchy in the sense of non-rule.

Where animals were concerned, the state of amicable coexistence applied to the entire species. In the case of man, it was confined to specific social groups, or nations. This was a gratuitous assumption on Saint-Just's part; he could equally well have argued that wars between states were a consequence of human corruption that had no place in natural society. Instead he chose to assert that each human society was totally independent of any other and had no moral responsibility towards it. Relationships between different societies, in a state of nature, might therefore involve armed struggle for territory or resources. Each society, in consequence, was liable to need physical force – which implied military leadership – for its self-defence. Saint-Just described the kind of organization that this implied as 'political' society, by which he meant any system of organization based on force. In his natural state man led a social life within his own community and a political life when that community had to be defended against other societies.

Everywhere in the world this original natural society had been undermined when the political had invaded the social. Military chiefs had used the power entrusted to them for national defence in order to achieve domination at home. All known societies, past and present, were therefore political rather than social and all were equally bad. Even Sparta had had its helots. 'I make no distinction between all the forms of legislation [i.e. governments], whether the people are subject to one man, to several or to themselves.' What mattered was not monarchy or democracy, but the fact that, in both, power rested ultimately on force, and order was maintained by repressive laws. Since these circumstances had prevailed from the beginning of recorded time, the prior existence of natural society was a matter of faith. Saint-Just described the political state as one of savagery. Its subjects were not merely oppressed but corrupted by its reliance on force, to such an extent that political theorists had come to believe that men were naturally cruel, selfish and aggressive. In a sense they were right, since human nature had itself become perverted. 'Social man is a simple being, a friend to his fellow-men. Savage or political man is a cruel animal. The force of the law [he really meant laws based on force] has altered his nature and stolen him from himself.' Saint-Just therefore agreed with Hobbes's pessimistic view of human nature as it existed. Hobbes's mistake had been to assume that this was the natural state of the species rather than the product of history. 'He thinks he is describing natural man when he is actually describing man who has become savage.' 'Crime is the product of force. It is not in men's nature to do evil, but it is in the nature of the slave to rattle his chains and pervert himself.' This was uncomfortably close to his account, in the *Esprit de la révolution*, of what had happened in Paris in July 1789.

In other words, all previous reasoning about political theory had been based on false premises. Saint-Just realized that this was a bold conclusion but he did not shrink from it. 'If what I have said is true no one, so far as I know, has suspected what nature really is.' The social contract which, for Rousseau, was both the foundation-deed of society and the means by which man transformed himself from a kind of superior animal into a moral being, was in actual fact the means by which a political – i.e. savage – society tried to regulate the use of force. It was not merely illegitimate but the source of further corruption. 'Men are civilized (*polices*) so long as they follow their inclinations; they become savages when political laws take the place of these inclinations.' Rousseau had had the right intuition about what was wrong with contemporary society but his mistaken remedy would only make things worse. 'He is looking for an independent society but that is irreconcilable with the vigorous government that he invokes. He strangles liberty with its own hands and the more he sets up safeguards against slavery, the more arms he forges for the service of tyranny.' This was well observed, so far as Rousseau was concerned, but it would not necessarily preserve Saint-Just from doing the same thing.

The political state had to be repudiated lock, stock and barrel – its dependence on force makes the military metaphor unusually appropriate. All previous revolutions, however, had been mistaken attempts to provide violent remedies for ills which arose precisely from the fact that societies were based on force. All such revolutions had therefore been doomed from the start – and that presumably applied to 1789, about which Saint-Just had always had his reservations. 'All the revolutions in the world have had a political point of departure; that is why they have been full of crimes and catastrophes. Revolutions born of good laws and conducted by skilful hands would change the face of the world without unsettling it' (*sans l'ébranler*). If Saint-Just's reasoning was correct, it might take rather more than 'good laws and skilful hands' to succeed where everyone else had been failing for over two thousand years. What was needed was obviously a new kind of revolution and this presented him with more problems than he realized.

One consequence of men's false ideas about their own true nature was that, the more intelligent and concerned for the moral regeneration of society they had been, the more damage they had done, since their acute awareness of the prevailing evil had led them to propose draconian ways of correcting it. '*Vertu* itself is no longer innocent' in the sense that those who invoked it were thinking in terms of a conscious effort of will, when what was really needed was a kind of benevolent instinct.

Saint-Just looked briefly at two specific aspects of contemporary corruption: commerce and religion. As a result of the growing complexity of an increasingly technological society, civil laws had equated men with things and reduced them to commodities. Unlike Rousseau, he did not believe that this was an inevitable product of human interdependence, since men were naturally social animals who could co-operate with each other. He thought it possible to base any society, primitive or economically developed, on natural laws, although he was content to state this as an axiom without exploring its implications.

Religion in natural society was a spontaneous feeling of love for one's Creator. In political society it had been captured by hypocritical priests who had turned it into a thing of fear, in order to carve out positions of power for themselves. Saint-Just was particularly hard on Moses ('the deepest and most skilful of men – and also the most wicked') and Mahomet. These were the men who, with Calvin, had been cited by Rousseau as models of the providential Legislator. Saint-Just's own heroes were Minos, Solon and Christ, the first two of whom had the advantage of being more or less mythical, so that they could be made to dance to any tune he wanted. Sophisticated societies, like those that evolved in Greece and Rome, outgrew the primitive religious ideas of their beginnings: 'Rome ended Stoic and Greece *philosophe*.' This was a typical example of Saint-Just's tendency to flit from one rhetorical assertion to another, without trying to organize his perceptions into any coherent system. Elsewhere he was equally emphatic that Rome had declined from its primitive virtue and become thoroughly corrupt. It would have been possible for him to combine the two ideas, in a vision of reason refining the basis of men's thinking, without being able to rescue them from the consequences of founding their societies on false moral premises, but Saint-Just was the man for perceptions rather than for syntheses.

His attitude to life had something in common with that of Blake. Both men saw social existence in terms of a black and white contrast between what was and what might have been, between an infernal present, where everything was regulated by coercive law, and a possible alternative of spontaneous co-operation.

Cruel works
Of many Wheels I view, wheel without wheel, with cogs tyrannic
Moving by compulsion each other, not as those in Eden which,
Wheel within Wheel, in freedom revolve in harmony and peace.

There had been some kind of Fall which had transformed human nature itself.

> For Mercy has a human heart,
> Pity a human face,
> And love, the human form divine,
> And peace, the human dress.

That was how things should be. In the actual world,

> Cruelty has a human heart,
> And Jealousy a human face,
> Terror the human form divine
> And Secrecy the human dress.

In the case of Blake, this fall from grace was associated with the adoption of the mechanistic philosophy of Newton and Locke and perhaps with its material realization in an increasingly mechanical society. This raises the question of whether or not Saint-Just's vision of what had gone wrong implied a similar critique. Abensour, in search of grist for what he took to be a Marxist mill, argued that Saint-Just's ideas were at bottom determined by his rejection of nascent capitalism and his attachment to the values of the pre-industrial peasant society that he had known in Picardy, 'the ideal of a society that was not torn apart or menaced by any social antagonism, a place of harmony and equality', that was threatened by 'social elements that wanted to break the feudal frame in order to liberate modern capitalist society'.[4] He was therefore a tragic figure, holding up his hand to history and ordering it to stop, and it was this that explained his ultimate failure. This is more ingenious than convincing. There was not a great deal of 'capitalism', in Abensour's sense, in pre-revolutionary France, and none at Blérancourt. Saint-Just knew quite enough of the 'pre-capitalist' goings-on of Gellé and his like, to have no illusions about the social harmony of the 'good old days'. If he considered this society in abstract terms at all, he probably thought of it as resting on iniquitous feudal foundations for which he hoped that the revolution would substitute more fraternal relationships.

He *had* defended the poorer peasants at Blérancourt, and there was an element of pastoral whimsy about his thinking that was to become more pronounced over the next couple of years, but what he wanted was not to preserve the past but to transform it. In *De la nature*, he insisted that there must be an upper limit to the amount of land that anyone could own. Property rights were sacrosanct, so that those whose land exceeded the permitted acreage would merely have to sell the surplus. He did claim that, in the political state, men were treated as commodities, but he specifically denied that this was a necessary consequence of the development of commerce. If the moral foundation of society was restored, 'industry and commerce will discover laws in accordance with nature.' Equality was a matter of personal independence and of all men being equally secure in their possessions, not of their owning equal amounts. He rejected the Roman concept of a *loi agraire* which provided for the periodical redistribution of land, not merely because it was impracticable but because the confiscation of property was against the law of nature. 'The man with less has

---

[4] Abensour, 'La Philosophie politique', pp. 354–5.

no claim against the man with more since ownership is inviolable.'
He was not, consciously or otherwise, arguing for or against any
kind of economic system and his conception of the relationship
between superstructure and infrastructure was the opposite of that
of Marx. All economic systems were equally invalid if they were
founded on the laws of force that governed political society. Once
human relations had been put on the right moral foundation, any
kind of economy would run itself on principles of co-operation
rather than of exploitation.

Saint-Just's vision of heaven and hell was essentially static.
There had been a Fall, before the beginning of historical time, but
since then nothing essential had changed. When it came to
explaining how things had gone so tragically wrong and how they
could be put right, his scrappy and superficial comments come as a
shock. As he himself seemed at times to suspect, his vision was a
daydream, a fantasy world that could not be connected to
historical or political reality. He had a clear, if simplistic,
conception of the consequences that had ensued from the
corruption of a community by the political relationships that
should only have applied to its contacts with other societies. When
it came to describing how a self-regulating society, at peace with
itself and with what he insisted was an inbuilt tendency towards
self-preservation, should have allowed this to happen, he was
quite extraordinarily casual. His chapter 'On the origins of the
savage state' consisted of two short paragraphs, the first of which
was devoted to arguing that a social contract presupposed the
existence of political society. The second was limited to three
sentences.

> This is how the savage state comes into being: initially peoples
> had no governments but only [military] leaders; the ancient
> Franks and Germans, our near neighbours, had no *magistrats*.
> The people themselves were both prince and sovereign, but
> when the peoples lost their taste for assemblies, in order to
> trade, cultivate the land and conquer, the prince detached
> himself from the sovereign. This was the end of social life and
> the beginning of political life based on contracts.

As an explanation of why, all over the globe, human societies had degenerated from the social to the political, this left rather a lot to be desired. To ridicule Saint-Just's somewhat condensed universal history is not a matter of academic pedantry. If it was so easy to fall from grace that all known societies had taken the primrose path, there did not seem much point in trying to redirect one of them back on to the right road, which it was unlikely to follow for very long.

When it came to the – rather important – question of exactly what action was needed to restore a society to a state of nature, Saint-Just's conflicting views produced total confusion. On the one hand, 'this state of war between men has withered their souls; none is happy, all waste away.' That might suggest that they would welcome a change. But 'Man ignores his own nature and, consumed with pride in the false nature that he has made for himself, how can he rediscover the true one? That posed rather a problem: the same problem that had led Rousseau to import a semi-divine Legislator to convert people to ways of *vertu* that they were incapable of conceiving, let alone following, by themselves. Saint-Just had no use for semi-divine Legislators ('The worst Legislators of all have been the prophets') but his whole system implied the existence of privileged people who had somehow transcended the social conditioning that had reduced the rest of the population to the condition of slaves who gloried in their chains. Persuading people – it had all to be done by persuasion since force belonged to the very political society that was being repudiated and even leadership was evidence of illegitimate hierarchical authority – to opt for a kind of society that they were incapable of perceiving to be preferable to the existing one, was going to call for considerable ingenuity. Saint-Just did not seem to think so: 'Simple laws would restore people to nature and hence to *vertu*.' It was as easy as that.

Leaving the uncongenial subjects of how humanity got into its present mess and how it was to get out of it, Saint-Just devoted most of Book II to an examination of what he called civil society, in other words, an exposition of how social relationships should be regulated within a regenerated community. Natural society

67

was based on interdependence and exchange, arising from human needs. Each citizen enjoyed both property (his right to personal independence together with whatever land he owned) and possessions which he exchanged with others. This distinction between the ownership of land and the mere possession of commodities such as crops may well have owed something to the traditional perceptions of Picard peasant society. Since landed property was an essential constituent of a man's independence, everyone was required to own a moderate amount. Those with more had to convert the surplus into commodities; those with less, or none at all, were excluded from the community.

When he dealt with women and marriage, his tone was very different from the condescending platitudes about women's 'faiblesse intéressante' in the *Esprit de la révolution*. With sober conviction he argued that both sexes should be treated as equal, at least where property was concerned, even if there might need to be some differences in the laws relating to possessions. In a revealing sentence, he challenged the reader who might be disposed to tell his 'beloved wife' that she was his inferior, to dare to say the same thing to his mother. If the mother happened to be the formidable Mme Saint-Just, it might indeed have been inadvisable. His views on marriage were followed by a curious chapter in which he argued that although incest was not likely to happen in the normal course of things, it was not contrary to nature, and the prejudice against it was a sign of corruption. Egyptians, Persians, Assyrians and Scyths, who married their sisters, 'must have enjoyed '*moeurs* of singular purity'. This seemed to imply that not all 'political' societies had been equally degenerate, but he had no time to linger over such niceties. Men who refused to marry were expelled from the community on the ground that they had no interest in defending it, which seemed rather illogical, if they were landowners. One thing at least was clear: the ideal society might have no *magistrats* but it was emphatically not a place where one could do as one liked and the rules of sociability could be more intrusive than political laws.

Exile was the penalty for three offences: committing a crime, owning less than the required minimum of land, and refusing to marry. This was scarcely practical politics – or rather, sociability – since it implied an exceptional equilibrium between the sexes, and townsmen might not care to be encumbered with estates that they had no time to cultivate and no freedom to sell. It also had a more sinister side. Excluding someone from a community whose moral norms he rejected did not sound either harsh or unreasonable – unless one remembered that, in Saint-Just's world, the obligation to treat one's fellow-men with humanity applied only within a given community. Exile was therefore tantamount to outlawry and if the whole of humanity were to be regenerated, criminals, bachelors and the landless would become Flying Dutchmen with no place in which they could settle. The social order might proscribe the use of force but it left plenty of room for moral blackmail.

Readers who were understandably curious to learn of the political arrangements that were to regulate a non-political society were presumably to be enlightened in Book III, 'On the City', which did not get beyond the first chapter. This informed them that the social body consisted of a legislator, a 'king' and the sovereign people. These three formed a kind of trinity in the sense that they constituted a single whole, whose attributions could manifest themselves in diverse forms. Saint-Just insisted that law was determined by nature and not by human will. That was all very well but nature could not speak without an interpreter and some people would have to inform the rest of what natural law implied. Some people, in other words, were more equal than others, and he was the most equal of all: 'If what I have said is true, no one, so far as I know, has suspected what nature really is.' In the summary of the contents of Book III one chapter carries the ominous title 'On the death penalty'. It is impossible to predict what Saint-Just intended to write, but it is a reasonable inference from what he did write that Book III would not have given the individual much scope for disagreement with the society in which he found himself. Book IV, whose list of contents treats the 'king' as a figure of speech for the executive, makes it clear that this institution was to be no more than an administrative machine for implementing the decisions of the legislature, which is how Saint-

Just had described Louis XVI in the *Esprit de la révolution*. The title of chapter 6 insisted 'that the king does not represent the sovereign'. In a Europe that contained a few republics – not to mention the one across the Atlantic – it was odd that Saint-Just should have chosen to refer to a king at all. Even the Constituent Assembly had been in the habit of referring to Louis as the 'executive power'.

Saint-Just's second version, at the end of his notebook, attached nature much more specifically to God. It also included an invocation in marked contrast to his usual impersonal and didactic style: 'O Supreme Being, receive in thy bosom an ingenuous soul that comes from thee and aspires to thee.' After repeating his familiar argument that the social contract was no substitute for the spontaneous harmony of nature, he wrote and then crossed out, 'I know very well that all this is only a dream, but a dream is always the sentiment of a truth that exists no more.' When he contrasted the political life with the life of nature he now conceded that reason, *vertu* and the rights of man were not entirely worthless, even if they were no more than a mistaken attempt to make the best of a bad job. In the last of his three chapters he reaffirmed his conviction that what people called a social contract was actually a political one and that in political society men lived in a state of savagery that was both a product of force and a source of continuing repression. If critics should ask how fallen man could have retained the faculty of reason, his answer was that reason, as his contemporaries understood it, was not a natural faculty at all but the degenerate form of natural intelligence, by which he seems to have meant some kind of instinctive wisdom peculiar to homo sapiens. He took a last shot at Rousseau, for sharing Hobbes's view that *homo homini lupus* referred to man's natural state, but when he wrote that 'happy man passed his social life in the forest' he seemed, like Rousseau, to be equating the ideal society with economic primitivism. He agreed with Rousseau that technology was suspect, as the desperate remedy by which fallen men tried to ensure their self-preservation. 'If you imagine innocent beings, they would need little by way of enlightenment.'

Throughout his manuscript Saint-Just had kept up a running

argument with Rousseau, stressing their points of disagreement. Where political philosophy was concerned these were indeed substantial. For Rousseau, man was naturally a solitary animal. His decision to unite with his fellow-men in society was due to a rational calculation of his advantage. Previous to this he had led an amoral life, and morality was therefore something brought into being by the social contract. The new society was, or ought to be, regulated by the sovereign will of its members, which implied their making deliberate rational choices. To initiate them into habits of *vertu* and to guide them in their decision-making, they needed Legislators who wisely pretended to divine inspiration, in order to win the assent of those who could not understand what was in the interest of the community and therefore to their own long-term advantage. A regenerated society rested on *vertu*, which implied the subordination of immediate self-interest to the collective good by a conscious effort of will.

All this Saint-Just denied. Man was a social animal whose natural state was one of spontaneous social integration. This implied the existence of private property and could encompass a developed economy based on the division of labour. Since the social state was the natural product of man's benevolence and of his needs, it had no room for contracts, Legislators and acts of will.

Nevertheless, when it came to political action, both men found themselves facing in the same direction. They agreed that contemporary society was a travesty of what ought to be, since it was morally corrupt. The objective of political action should therefore be moral regeneration, which was not to be achieved by tinkering with constitutions. The goal was a unanimous community from which no one would want to dissent. Those who rejected the tenets of Rousseau's civic religion were to be deported and those who resisted the general will would be 'forced to be free'. Saint-Just was in favour of exiling those who deviated from social or economic norms. Both agreed that, as things were, the over-whelming majority in every existing society (with the partial exceptions of Poland and Corsica in the case of Rousseau) had been so corrupted by their environment that they were incapable of understanding what was actually good for them. Rousseau accepted their need for guidance from above. Saint-Just rejected it in theory, but his moral revolution could scarcely take place unless it happened in practice. Both associated equality with economic independence and both based their ideal societies on conscience rather than on reason. They were equally suspicious of intelligence and of technology. Each located social morality within a particular community – the focus of sociability for Saint-Just and the home of the general will for Rousseau – that had no moral obligations towards its neighbours. They were equally hostile to any concept of a pluralist political system, based on the balanced representation of necessarily divergent values and interests, in which the citizenry would enjoy a degree of autonomy that would allow them to challenge the political attitudes and moral norms of the majority. Since the object of political action was the moral transformation of the community in a way that would be to its collective benefit, dissent on major issues of policy would inevitably be equated with self-interested resistance to the common good. One does not – or at least one ought not to – compromise with sin. 'Nature', like the 'general will', ultimately meant what the writer believed it to mean. There was no way, when it came to making actual choices, of proving that it pointed in one direction rather than in another, and it was never to be equated with the wishes of the majority. However far it may have been from the intentions of either of them, any attempt to put their principles into practice could only imply direction from above. Saint-Just could see this mote in Rousseau's eye but not the beam in his own: 'no one, so far as I know, has suspected what nature really is.' Only one man was fit for the job and they were all out of step except Antoine.

The impatient reader may well be wondering why it was necessary to examine at such length the incoherent and impractical daydreams of a clever young man who was not very good at the systematic development of his ideas. The explanation is simple. The young man happened to be Saint-Just, who was soon to find himself a member of the Convention and, before long, of its Committee of Public Safety. What he thought, was to be a matter of life and death to a good many people, beginning with the king.

As the rest of this book will demonstrate, his choice of political options was to be consciously motivated by an attempt to bring into being the ideal society that he had tried to describe in *De la nature*. Understanding what was at the back of his mind is the essential preliminary to the comprehension of what he was trying to do, first of all as a deputy and then as a member of the government, and these policies were to have a significant influence on the course of the French Revolution.

5

Creating a Republic

When Saint-Just moved to Paris the political situation had been transformed by the events of the summer. In April 1792 France declared war on Austria, which led Prussia to intervene in Austria's support. The first result of the argument about whether or not it would be to the advantage of the revolutionaries to provoke a war, had been to divide what had hitherto been a reasonably united group of radicals whose aim had been to reduce the king to a cipher and make France a republic in all but name. Brissot and his allies believed that war would force Louis XVI off the fence and make him declare himself either for or against the national cause. Robespierre, together with a considerable number of the members of the Jacobin Club, the home of the radicals, replied that to gamble on war was to risk the entire fate of the Revolution, whether the victorious allies restored the monarchy or a grateful country threw itself at the feet of some victorious Caesar. Since they occupied the uppermost seats in the assembly they called themselves Montagnards.

The war itself, which might have been expected to reunite the two groups, since both were agreed that defeat must be avoided at any cost, soon had the opposite effect. The demoralized and undisciplined French forces offered no effective resistance to the allies, and by the end of July a Prussian army was ready to invade. The Legislative Assembly, although it deplored the way that things were going, was the prisoner of its own sense of legality and would not violate the constitution, even though it suspected the king of being ready to help the progress of those who claimed to be coming to his rescue. This time it was Robespierre and those who thought like him, who braced themselves to gamble on overthrowing the monarchy by force. Brissot, who believed that the mere threat of insurrection would be enough to make the king capitulate, tried to prevent what he saw as a dangerous and unnecessary appeal to arms.

The insurrection of 10 August that captured the royal palace of the Tuileries after heavy fighting, was not a purely Parisian affair. The National Guards of the forty-eight sections of Paris were reinforced by battalions of volunteers from Brest and Marseille which had come to Paris on their way to the front. It could therefore be presented, with enough plausibility to satisfy those eager to be convinced, as an example of the sovereign people exercising its inalienable right to overthrow a government that no longer represented the general will. The king was suspended, and the deputies voted to end their session as soon as a convention could be elected to draft a new constitution. This produced a kind of interregnum. The assembly insisted that it alone represented the national will. Friends of Brissot took over all ministerial posts except Justice, which went to Danton, who was trying to keep in with both sides. The Brissotins, or Girondins as they were sometimes called since some of their leaders came from Bordeaux in the Gironde, thus picked up most of the winnings from an insurrection that they had tried to prevent. Robespierre and the members of the insurrectionary Paris Commune that had been created on the night of 9–10 August, saw things differently. For them, the rising had implied the repudiation of the assembly as well as the king. Until a convention could be elected, Paris, as represented by its Commune, was the provisional executor of the general will, and the resolutions of the Commune had a kind of legitimacy that did not apply to the decrees of the assembly.

Throughout the rest of August the assembly legislated and the Commune tried to bully it. It was the latter that insisted on treating Louis XVI as a prisoner and on creating a special revolutionary court to try those who had been most active in defending the royal cause. In the meantime the Prussian army crossed the frontier, the forts that should have held it up until the end of the campaigning season surrendered with virtually no resistance, and by the end of the month it began to look as though Paris might soon be in danger. The Commune closed the gates of the capital and began night-time searches for arms and suspects, while an emotional recruiting campaign contributed to the sense of panic. Encouraged by the radical journalist, Marat, groups of fanatics who had been persuaded of an aristocratic plot to open the prisons and seize Paris while all true patriots were at the front, occupied the prisons and butchered over a thousand of their inmates. Robespierre and his colleague on the Commune, Billaud-Varenne, chose this time, when to be arrested was to risk being massacred, to denounce Brissot and some of the Girondins to the Commune.

In Paris the September massacres coincided with the beginning of the elections to the Convention. These were conducted on the basis of universal suffrage, but since voting was public it was easy for any locally dominant faction to impose its own candidates, as happened in various parts of France. The elections in the capital were efficiently managed by the Commune and the Cordelier Club, the fief of Danton. That meant the elimination of the Girondins who were forced to get themselves elected in the provinces.

The result of all this was to generalize and intensify conflicts that had previously involved only a score or so of people on either side. The Girondins, like the Montagnards, had tended at first to see the prison massacres as a regrettable piece of hysteria that had to be overlooked in the interests of national unity. Ejected from Paris, where the lives of some of them had perhaps been in danger, they now began to denounce the Commune and the Paris deputies in the Convention as blood-soaked anarchists. They turned for support to the provinces, stressing the need for law and order, even within a revolution. Their opponents, threatened by a Girondin attempt to have Robespierre, Marat and Danton expelled from the assembly, turned for protection to the Commune and the Parisian sans-culottes.

There was virtually nothing to divide Girondins and Montagnards where political principles were concerned. Both were democrats, republicans, economic liberals · and anti-clericals. Despite their initial disagreement over the advantages of declaring war, by the end of 1792 both championed an ideological crusade against the crowned heads of Europe. What separated them was power, in the sense that the Girondins were greedy for office and the Montagnards morbidly suspicious of anyone who was trying to govern. It was largely tactics that inclined the Girondins towards conservative (but still republican) opinion in the provinces and forced the Montagnards into a measure of dependence on the sans-culottes. The two sides united briefly when the Convention met and declared France a republic, but the Girondins then began a bitter struggle that gradually dragged in more and more of the provincial deputies.

No political situation during the French Revolution was without its ideological dimension, which was often responsible for making differences insoluble. Most of the leading Girondins and Montagnards were Rousseauists of a sort, who believed in popular sovereignty and its manifestation through the general will. In practice this meant a conviction of their own rectitude, if not infallibility. Each side was convinced that its policies were – to use the language of more recent cant – 'objectively' in the interests of the nation as a whole. Since they believed their opponents recognized this too, any opposition was therefore a matter of defending vested interests, to the national detriment, by people who were well aware of what they were doing. This did not make for concession or compromise.

Ideology affected men's thinking in another way. It was from Montesquieu rather than Rousseau that the revolutionary generation had learned that republics were different in kind from monarchies. The latter were sustained by a sense of honour that inclined nobles naturally to offer their services to the king in return for titles, decorations and his respect for their dignity. In a republic, on the other hand, the entire population had to be motivated by a sense of *vertu* that led them to seek their personal fulfilment in the discharge of their civic obligations. As Montesquieu had recognized, this was asking rather a lot: 'Political *vertu* implies a renunciation of self that is always a painful thing.' Robespierre recognized that the French had put the cart before the horse, in the sense that people who had grown up conditioned by the evil influences of monarchy suddenly found themselves living in a republic. What should have been the product of *vertu* would have to become its cause. As he put it, 'To shape our political institutions we ought to have the *moeurs* that they will eventually create for us.'[1]

In theory, this should have been less of a problem for Saint-Just. He had explained in *De la nature* that all political societies were equally bad, a republic was no better than a monarchy and all revolutions in history had merely substituted one kind of exploitation for another. It was one thing to offer this sort of comment from the Blérancourt touchlines; things looked rather different when he found himself in Paris as a member of a national parliament. His confidence in his own rectitude convinced him that he could not be merely a party to the age-old confidence trick, and if that applied to him it was equally true of those who agreed with him or took his advice. Inevitably his perspective changed and he soon adopted Robespierre's view that *this* revolution was a providential moment that had allowed France to break away from the treadmill of history and by its example to offer to the benighted nations the key to their own salvation. The republic therefore became the sign that the change had been positive. In the language of *De la nature* it had substituted the social for the political state. Its survival therefore demanded the transformation of all France's institutions which had been created to serve the corrupt purposes of monarchy.

Where politics was concerned, Saint-Just was not committed to either party when he was elected. He had once expressed his

---

[1] *Lettres à ses commettants*, no. 1 series 1, 19 October 1792, in *Oeuvres complètes*, vol. V, ed. G. Laurent (Paris, 1961).

admiration to Robespierre, when he hoped to enlist his help, and he had been on cordial terms with Desmoulins, although he had subsequently denounced him in the letter to Daubigny.[2] Both of these men were now prominent Montagnards. On the other hand he had never been unduly impressed by the revolutionary efforts of the Parisians, and if he had been revolted by the isolated atrocities that had accompanied the insurrection of July 1789 he might have been expected to be outraged by the September massacres. His elevated sense of his own vocation for leadership would not incline him to listen patiently if the Parisian sans-culottes tried to impose their views on the Convention in the name of popular sovereignty.

He remained aloof from the exchange of personalities in the Convention when the Girondins took advantage of their initial superiority to pack its committees with their own men. It was not until 22 October that he made his first speech, not in the assembly itself but in the Jacobin Club which was becoming a Montagnard stronghold. Its subject was the question of whether or not the assembly should surround itself by National Guards drawn from the provinces, in order to protect it from intimidation by Paris. This had been proposed by the Girondin, Lanjuinais, on the 5th. Two days later the assembly received a threatening message from the Gravilliers, one of the most radical of the Paris Sections: 'The men of 10 August will not allow those whom they have invested with their confidence [i.e. the deputies] to ignore for a moment the sovereignty of the people . . . it is right to resist despots in whatever disguise they appear.' This brought a surprisingly moderate reply from the Girondin, Buzot. Saint-Just must have nodded his approval when Buzot said that a new order had begun, which implied the annihilation of everything selfish or vicious. He agreed with Buzot's definition of the republic as 'a holy confederation of men who recognize each other as their equals and brothers, men who are equal and independent but prudent, who recognize no master except the law that emanates from the general will, freely expressed by the representatives of the nation as a

[2] See above pp. 28 and 33–4.

whole'. Buzot even echoed the language of *De la nature* when he said that, in the social order, the happiness of each was indistinguishable from that of all. He conceded that Paris had overthrown despotism and made the revolution – but only with the help of the provinces. A provincial guard, according to Buzot, would be a moral link between the capital and the rest of the country. It could be opposed only by factious men intent on creating a new aristocracy to their own advantage.

Relations between Paris and the Convention became more heated in the middle of the month when the Marseille Section – the home of the Cordelier Club – challenged the attempt of the assembly to stop it voting in public. This induced Buzot to change his line of approach, and to assert that obedience to the assembly was to be found only in the provinces. On 19 October the forty-eight Sections presented a joint address in which they said that if the deputies surrounded themselves with an armed guard they would be tyrants. 'Paris has made the revolution. Paris has given liberty to the rest of France.' It was at this stage that Saint-Just rose to make his maiden speech to the Jacobins on the 22nd.

He had changed his ground since he described the insurrection of July 1789, in the *Esprit de la révolution*, as a slave revolt. He now said that the French were a great people who had made three revolutions in three years. They must therefore be governed by gentle means and not by force. At the back of his mind were the ideas he had expressed in *De la nature* that the social order must be based on consent. 'You have not got a political existence, which means one based on force.' The destruction of the monarchy meant the end of any system based on violence, which was merely monarchy in another form. The republic, in other words, had been equated with his ideal 'social' state. If protection from anarchy and disorder was needed, it must be secured by peaceful means and not by arming the *magistrat*, which would create two hostile forces within society. This implied an acceptance of the Montagnard attitude that the Paris militants were good republicans whose claims to monopolize the general will were not to be taken too seriously. This was perhaps optimistic, but Saint-Just's attack on the arguments of his opponents was eminently sensible. He thought that the danger from his old bogey, the intrusion of the military into the civil, came more from a departmental force than from the Paris Sections. Creating such a guard would provoke the agitators in the capital without intimidating them. If these agitators could win over the population as a whole, the guard would not dare to open fire; if they could not, it was unnecessary. There was no guarantee that, once settled in Paris, it would not be persuaded to change sides, in which case the assembly would be in a worse predicament than ever.

Saint-Just was courteous towards Buzot – at a time when Montagnards and Girondins were already denouncing each other as hypocrites and would-be tyrants – but he dropped unspecified hints about those who were aspiring to attain personal power by legal means. In a significant revelation of his sense of his own importance, the 25-year-old deputy reassured his colleagues, many of whom were revolutionary veterans who had served in one of the previous assemblies: 'One must allow crime to mature and I am waiting for it.' 'You must have the courage to listen to what I say. It is less deadly than your lethargy.' The real danger came not from sans-culottes but from royalists, and the best preservative against that was to punish 'a criminal family'. The fate of Louis XVI was soon to become the main bone of contention between the two rival factions, but at the time he spoke Saint-Just may have believed that making the king a scapegoat might serve to unite them. His speech went down well with the Jacobins, who ordered it to be printed. He was off to a good start.

Within the Convention the party battles became increasingly acrimonious. The Girondin, Louvet, made a full-scale denunciation of Robespierre who replied on 4 November with a defence of his revolutionary career. Saint-Just had put himself down to speak in the debate but the assembly was tired of personalities and moved to other business, and he had to deliver his speech in the Jacobin Club that evening. In a manner that was to become familiar, he invited his audience to get behind the symptoms and go for the basic problems. 'The cause of all our misfortunes is the political situation.' When governments dissolved they became 'as full of rascals as a corpse is full of worms'. This implied that he was changing his mind about the last revolution having created a 'social state' that was threatened only by the king and his partisans. There was still something rotten in the state of France. In the spirit of *De la nature* he condemned the Girondins for speaking the language of power and trying to destroy the Montagnards and Robespierre. 'What a government that plants the tree of liberty on the scaffold and thrusts an axe into the hands of the law!' He rather spoiled the effect of this by himself inviting the Jacobins to denounce all 'traitors'. By now he was firmly aligned with the Montagnards, but they were unlikely to find him an easy bedfellow.

It was not until 13 November that Saint-Just made his maiden speech in the Convention itself, when he intervened in the debate about the way to deal with the king. The proclamation of a republic had deprived the Bourbons of their status as a ruling dynasty but said nothing about what was to be done with them. Louis was an embarrassing relic of a repudiated past. He had long since forfeited the affection and respect of 1789, when the Constituent Assembly had voted to put up a statue to him as the restorer of French liberty. He was now regarded by virtually all the deputies as a man who, unable to defeat the Revolution by force, had tried to subvert it by intrigue. This impression was to be strengthened in late November by the discovery of a safe in the Tuileries containing evidence of his secret correspondence with some of the early leaders of the Revolution and with royalists who had left France in the hope of raising an army of liberation with the help of foreign princes. The prisoner in the Temple was no longer in a position to oppose anything, but he remained a powerful symbol of monarchy and the passive focus of royalist aspirations. The constitution of 1791 had declared him to be personally unaccountable for his actions, and since the repudiation of the constitution he had not been able to perform any. Whatever the Convention did to him could have no legal foundation, and it was likely to be denounced as either pusillanimous or vindictive.

There could be no question of holding a referendum on the overthrow of the monarchy, since a vote that went the wrong way would mean restoring it. At the same time, the outcome of the fighting had to be legitimized by an appeal to some kind of principle. If the insurrection had been an anticipation of the general will it needed confirmation by the sovereign people as a whole. This raised the question of whether or not the elections had transferred the exercise of popular sovereignty to the Convention. The Girondins, confident of having a majority in the assembly, insisted that it had. The Montagnards, who did not want to rule out the possibility of a subsequent movement in their favour, asserted that nothing could deprive the sovereign people of its ultimate right to revolt. Both sides accepted the sovereignty of the general will and since there was no way of determining what it was, each was convinced of its own rectitude and each believed the other to be prostituting the sacred principle in support of its self-interest. At a less exalted level, both of them had to tackle the problem of finding the most effective way to make the republic secure and to eradicate royalism. The unfortunate Louis now became a political football whose fate depended on the outcome of the struggle for power in the assembly. The Montagnards regarded his death as essential to the survival of the republic, although they had doubts, about the best way to kill him without making a martyr of him. The Girondins were unable to agree on any policy. A few of them agreed with the Montagnards. The majority, whilst accepting the king's guilt, recoiled from putting him to death, for a variety of reasons. Something had to be done and the argument over what it should be offered a fertile ground for ideological ingenuity, political double-talk and hypocrisy.

On 7 November Mailhe, for the *comité de législation*, opened the debate with the argument that Louis had forfeited his inviolability by himself breaking his constitutional oath. The rising of 10 August had been an assertion of national sovereignty, and since the king had been overthrown by the nation he should be judged, not by a court of law, but by the Convention, which was the personification of the nation. If found guilty, his fate should serve as an example to the world. On 13 November Pétion, while rejecting the king's inviolability, demanded a full discussion on whether or not he could legally be tried. He was followed by Morison, another Girondin, who said that the people, although sovereign, had bound themselves by a decision to punish only those who had broken an existing law. Louis was undeniably a traitor, but while the Convention was entitled to abolish the monarchy it had no power to judge a king who was protected by his constitutional privilege.

Saint-Just, who spoke next, began by rejecting the opinions of both Mailhe and Morison. 'What I say is that the king must be judged as an enemy, that it is not so much a matter of judging him as of fighting him.' His proposal rested squarely on the argument that he had worked out in *De la Nature*. Between a king and a people there could be no natural relationship. The very concept of kingship implied the invasion of the social by the political, and any king, by the mere virtue of his office, was guilty of the worst of all crimes. Monarchy was an offence against the law of nature. 'On ne peut régner innocemment.' Since the law of nature was the ultimate criterion of human conduct, the general will itself could not legitimize anything contrary to nature and, whatever the decision of the Convention, any citizen would be entitled to murder Louis, since criminals excluded themselves from the city and their relationship to it was that of foreigners. In terms that must have been more comprehensible to him than to his audience, Saint-Just went on to argue that the proclamation of the republic had meant the restoration of that 'social' order whose world-wide demise he had lamented in *De la nature*. 'We shall have no sort of republic without those distinctions that regulate the natural movement of all parts of the social order.' Louis should therefore be treated as a foreign prisoner of war.

Consistency was never Saint-Just's strong point, and after asserting that there could be no pact between a king and a people he then said the opposite: there *had* been a contract, by which Louis undertook to protect his people. Since he had done the contrary he could not invoke the protection of the law that he himself had violated. This was to return the argument to the political arena, which allowed of endless equivocation about what the contract was and who should determine whether or not it had been broken, but Saint-Just brushed aside all such legal niceties: 'This man must either rule or die.'

When it came to opposing the inconsistencies of others, he was fairly devastating. If the king was indeed inviolable, it had been a crime to overthrow him. To try him would be to put the general will itself in the dock, and his acquittal would make everything that had happened since 10 August illegitimate. For those who were his accusers to constitute themselves as his jury was a denial of the most elementary principles of justice, and whatever legal forms were introduced would be mere refinements of hypocrisy, designed to give an air of judicial respectability to what could be only a political act. He was always better at exposing the flaws in others' arguments than at understanding how tenuous were the premises of his own.

Saint-Just's speech made a deep impression on the Convention. What is most appalling about it to the modern reader is its tranquil inhumanity. Morison, who had argued that the king could not be tried, had nevertheless worked himself up about Louis's 'crimes'. Saint-Just scarcely mentioned them since they were irrelevant to his main argument. He was prepared to immolate Louis – and there was no reason to stop at the king – in the name of a purely personal conception of nature that he assumed the right to impose on everyone else. If the peaceful and harmonious social state was to be inaugurated with an execution, one could guess how it was likely to develop. The people, in the abstract, might be sovereign, but people as actual men and women simply did not matter. They were terms in an equation, to be subtracted as necessary in order to solve it. He was never to lose his belief that the Revolution had inaugurated the ideal 'social' state in which the virtuous were sovereign and governments suspect, but it became increasingly irrelevant as he concentrated more and more on destroying the unregenerate – and they were eventually to comprise the majority of the population. It was logical, in terms of his own political theory, to describe Louis as a foreign prisoner of war, but civilized states did not execute their prisoners of war. The logic did not stop at Louis: anyone who refused to accept the republic, as defined by Saint-Just, was liable to find himself excluded from French society and treated as an outlaw. He ended his speech with the threat of a new insurrection: 'People, if the king is ever absolved, remember that we are no longer worthy of your confidence and you will be able to accuse us of perfidy.' What he had done was to anticipate the mentality of the Terror, with its cold-blooded extermination of opponents in the name of *vertu*, the insurrection of 2 June that destroyed the Girondins, and the decree a year later that all British and Hanoverian prisoners were to be put to death. The Convention was not yet prepared to acquiesce in this nightmare of blood and vengeance, but it was a world in which Saint-Just already felt himself impassively at home.

His speech was interrupted by frequent applause, and the deputies had it printed, although they had no intention of following his advice. Incredibly enough, the Girondin Brissot awarded it is his rather patronizing praise in his newspaper. 'Amongst some exaggerated ideas that betray the youth of the author, there are some brilliant details, a talent that may yet honour France.' What must have given Saint-Just particular pleasure was the fact that he converted Robespierre, the ideological standard-bearer of the Montagnards. When Robespierre joined in the debate, on 3 December, his tone was more emotional and his speech better constructed, but many of his arguments were borrowed from Saint-Just. Not having read *De la nature*, Robespierre was more concerned about the problems of making the republic secure and preventing the king's trial leading to a resurgence of royalism, than with the relationship between 'political' and 'social' states, but on the central issue he repeated what Saint-Just had said. The fate of the king was a political rather than a judicial matter; the deputies were confusing the rules of positive civil law and international relations; the 1791 constitution had been replaced by laws of nature that formed the basis of civil society. Unlike Saint-Just, Robespierre insisted that it was for the Convention to direct public opinion rather than to follow it. It would be the fault of the assembly if the people became depraved. It would take Saint-Just some months to come round to this view of political leadership. Robespierre's conclusion was the same as that of Saint-Just, but he did at least claim to regret the need to kill Louis in order to make the republic secure, which probably looked to the younger man like an unnecessary concession to sentimentality.

Saint-Just intervened in the debate again on 27 December, when he showed that he knew how to put ideology to one side in order to get his audience to do what he wanted. This time he abandoned the cold exposition of principle for more conventional rhetoric. He began by explaining to the deputies that if they had got themselves entangled in a thicket of legal complications this was because they had failed to take his advice. 'I told you, Citizens, that a king was no part of the state . . . and nevertheless you have set yourselves up as a civil court . . . I don't know where this travesty of the most transparent ideas of justice is going to lead you.' After getting this off his chest he developed a conventional political argument that the king's crimes, rather than his royal status, were the reason why he should be found guilty. 'If he is innocent the people are guilty.' A referendum on the nature of his punishment – even before his trial was over everyone took the verdict for granted – would imply the risk of his restoration. This suggested that Saint-Just, like Robespierre, believed that popular sovereignty did not necessarily involve doing what the majority of the population actually wanted. He insinuated that those who disagreed with him were trying to restore Louis to his throne and those who wanted a referendum had perhaps been bought with foreign gold. By his own standards this was fairly conventional stuff: He did not disagree with it, but it was what his audience wanted to hear rather than the way in which he himself actually saw the situation. The Montagnards got their way. Louis was tried by the Convention, found guilty, and executed on 21 January 1793.

In the meantime Saint-Just had distinguished himself by another speech in the Convention that won him Brissot's praise once again. 'He deployed wit, warmth and philosophy and did honour to his talent in defending freedom of trade.' The question at issue was the explosive one of food supplies, threatened by both scarcity and inflation. On 29 November the Paris Commune demanded the introduction of price controls in the interest of the urban consumer. A committee of the assembly recommended the imposition of the traditional measures to guarantee that the markets were supplied and private consumers had priority over wholesalers.

Saint-Just once again began by disagreeing with the committee and claiming to think everything out afresh from the first principles of a republic.[3] Resorting to the old-fashioned controls of the monarchy or exhorting everyone to behave disinterestedly were equally useless. The consequence of the Revolution had been to substitute conditions of anarchy for an economic system that had no doubt been corrupt and oppressive but had at least functioned. In the present confusion and uncertainty everyone naturally consulted what he believed to be his own self-interest. Saint-Just did *not* imply that all the trouble was due to the turpitude of the rich.

Various factors had upset the equilibrium of the French economy. Luxury trade had been virtually annihilated by the Revolution, since many wealthy people had left the country and those who remained were in no mood for conspicuous consumption. Unlike the Rousseauists of the strict observance, Saint-Just did not applaud this as a preservative against vice. 'Someone here has complained about the luxurious life of the yeomen. I am not offering any opinion on whether or not luxury is a good thing in itself, but if we were lucky enough to have yeomen who liked luxuries they would have to put their grain on the market in order to buy them.' Since French trade had been mainly in luxuries it had been crippled by the collapse of the luxury market. Farmers had not been in the habit of buying much but they had liked to accumulate gold, for which they had to sell their food. They were not interested in amassing paper currency and, unlike merchants who had to trade in order to live, they had few needs, could feed themselves and keep their capital in the form of hoarded grain rather than money. It was this, rather than a defective harvest, that was creating scarcity in the towns. What was needed therefore was not to tinker with controls but to create a new economic system in which the extinct luxury trade could somehow or other be replaced by 'the simple correlation of individual needs' and incentives provided that would induce the farmers to bring their

[3] For a discussion of this speech, see C. A. Michalet, 'Economie et politique chez Saint-Just: l'exemple de l'inflation' in *Actes du Colloque Saint-Just* (Paris, 1968).

food to market. What was required was intelligent planning rather than exhortation or coercion. 'You need some luxuries in your republic, or else violent laws directed against the farmer, which would destroy the republic.'

This problem had been compounded by the excessive printing of paper money which had been covered in theory by the sale of Church lands to an equivalent value. This had been a mistake. What should have constituted the balance between goods and currency was not the value of the land itself, since this did not influence food prices, but that of its annual produce. In consequence, the country had been flooded with *assignats* to about thirty times the value of the commodities that were supposed to counterbalance them. Saint-Just might have added that this problem had been accentuated by the facility for buyers to pay for Church lands in annual instalments.

He went on to make some well-informed remarks about the decline in pasturage and the general obsession with cereal production. This had nothing to do with the Revolution. Saint-Just blamed it on the royal edict of 1763 which had facilitated enclosure and the division of common land, on the initiative of the lord of the manor, who was able to help himself to a third of it. The consequent decline in French livestock had affected trade in meat, wool and hides and had also reduced the cereal crop, which was dependent on animal fertiliser.

The decline in the French export trade had led to an unfavourable balance of payments. France was therefore having to pay for indispensable imports in cash, just when the excessive issue of paper currency and the growing reluctance of foreigners to accept it was producing a deterioration in the rate of exchange.

All these problems tended to reinforce each other, and their solution therefore called for a new kind of economic policy that would make the pursuit of private benefit serve the purposes of public need, so as to do away with coercion and make exhortation unnecessary. This was compatible with Saint-Just's conception of the social state, but he now saw 'natural' economic relationships as the product of political action from above. What was needed was to put an end to the emission of paper money, to pay the state's creditors in land or annuities, rather than reimburse them in lump sums, to exploit the occupied territories, which must be made to pay for their 'liberation', and to make all land taxes payable in kind into public granaries. Only when all this had been done would it be legitimate for the republic to insist on freedom of trade, which would then be a natural source of exchange rather than a source of speculation for those with stocks of food or money. This was conditional liberalism, but Brissot was right in seeing the speech as a defence of free trade, in the sense that Saint-Just wanted to base economic relations on consent rather than control. He was not a pure economic liberal since he believed it to be the responsibility of the state to regulate the functioning of the economy, but it should do so in such a way that individuals, in the pursuit of what they saw as their self-interest, would automatically contribute to the harmonious functioning of the system as a whole. There would still be what Adam Smith and others had described as an 'invisible hand', but it was that of the legislator rather than of Providence. Saint-Just made it clear that he was opposed to controls in principle. 'People are asking for a law on food supplies. A positive law on that subject will never be wise.'

He was better at describing what was wrong than at seeing how to put it right. His analysis of French economic problems was acute and realistic. It is a reminder that his exalted opinion of his own talent rested on a substantial foundation. His solutions, as tended to happen, made light of difficulties. One of the main reasons for inflation was the cost of the war. During the next few months France was to extend this to England, Holland and Spain – without any protest from Saint-Just – and to order the levy of 300,000 men for the army. War expenditure on such an unprecedented scale could never be financed by taxation. Saint-Just was continually grumbling about the excessive resort to paper money, but in April 1793 he was to propose that the Convention should vote the liberation of the world. State granaries would take years to organize, when the demand was for immediate action. Former attempts by the monarchy to regulate the grain trade had always generated suspicion that the government was speculating in public misery. If Saint-Just thought that could never happen in a republic he did not know much about peasants, who were not going to make subtle distinctions between Church tithes that had been abolished and new tithes that were all for their own good. Whatever the republic did, the government would be as helpless as the monarchy before it to procure the free circulation of grain in times of scarcity without the use of force.

The deputies once more applauded Saint-Just, voted to print his speech, and did nothing about it. Its historical interest lies in what it tells us about his thinking. His approach to every problem was to look for 'republican laws' that ought to create the kind of harmonious, self-regulating system that he believed to be characteristic of civil society. Everything ought to be based on co-operation rather than coercion. Unlike Robespierre, who saw this as some kind of moral victory of *vertu* over inclination, Saint-Just believed that it would happen spontaneously if society were once set on the right lines. Both were agreed that anyone who aspired to sabotage the New Jerusalem must be destroyed as a public enemy.

Throughout his speech Saint-Just had referred to *laboureurs* – in other words, yeomen farmers – rather than to peasants in general. He was thinking of the minority of relatively well-off men who produced for the market, rather than of the rural community as a whole. In *De la Nature* he had made the ownership of a minimum amount of land a qualification for citizenship, and he was now more concerned with problems of supply than of distribution. Whatever his intentions, he had not found any magic solution to problems that derived from inflation, low productivity and over-population, and were soon to be exacerbated by total war. The gap between his theories and peasant ways of thinking was unbridgeable, and if any attempt was made to put them into practice, the effect of their republican label would be to turn large elements of the rural population against the republic.

If he tried to draw up any sort of balance sheet of his progress, at the end of 1792, Saint-Just could feel pleased with himself. He had arrived in Paris as an unknown youth and he was already respected – by both sides – as one of the outstanding members of the assembly. The Jacobins had put him on their constitutional committee even before his first speech to the club, and they made him president on December 19. The Convention chose him as one of its secretaries at the end of November. His speeches were applauded, printed and praised in the press. Robespierre himself had followed his lead over the king's trial. It all added up to a very promising start.

In February 1793 he received a nasty jolt that followed directly from his speech on the economic situation and was, in a way, an embarrassing tribute to the extent of its influence.[4] A radical movement had developed in Paris amongst sans-culottes, who made no distinction between Girondins and Montagnards but accused both of paying lip-service to a 'people' whose sovereignty they proclaimed in theory and ignored in practice. When a deputation from the Paris Sections was denied a hearing on the 11th it wrote a stiff letter to the president of the assembly which included an oblique reference to Saint-Just: 'You have been told that it is impossible to frame a good law on food supplies . . .' On the following day the deputation was allowed to present a petition for a nation-wide maximum to be imposed on the price of grain. One of its members, Heudelet, made the mistake of claiming to address the assembly 'in the name of all our brothers in the departments'. This provoked a somewhat hysterical storm of abuse from deputies of both factions who scented a challenge to the status of the Convention. A Girondin described the petitioners as vermin, and Marat, supported for the only time in his life by Buzot, demanded their arrest. When the unfortunate Heudelet was at last allowed to speak he explained that when the deputation had come to the Convention that morning, a deputy had advised it to demand that the assembly should drop all other business in order to pass a law on the regulation of food supplies. Ordered to name the man responsible, he said that he understood him to be called Saint-Just.

Saint-Just's version of the incident was naturally rather different. He told his colleagues that a pamphlet published that morning had

[4] The account by A. Mathiez in *La Vie chère* (Paris, 1927), pp. 140–3, differs in some respects from the report in the *Moniteur*.

denounced deputies who 'make fine speeches to the Parisians – and eat well every day. Amongst them is the deputy, Saint-Just.' He had therefore gone to meet the petitioners and asked them if he had lost their confidence. On being assured of the contrary, he had advised them to avoid violence and to request a general law from the assembly. 'If the Convention adjourns your request, I will ask permission to speak and follow the thread of the view that I have already expressed.'

It is difficult to know what to make of this curious little incident, especially since Saint-Just may well have 'rectified' what he actually said to petitioners who were not going to contradict him when he was ensuring their safety as well as his own. If what he said about the pamphlet was true, the Parisians sans-culottes did not exactly regard him as one of their heroes, and another speech along the lines of his previous one would not have done much to make them change their minds. The deputies, unusually united in defending the assembly against what they saw as a challenge to its authority, were in no mood to pick a quarrel with one of their own number. They did not take up the question of what Saint-Just had actually said to the petitioners, and the affair did his reputation no harm. It should at least have warned him that abstract theorizing about food shortages was liable to be misinterpreted by the hungry and the ignorant.

During the first months of 1793 he devoted most of his attention to military matters. After the initial defeats of the previous year, things had gone surprisingly well for the French. The Prussians had been checked at the battle of Valmy on 20 September and had withdrawn across the frontier. On 6 November the defeat of an Austrian army at Jemappes allowed the republicans to occupy the whole of Belgium. This was too good to last. Many of the volunteers who had rushed to the colours to defend the country against invasion, considered that their job was done and returned home. By early 1793 the size of the French army had fallen from just over 400,000 to not much above half that number. The War Minister, Pache, in an attempt to put an end to the peculation of private war contractors, replaced them by an army purchasing commission. Dumouriez, commanding the army in Belgium, complained that the ensuing anarchy had deprived his men of food and equipment. The extension of the war to Spain, England and Holland, opened up a new military frontier along the Pyrenees, hundreds of miles away from the other French armies. With the campaigning season approaching, there was everything to be said for overhauling the French war machine.

On 25 January Sieyès, for the *comité de défense générale*, presented a plan for the reorganization of the War Office. He claimed to have deduced it from *la nature des choses* rather than from precedent. Dividing his subject into munitions, ministerial control and field command, he opted for the most rigorous centralization in every case. There should be one supply department for the whole country, under the exclusive direction of the Minister of War, who should exercise undisputed personal control over the entire war effort. Commanders-in-chief, who might be required to take emergency action to deal with unpredictable crises, had to be entrusted with a kind of 'temporary despotism' that freed them from civilian control.

The trouble with *la nature des choses* was that it meant whatever one wanted it to mean. When Saint-Just opened the discussion on Sieyès's proposals three days later, he disagreed as usual. When it came to deducing policy from first principles, he was a match for anyone, but his principles were rather different. He did agree with Sieyès that, as Saint-Just expressed it more pithily, 'the present order is disorder expressed as law.' As in the case of the economy, a rational but vicious kind of order had been replaced, not by a republican way of doing things, but by anarchy, with no one in control, no clear principles, and waste and fraud everywhere. For Saint-Just is seemed that order took precedence over liberty. 'The principles and the ideas of liberty are no substitute for harmony within the government . . . nothing can take the place of order.' It all depended on what kind of order. Sieyès was right to want to centralize army purchasing, but where the powers of the Ministry of War were concerned, he had not adjusted himself to the ethos of a republic.

Centralization of the kind he advocated might work well

enough under a monarchy but it was inappropriate to the new order. Rather grudgingly, Saint-Just admitted that there *might* be a case for a balance of power between legislature and executive in civil matters, at least in certain cases. The War Office was different: 'If one looks for the main cause of the enslavement of the world it is because the government, amongst all peoples is in control of armed force.' This harked back, as usual, to *De la nature*. Civil society was always at the mercy of the ambitious warlord. Royalism was not merely a matter of being ruled by a king; it meant any kind of regime in which the executive was independent of the legislature. This was especially the case where the armed forces were concerned since war was a special kind of activity that was not part of civil law. The 'civil order' which was regulated by the *magistrat*, was distinct from external relations, which could be safely entrusted only to the sovereign people or its representatives. Sieyès's solution was therefore monarchical in inspiration. In a republic, control of the army should be vested, not in a minister but in the legislature itself, with the War Minister responsible only for the execution of orders given by the assembly. In terms of Saint-Just's political theory, this was perhaps logical. In actual fact the Convention was paralysed by its divisions and suspicions, and to have made it responsible for strategy might have been a recipe for disaster. It was perhaps with this in mind that he concluded his speech with a plea for unity. 'If we do not conquer together we shall die together.' He kept clear of the personal abuse that Girondins and Montagnards loved to heap upon each other, and perhaps felt entitled to remind his audience that the pursuit of individual interests violated the social order. This inclined him towards rather sanctimonious preaching: 'Forget yourselves . . . your own interest commands you to forget your self-interest; you can find you own safety only through public safety.' When speaking of the Convention, he generally said 'you' rather than 'we'. He was the one who showed the way and it was for others to get back on to the right road.

He intervened again on a military subject, this time on 11 February, the day before his encounter with the deputation from the Commune.[5] For the first time he actually spoke in support of one of the assembly's committees. Dubois-Crancé, in the name of the *comité militaire* put forward a plan for what he called the 'nationalization' of the army. The French army was so far short of the target of half a million men adopted by the Convention that the assembly had voted to raise another 300,000 troops. It would be impossible to persuade many people to join the regular army when volunteers enjoyed better terms of service, including the right to elect their officers. Dubois-Crancé therefore proposed to fuse the two services in a single national force, one-third of whose officers were to be promoted by seniority and the remainder by election. This was intended to destroy the particularist esprit de corps of the regulars and, since the volunteers outnumbered them two to one, to infuse the whole integrated army with the republican principles of the latter.

Dubois-Crancé's proposals were very much in line with Saint-Just's own ways of thinking. He stressed the need to combine discipline with the republican spirit; otherwise a powerful regular army would be equally dangerous in victory or defeat. What the committee suggested was the republican way to deal with the problem. 'If you want to establish a republic, take away as little power as possible from the people.' He therefore approved of the general principle of the election of officers but, always on his guard against the intrusion of military power into civil society, he proposed to make an exception in the case of generals, who should be appointed not by the people but by their 'legitimate representatives', the Convention. He realized that what was at issue was the substitution of a new sense of patriotism for what he called 'a false conception of honour and exclusive pride.'[6] This nationalization of honour was destined to have a long and bloody future that was already implicit in Saint-Just's prophetic language. 'One does not make revolutions by halves. It seems to me that you are destined

---

[5] C. Vellay, in his *Oeuvres complètes de Saint-Just*, 2 vols (Paris, 1908), vol. I, pp. 412–16, mistakenly dates this speech 12 February.

[6] See N. Hampson, 'The French Revolution and the Nationalization of Honour' in M. R. D. Foot (ed.), *War and Society: Historical Essays in Honour and Memory of J. R. Western* (London, 1973), pp. 199–212.

to change the face of the governments of Europe. You must not rest until it is free. Its liberty will guarantee yours'. The Brezhnev doctrine has a long pedigree. It was already clear that Saint-Just's conception of liberty meant satisfying the 'real' needs of the people, as defined by its 'legitimate representatives' rather than giving them what they actually wanted. It had a Spartan side to it that might not be to everyone's taste. Since 'the foundation-stone of liberty is pure love for one's *patrie*', Saint-Just objected to the committee's plan to give volunteers an increase in pay if they agreed to serve for more than one campaign, and even looked forwards to a time when all ranks would receive equal pay. 'The only way to create a republic is by frugality and *vertu*.' This was Robespierre's old dilemma: it was habits of frugality and *vertu* that ought to have created the republic, and trying to do things the other way round was liable to prove unpopular.

In order to supervise the raising of the 300,000 new recruits the assembly despatched pairs of deputies into the departments, with powers to requisition men and supplies and to suspend and arrest suspect local authorities. Saint-Just and Deville, a lawyer from Reims whom he had known before the Revolution, were sent to the Aisne and Ardennes, their home territory, although they seem to have confined themselves to a brief tour of the Ardennes.[7] They were shocked by the state of the frontier defences, which they reported to the Minister of War, Beurnonville, who had replaced Pache in February. In marked contrast to Saint-Just's later missions, they made very little use of their extensive powers. Their only known action was to have authorized local authorities to requisition seed corn, in return for payment, from the granaries of *émigrés*. Saint-Just was away from Paris from 9 March until towards the end of the month. He seems to have cut short his mission and returned to the capital in order to report his concern about the condition of the frontier. On 31 March he described the unsatisfactory state of affairs to the Jacobins and denounced Beurnonville as a traitor since he had not replied to Saint-Just's letters of complaint. 'There is not a single good man in the

[7] See J. P. Gross, *Saint-Just, sa politique et ses missions* (Paris, 1976), ch. 2.

government.' For him the legislature was the personification of the sovereign people, and all ministers, even republican ones, were something alien, at best an unfortunate necessity, at worst the men who were trying to impose their own political order on civil society. It was to take him rather a long time to realize that the only way of dealing with this problem was to entrust one of the committees of the assembly with the powers of government.

As spring approached, the tensions within the Convention became uncontrollable. The campaign opened disastrously. The main French army was defeated on 18 March and forced to evacuate Belgium. Its commander, Dumouriez, tried to negotiate an armistice with the Austrians so that he could march on Paris, and when his army refused to follow him, fled to the enemy, leaving his troops leaderless and demoralized. Faced with treason and defeat, the assembly created the institutions that were eventually to provide the machinery for both victory and the Terror: the Committee of Public Safety and the revolutionary tribunal. The deputies, in May, gave the sans-culottes the price controls on grain that had been so indignantly refused in February, but they were incapable of providing the country with effective leadership. Every debate degenerated into an exchange of abuse between Girondins and Montagnards, who were too suspicious of each other to unite in self-defence. Things could not continue in this state, and the way in which the conflict was resolved would determine the political future of Saint-Just.

6

Making a Constitution

When the Convention assembled in September 1792 its essential
purpose was assumed to be the drafting of a new constitution,
since the old one had become obsolete with the overthrow of the
monarchy. One or two decisive votes were carried at once. On 21
September the deputies proclaimed France a republic and voted
that the future constitution would be submitted to a referendum.[1]
They rejected a proposal to hold a referendum on the abolition of
the monarchy. This made good political sense but it exposed a
logical dilemma from which the Convention could never escape.
The people were sovereign but there were some things that their
representatives would not allow them to do and some opinions
that they were not allowed to hold. Robespierre and Saint-Just
tried to get out of this predicament by arguing that those who
were not republicans were not entitled to a voice in the republic.
This, however, raised the question of how and by whom
republicanism was to be defined. If it was permissible for the
assembly or the revolutionary government to outlaw opponents
as royalists, this opened up a nightmarish prospect of an ever-

[1] For the political background to this chapter, see A. Aulard, *Histoire politique de la
révolution française* (Paris, 1901), Part II, ch. 4.

diminishing body of citizens, which might eventually exclude most of the people who actually lived in France. For the moment, the deputies had some justification for assuming that they really did represent the will of the majority; they had, after all, just been elected by a democratic vote, even if the low poll had been due to the abstention of those who did not think it safe to reveal themselves as monarchists.

The Convention soon became a battleground between the two rival factions. The Girondins, smarting from the failure of their leading men to win any of the Paris seats, tried unsuccessfully to have Robespierre, Danton and Marat expelled as would-be dictators. The majority of the deputies remained aloof from both sides, but as the Girondins gradually discredited themselves by their vendetta against Paris and their failure to unseat the leading Montagnards, the latter picked up more and more support.[2] Debates degenerated into noisy slanging matches and any proposal by one side was automatically denounced by the other.

Military victories at the end of the campaigning season of 1792 at first allowed the deputies to quarrel with each other, without doing much harm to anyone except the king. The disasters of the spring of 1793 put an end to all that. A massive revolt broke out in the conservative west, and the main French army was defeated by the Austrians in Belgium. When Dumouriez failed to persuade his men to march on Paris, that averted the worst, but France was soon to be invaded and, with a long campaigning season ahead, the military situation was more dangerous than that of August 1792, which had provoked the revolt that overthrew the monarchy. Instead of persuading the deputies to sink their differences in self-defence, the crisis exacerbated their mutual suspicion and hatred. Each side maintained that Dumouriez had been secretly concerting policy with the other. It was in this poisoned atmosphere, with the survival of the republic looking increasingly problematical, that the Convention began to debate the constitution.

On 15 February 1793 Condorcet presented a draft in the name of the constitutional committee. Since this was eventually rejected

---

[2] See Alison Patrick, *The Men of the First French Republic* (Baltimore, 1972).

and the Montagnard constitution that was finally voted was never actually implemented, the reader may be spared a detailed examination of all the proposals and counter-proposals. The objectives of all of the deputies were very similar. They wanted a democratic republic in which popular sovereignty would be more than the polite fiction embodied in the 1791 constitution. Subject to the final arbitration of the 'people', effective power should be concentrated in a single elected assembly. There would have to be some kind of executive authority, also responsible to the 'people', but it must be subordinated to the assembly. 'Minister' was still something of a dirty word, with its connotations of 'ministerial despotism' and royal absolutism from the years before 1789. If one disregarded the political infighting, the disagreements over the constitution concerned means rather than ends.

On 16 February the Convention voted to print at the public expense any deputy's alternative to Condorcet's draft. The original committee had resigned after presenting its proposals, and a new one was elected to report on the suggestions that came pouring in. One or two advocated votes for women, which the committee considered to be unwise, 'at least for a few years' until better provision had been made for women's education.[3] In the event, French women had to wait until 1945. The assembly then decided to get down to the serious discussion of the various proposals, setting aside three days a week for debates on the constitution. These discussions lasted from mid-April to the end of May, without making much headway. On 24 April Saint-Just joined in with proposals of his own, prefaced by a long statement of principles. Although he criticized Condorcet's draft, he did so without acrimony, in marked contrast to Robespierre, who was forever accusing his opponents of sacrificing the public good to party advantage. 'In the constitution offered to you [by Condorcet], without impugning its merits, which I am incapable of flattering or abusing, there are perhaps more precepts than laws, more powers than harmony, more agitation than democracy.'[4]

[3] Aulard, *Histoire politique*, p. 289.
[4] For Saint-Just's speech, see C. Vellay, *Oeuvres complètes de Saint-Just*, 2 vols (Paris, 1908), vol. 1, pp. 418–54.

His own draft opened with the proposition that in a republic with a representative constitution, what was represented was people rather than territory. This served two purposes. It allowed him to disregard inconvenient Frenchmen, such as monarchists, and it was a safeguard against any assertion of sovereignty by the inhabitants of a particular region. The French people constituted a single society and the general will was the communal will of that society as a whole, and not the sum of its constituent parts. This will was expressed through deputies who were the elected representatives of the sovereign people. All the agents of the administration, from ministers downwards, were merely appointed to implement what had been decided in the people's name.

Much of what Saint-Just proposed, such as universal male suffrage, equal eligibility for employment, and the right of petition, was common to most of the draft proposals and does not tell us much about his own particular views. He was in favour of public voting, when some people favoured a secret ballot, but he did not give his reasons. He advocated a relatively small assembly of 341 members, sitting for two years, when Condorcet had thought in terms of a larger one, elected annually. Where Saint-Just was original was in his proposals for its election. True to his belief that what was represented was the people *en masse*, he proposed that on polling day each citizen should cast his vote in favour of one candidate. When the votes of everyone in the country had been counted the 341 men with the most votes would be declared elected. Saint-Just was never much concerned with the logistics of anything and he did not stop to consider how long it would take to collect, transmit and count several million votes, distributed amongst several thousand candidates. All that concerned him was the accurate representation of the general will. The result of his electoral system would have been to eliminate all local candidates and to create a political class of former deputies, journalists and men with a national reputation, which was scarcely what he intended. It was likely to favour the Girondins rather than the Montagnards. Equally unrealistic was his proposed ban on the formation of specialist committees within the assembly, which may have reflected a Rousseauist suspicion of intermediate bodies as breeding grounds for faction.

In harmony with what he had said earlier in the year about the War Office, he wanted the assembly to be responsible for the selection and dismissal of generals and admirals, and for the impeachment of ministers. He believed that any corporate governing body was potentially despotic. He therefore proposed that each of France's eighty-five departments should elect one man to an executive council. This council would be collectively responsible for administering the country and enforcing the laws voted by the assembly but it would not control any government departments. These were to be handed over to nine ministers, who were never to concert policy together and would be, in effect, heads of civil service departments. This would have entrusted the government of the country to a kind of Upper House, with collective responsibility but no corporate identity and selected in a way that would emphasize regional diversity. It might guard against the threat of an over-mighty executive but it seemed unlikely to do much else.

Saint-Just was no parliamentary draftsman and his account of the division of power between council and assembly was somewhat vague. He seemed to imply that normal legislation was the exclusive business of the assembly. The council, however, could demand a referendum on any bill that appeared to contravene the declaration of the rights of man. If the assembly's bill was approved by a majority of the population, or if most of the constituencies favoured some change in the constitution, a special convention would be elected for this purpose.

The second part of his proposed constitution set out the basis of a new legal system. This was largely technical in nature, but one curious clause anticipated the way in which his thinking was to evolve in the coming year. Maintenance of public order was to be entrusted to 'elders accredited by their virtues', who were to wear tricolore scarves and white plumes. 'When they appear in their insignia the people are silent and arrest anyone who provokes a disturbance.' This had more to do with a romanticized vision of Athens and Sparta than with eighteenth-century France, and one cannot help wondering how it would have worked on 14 July 1789. A rather more sinister clause excluded traitors from the general ban on retroactive legislation. In other words, one could be arraigned for an action that had been legal at the time but was subsequently judged to be treasonable. This would have allowed Saint-Just himself to be prosecuted for his defence of constitutional monarchy in 1791. A final chapter saw him at his most naïve and hyperbolical. The Republic 'will conclude no treaties that do not have peace and the welfare of the nations as their object. The French people votes the liberty of the world.'

The less extravagant parts of Saint-Just's draft were similar to many of the proposals that were coming from other deputies and his suggested constitution does not seem to have attracted any particular attention. Of much more interest in tracing the development of his ideas is the speech that introduced it. This looked both backwards and forwards. His basic attitude towards politics was the one that he had tried to work out in *De la Nature*. The essential objectives of a republican government must be to move society in the direction of that 'social state' in which coercion had no part to play. The problem was how to get there, starting from a flawed society in which men had been corrupted, or at least persuaded to believe that they were naturally wicked. Where the policies appropriate to this transitional state were concerned, he was beginning to move away from the position he had previously adopted, in the direction of the 'vigorous methods' of Rousseau that he had formerly condemned.

For him, as for Robespierre, the Revolution had become *the* turning-point in the history of the human race. 'Europe will demand peace as soon as you provide France with a constitution. On that day divisions will cease. Faction will be overwhelmed and yield beneath the yoke of liberty; citizens will return to their workshops and their labours; peace, reigning over the republic, will make the monarchs tremble.' This seemed to offer the Girondins a place in the New Jerusalem, even if it held out the prospect of rather less exciting times for the 'citizens' than for people like himself. What was needed, in peace or war, was 'vigorous government'. 'Peace and plenty, public virtue, victory, everything depends on the vigour of the laws; outside the laws everything is sterile and dead.' He had travelled a long way since he wrote that laws were responsible for crime since they perpetuated a 'political state' that was founded on force. The French people should not be wearied by being too heavily involved in public affairs. They must be ruled without weakness and without constraint. Whatever that meant, it was easier said than done but it was already clear that Saint-Just was thinking of the rulers as 'we' and of the French people as 'them'.

He then suddenly reverted to the ideas of his more anarchic days. 'Nothing is ordered except that which moves itself and obeys its own harmony; the only role of force is to exclude what is alien to that harmony . . . Laws merely repel evil; innocence and virtue walk in independence in the world.' This led him to reminisce about his former theorizing, in terms that must have mystified his colleagues, who were not familiar with the argument of *De la nature*. 'I though that the social order was inherent in the nature of things . . . that man was born for peace and freedom and was made wretched and corrupt only by the invidious laws of domination. I imagined that if one gave man laws appropriate to his nature and his heart he would no longer be wretched and corrupt.' The fact that he put this in the past tense need not mean that he no longer believed it.

Such laws would lead men to identify justice with self-interest, which suggested some lowering of the moral tone. He then treated his colleagues to a paraphrase of *De la nature* on the social and political states, the former applying within a society and the latter regulating its relationship towards other societies. The present unsatisfactory state of affairs was due to the machinations of rulers who had managed to deceive their docile subjects into believing that the ferocity of subjects could be restrained only by repressive laws. Perhaps remembering what he had been saying a few minutes before about everything depending on the vigour of the laws, he then pulled himself up. 'I will not deny the law the force it needs, taking man as he is now . . . One must not think in terms of the politics of natural man and that is not my intention.

Despite this caveat, which must have made more sense to

himself than to his audience, he was off back to *De la nature*, with a rather crisper version of how the Franks and Germans had declined from the social to the political state. Switching abruptly to the present, he then said that if France was to escape the fate of Sparta, the essential thing was to produce a constitution that would be proof against the usurpation of power. This brought him round on a Rousseauist tack. Success or failure would depend, not on circumstances or the character of the people, but on the wisdom of the 'legislator'. 'It is useless for him to be weak; it is for him to will the good and to perpetuate it; it is for him to turn men into what he wants them to be.' (Rousseau had said 'into what he needs them to be'.) Society was inert until animated, for better or worse, by laws that engendered either virtues or crimes. Circumstances did impose a measure of restraint on what was possible: one had to take the French people as they were, respecting their weaknesses, and make laws to fit the people since it was not practicable to do things the other way round. He had picked that up from Montesquieu and it scarcely fitted the rest of his argument. Despite the need to tread cautiously, popular sovereignty did not mean giving people what they said they wanted, but what they would have wanted if they had known what was good for them.

Leaving his audience, one suspects, in even more confusion than himself, he then started off in pursuit of a new hare. All legislation was a matter of precepts or of laws. Precepts on their own were ineffectual unless there was some sanction behind them. This sounded suspiciously like the evil ideology of the 'political state'. There had been plenty of virtuous principles under the monarchy but they had been powerless to affect men's hearts. This sent him off in yet another direction. 'The French monarchy perished because the rich imparted their distaste for work to the poor.' He could never resist the sparkling aphorism, even if it was nonsense. With a sudden touch of Samuel Smiles, he identified the health of a state with the amount of productive activity that went on inside it. A case could have been made out for this – but not one that would have been appreciated in Sparta, where the work was done by helots.

Saint-Just then came down to earth with a practical discussion of Condorcet's proposal, which he suspected would pave the way for the usurpation of power by the executive. According to Condorcet's draft, ministers were to be elected nationally and deputies locally. The former would therefore have a better claim to embody the general will of the people as a whole. Sitting as a cabinet, they could concert policies and enforce them by means of the government departments that they controlled. The result would be to create, within a generation, a patriciate in which power was monopolized by a few families. Had he been a man like Robespierre, he would have insinuated that this was Condorcet's secret intention, but he kept his own criticism free from personalities.

Somehow or other he then found himself expounding the nature of the general will, which he defined as 'the majority of particular wills, individually communicated, without any external influence'. This, of course, corresponded to Rousseau's 'will of all', which Rousseau specifically distinguished from the general will. The latter was what was actually good for a society, whether or not its members appreciated the fact, but Rousseau was both ambiguous and contradictory, and there were times when he too located the general will within the majority. This was much more than a technical quibble. If the general will was what was best for society, it was what everyone ought to have wanted, and morally incumbent even on those who, perversely or from ignorance, had voted for something else. Forcing them to subscribe to it, as Rousseau had said, was merely forcing them to be free, since it was what their better natures 'really' wanted. Saint-Just and the Montagnards in general were inclined to assume that any vote of the majority embodied the moral sanction of the general will. It was not merely a verdict that a democrat had to accept until he could rally enough support to get it reversed, but a pronouncement about the real interest of society that he was not free to oppose and ought, indeed, to prefer to his own subjective judgement. For the time being Saint-Just had no need to explore these dangerous implications. What he actually did was to accuse the constitutional committee of thinking of the general will in purely intellectual terms, unlike Rousseau who 'wrote from his heart and wanted to bestow on the world all the good that he could only express in words'. This was a good deal warmer than the tone in which Saint-Just had formerly written about him.

Rather unfortunately, he invoked the example of an imaginary sultan who might say to his people, 'If one of you offends my will to make you free, I will have him put to death.' This seemed to Saint-Just to be self-evidently absurd but it was not a bad anticipation of the way in which his own thinking was to evolve within less than a year.

Towards the end of his introduction to the constitution he fell back on the kind of conventional platitudes that made nonsense of his previous argument. 'There are few men without a secret inclination towards wealth . . . few men pursue the general good for its own sake.' If this was actually the case, and not a myth that 'tyrants' had foisted on their credulous subjects, then the will of a corrupt majority would represent nothing more than their calculation of their self-interest. As such, it could have no moral authority over the virtuous minority. If men were 'naturally' good there were only two ways of explaining their actual behaviour. Either they had been mystified by their rulers into believing themselves corrupt, in which case all that one had to do was to reveal to them the truth about their real natures; alternatively, if they had actually been perverted by the evil influence of 'political society', the process could presumably be reversed. In the latter case they would not be likely to respond very enthusiastically to a vigorous course of moral regeneration and the practice of virtue and frugality. If people could indeed be redeemed by reversing the social pressures that had corrupted them, or led them to believe themselves corrupted, this would have to be done by the minority that had somehow or other managed to escape contamination. Saint-Just was confident that he himself was one of the elect, but he had not yet worked out the implications of being a member of the moral minority. Convinced that his own policies were the only ones that would lead to the redemption of society, he would be virtually bound to regard opposition as the work of evil men who were trying to perpetuate an unjust society for their own advantage. Society therefore consisted of three elements: the saints, the misled and the misleaders. If the misled were ever to be brought to recognize their inherent virtue – and strengthened against the forces to which they had succumbed in the past – the saints would have to eradicate the misleaders, who were entitled to no mercy since they were well aware of what they were doing. From Saint-Just's point of view, Louis XVI had been executed for the crime of being a king: 'one cannot reign innocently.' This had excluded him from the community of Frenchmen. Anyone who tried consciously to subvert the work of regeneration would be even more culpable since he would have chosen to wage war against the society of which he was a natural member. For the moment, Saint-Just was content to point out what he saw as the way towards the creation of a 'natural' society. If he were to find himself in a position of authority and French society failed to regenerate itself under the beneficent sway of a government that thought only of the general good, he would find it impossible to resist the temptation to destroy those who were subverting the redemptive process.

He intervened twice more when the Convention began the laborious business of arguing out the constitution, clause by clause. On 15 May he tried once again to convince his colleagues that, in a republic, what was represented was people rather than territory. Although a good many were inclined to see themselves as Spartans or Romans, his description of the French people as split into eight-five tribes', one for each department, must have seemed to them to be carrying antiquarianism rather far. His objective, however, was not merely to put Frenchmen into metaphorical togas. He had good political reasons for locating administration in geographical areas and defining representation in terms of people. The first of these concerned his suspicions of the executive, which were shared by most of the deputies. He repeated his argument that if the ministers were chosen by a national vote whilst deputies represented only their constituencies, the government would come to be seen, and would see itself, as the voice of the country as a whole, which would allow it to play off local interests against each other and to claim more and more authority as the personification of the general will. In the second place, if sovereignty rested on a territorial basis, there would be nothing to prevent sections of the republic from seceding. In this context he evoked the example of the Vendée, which considered itself to be in revolt against the republic and, in a rare reference to the United States, predicted the dissolution of the federal union. If, however, electoral divisions were no more than fragments of an indissoluble sovereign people, they could exist only as fractions of an indivisible whole. Even where administration, rather than representation, was concerned, he wanted to divide each of the departments into three, to discourage local particularism. He commented, in passing, that the 1791 constitution, which he himself had once praised so enthusiastically, had been *contre nature*. In other words, republican ideology had been promoted from being a particular political option, to the status of the only legitimate method of government for any state.

His second speech, on 24 May, had a more immediately political objective. Since their failure to win any of the Paris seats in the Convention, the Girondins had tried to present themselves as the spokesmen of the country as a whole and to resist what they denounced as a usurpation of power by Paris and its Commune. On 22 May one of them proposed that towns with a population of more than 50,000 should be divided for administrative purposes, and Buzot, Saint-Just's old adversary, specifically attacked the excessive influence of Paris. In his Blérancourt days Saint-Just might have sympathized with this point of view, but he had shifted his ground since his election to the Convention. He began his speech by making the general point that a municipality was an administrative rather than a political unit. It might contain several constituencies for voting purposes but it was a single entity where the regulation of the affairs of the local community was concerned. This led him on the defence of the role of Paris in the Revolution. 'This population constitutes no danger to liberty . . . Anarchy does not reside in the people, but in love of power or jealousy of those in authority.' This aligned him with the Montagnards in the party battle, but he still abstained from personalities and polemics. If his praise of Paris was not merely tactical it constituted another change of perspective. In the *Esprit de la révolution* he had dismissed the events of July 1789 as a slave revolt; when he now spoke of Paris he evoked the 'blood of its martyrs'.

However little his colleagues may have understood his fundamental political ideas, they seem to have appreciated his contribution to the debate. On 30 May he was one of the five deputies added to the recently created Committee of Public Safety for the specific purpose of preparing yet another draft text of the new constitution. That committee was was still a long way from constituting a *de facto* revolutionary government, but it was already the most important of the assembly's committees, and Saint-Just was moving steadily towards a position of political power.

All through the spring of 1793 radical agitators in Paris had been demanding the arrest of the leading Girondins. Robespierre and the Montagnards tried to restrain them, whether from constitutional scruple, because they feared the consequences of an unsuccessful insurrection, or because they were apprehensive about becoming the prisoners of a movement that was not under their control. An attempted insurrection on 10 March fizzled out when it failed to win the support of either the Jacobin Club or the Paris Commune. Matters were precipitated when, on 18 May, the Convention set up a Commission of Twelve to investigate the reports that another insurrection was being planned. The Commission set to work with a will, arresting leading radicals, including Hébert, the editor of the popular newspaper, the *Père Duchesne*, who was also the deputy *procureur* of the Paris Commune. This may have driven the Montagnards to the conclusion that if they allowed things to take their course they risked finding that the destruction of the Parisian extremists had left them exposed to their Girondin enemies.

What happened next has never been explained very satisfactorily.[5] A radical insurrection on 31 May seems to have disconcerted both the Montagnards and the Paris Commune. The latter was so

---

[5] The most interesting account of these events is still that in D. Guérin, *La Lutte des classes sous la Première République*, 2 vols (Paris, 1946), vol. I, ch. 2. Morris Slavin, *The Making of an Insurrection* (Cambridge, Mass., 1986) provides the fullest description of the course of events.

concerned to keep things under its own control that it applied the brakes too effectively, with the result that the assembly was not sufficiently frightened to agree to a purge of the Girondins. By 2 June the Commune had succeeded in taking charge of the movement. It surrounded the Convention with its National Guards and intimidated the deputies into voting to put a couple of dozen leading Girondins under house arrest. The immediate consequence of this was to transfer control over the Convention to the Montagnards. There is no evidence of what Saint-Just thought about it all. The immediate concern of the Montagnards was to secure general endorsement for what their opponents insisted had been an illegitimate purge of the assembly by Parisian violence. The best way to effect this was by the speedy adoption of a democratic constitution that would disprove the accusation that they were aspiring to some sort of a dictatorship. This was the task of the five deputies who had been added to the Committee of Public Safety just before the insurrection. Saint-Just claimed afterwards that the new constitution was essentially his own work. It was presented to the assembly by Hérault de Séchelles – another of the five – but the text owed a good deal to Saint-Just's influence. Its chapter headings were similar to those in his own draft and Hérault quite often borrowed Saint-Just's words.

There was, in any case, general agreement on the broad lines of the constitution, which must be democratic and unicameral, with all major legislation approved by referendum and the executive subordinated to the legislature. The committee endorsed Saint-Just's view that people were represented and areas administered, although it insisted on preserving the departments, which he had wanted to abolish as administrative units. It followed his lead in providing for the direct election of representatives, but not of administrative officials, although it rejected his impracticable plan for a single national constituency in favour of local elections. The final text allotted one deputy to each 40,000 voters, which would have produced an assembly about twice the size of that envisaged by Saint-Just. It contained no mention of his ban on specialist committees, and his proposal that any commune could, at any time, demand an explanation of his conduct from any deputy was also dropped. Nothing was said about Saint-Just's provision for the nomination and dismissal of generals and admirals by the legislature.

Where the executive was concerned, Hérault followed the general tenor of Saint-Just's thinking, modifying it in the interests of practicality. He accepted the idea of a collegiate council to oversee all government departments. The former ministers were to be replaced by civil servants, heads of separate departments who were not allowed to concert policy with each other. Where Saint-Just had opted for a frankly federal council of eighty-five members, each chosen by a particular department, Hérault provided for the legislature to select twenty-four men from the departmental nominees. This would have made for more cohesion and it would also have ensured the subordination of the executive to the legislature.

Both men favoured the right of the electorate to demand a referendum on important legislation and to propose the election of conventions for the revision of the constitution itself. In the final section, Hérault was much more cautious than Saint-Just. He dropped the clause about the French people voting the liberty of the world and added a pledge that France would never interfere in the government of other nations. This made a pacific foreign policy possible and, with a constitution as decentralized as this, it looked as though France would need one.

The new draft was completed within ten days, approved by the whole Committee of Public Safety and presented to the Convention on 10 June. It was finally voted after a fortnight's debate. If one recalls that it had taken two years to produce the constitution of 1791, it is impossible not to ask oneself if the new version was more than an exercise in public relations. That would probably be too cynical a view. The Convention had to hurry if it was to neutralize the effects of the coup d'état of 2 June and convince the country of its democratic good faith. Condorcet's original draft, which had not been influenced by tactical considerations of this kind, had also carried decentralization and popular consultation to equally impracticable extremes. The Montagnard constitution did represent a kind of republican dream of the way in which a free people would regulate its affairs in an ideal world. It was the events of the summer of 1793 that turned it into an extravagant irrelevance.

On 26 June the Convention voted to submit the constitution to a popular referendum and to dissolve itself as soon as the text had been approved. It was duly ratified by 1,801,918 votes to 11,610. One has to remember that royalists were unlikely to draw attention to themselves by public opposition, although one of France's 40,000 communes apparently did ask for the return of the monarchy![6] Almost all of those who voted had something to hope for from acceptance of the constitution. For the Montagnards it meant the legitimization of the coup d'état; it gave the Girondins the hope of returning to power by mobilizing their support in the provinces. It did not threaten anyone, and if it seemed too democratic to work, there was no alternative on offer.

The constitution was proclaimed on 10 August but its implementation soon raised problems. On the following day Robespierre persuaded the Jacobins that the military situation was too critical to permit of a general election. On the 28th Barère, in the name of the Committee of Public Safety, told the deputies that domestic opposition to the revolution was too dangerous for the 'simple execution of the constitutional laws'. There, for the moment, the matter rested.

[6] Aulard, *Histoire politique*, p. 310.

7

A Member of the Government

The insurrection that began on 31 May 1793 eventually came to be regarded, at least by the Montagnards, as the third turning-point in the onward march of the Revolution, a worthy sequel to the taking of the Bastille on 14 July 1789 and the overthrow of the monarchy in August 1792. Once again Paris had anticipated the sovereign will of the nation and earned the gratitude of all right-minded Frenchmen. To have any reservations about that glorious event was to confess oneself a crypto-royalist.

That was not how it appeared at the time. On 2 June, when the assembly had been surrounded, all the deputies except for a handful of Montagnards, led by their president, Hérault de Séchelles, had gone in solemn procession to break out of the encirclement, and been repulsed by the National Guards under the command of Hanriot. They bitterly resented this humiliation at the hands of the troops of the Paris Commune. The abbé Grégoire, as staunch a Montagnard as anyone, complained on 2 June that the assembly had been insulted. According to Garat, the Minister of the Interior, when the Girondins were arrested, 'consternation and indignation were the sentiments of almost all those in the Committee of Public Safety and the executive council.'[1] When on 6 June Barère, in the name of the committee, delivered what was supposed to be a report on the behaviour of the Girondins, it took the form of an attack on the Commune in the name of the nation. He demanded the replacement of Hanriot and denounced the Commune's interception of newspapers destined for the provinces. The Committee of Public Safety even offered to send its members to the disaffected south as hostages. Danton supported this, and Robespierre's ally, Couthon, offered to go to Bordeaux. On 11 June one deputy proposed the readmission to the assembly of all the arrested Girondins, and two days later another one called for Hanriot's arrest.

If the Girondins had played their cards more skilfully they might have reversed the situation. They still had plenty of supporters in the assembly. Even the more radical Montagnards were determined to put the Paris Commune in its place, and the uncommitted majority of the deputies would have followed a constructive lead. But the Girondins were never very good at tactics. With understandable, if misguided, indignation, some of the arrested deputies demanded an immediate report on their conduct or wrote to denounce the Committee of Public Safety. More disastrously, a score of them escaped from Paris and tried to organize a provincial revolt against the capital. From their point of view, the representatives of the nation had been the victims of an armed coup by the city responsible for the prison massacres of September 1792 that was determined to impose its will on the rest of the country. Their reaction was understandable but unwise. France was faced by a desperate military situation, and there was not much point in rescuing the Convention from Paris if this provoked a civil war, and the Revolution itself was destroyed by foreign armies. The deputies who continued to sit in the assembly, however resentful of the behaviour of the Commune, in a sense endorsed its action by continuing to legislate in the absence of their colleagues. Inevitably, they came to see the provincial revolt as a challenge to their own authority.

Gradually the pendulum swung, and throughout June and July

---

[1] D. J. Garat, *Mémoires* (Paris, 1862), p. 231.

the Convention, reassured by the shrewd docility of the Commune and out of patience with those who seemed to be putting their own interests before those of the nation, lost patience with the fugitives, who compromised what was left of the Girondin cause. On 13 June the deputies voted to put Buzot on trial for trying to raise Normandy, and four days later they charged Barbaroux, with doing the same in Marseille. Brissot was not involved in these insurrectionary plans. He was trying to escape to Switzerland when he was arrested at Moulins, but the assembly on 22 June voted to try him as well.

The Committee of Public Safety, under moderate Montagnard leadership, seemed reluctant to act against the Girondins. It had been in its name that Barère had denounced the Commune. When reports of the provincial revolts were referred to it, it took no action. On 13 June it merely suggested replacing deputies who were absent without leave, and a little later persuaded the assembly to expel deputies who refused to return to Paris when summoned. In the meantime it was preparing a second report on the Girondins. On 16 June this was entrusted to Cambon and Saint-Just, but Cambon withdrew a few days later.

If one is to understand what to make of Saint-Just's report, it must be seen in its political context. Most historians, impressed by its contrast with the speeches of proscription that he was to make in the following year, have expressed surprise at his 'moderation', without asking themselves how far he was given a free hand. Although nothing is known for certain, the report seems to have provoked a good deal of controversy in the committee. On 25 June it was said to be ready but when, on the next day, a deputy demanded that it be produced, Saint-Just snapped him into silence. He had already read it to his colleagues on the 24th, but they do not seem to have been satisfied with it. Couthon wrote to his constituents two days later that the committee hoped to approve the report that day. On 1 July Barère promised the assembly that it would be delivered the next day, but it was not until the 8th that Saint-Just actually read it to the assembly. What all this means it is impossible to say, but there were clearly disagreements, and Saint-Just, as a newcomer to the committee, was in no position to impose his own views. At one point in his speech his dissatisfaction with his brief almost came out into the open. He twice explained that no deputy was going to be prosecuted for his opinions, but only for his actions.

> One could say that the speeches of a representative *are* actions
> . . . Was there anything privileged about the opinion that
> condemned Socrates and made him drink hemlock? Is there
> anything privileged about the opinion that is responsible for
> the destruction of a people? However that may be, liberty
> will not be terrible towards those it has disarmed, who have
> submitted themselves to the law.

To a man like Saint-Just, opinions were almost more important than the actions that were bound to follow from them. To wait for the actions and then punish them was to behave like a policeman. The job of the legislator was so to influence opinion that the right consequences must follow. It is reasonable to conjecture that the final proposals, about who was to be outlawed, who tried and who acquitted, represented the views of the committee as a whole, whilst the elaboration of the charges was left to Saint-Just.

His problem was an unenviable one since he was not free to present the situation in its true light. Girondins and Montagnards had shared much the same political principles, even if tactics had eventually drived the former to appeal to the provinces in the name of law and order and forced the latter into an informal alliance with the Parisian sans-culottes. Their rivalry had paralysed the Convention, made effective government impossible and endangered the survival of the republic. The Montagnards had therefore reluctantly acquiesced in the forcible purge of the assembly. As one of them put it, 'The Convention was constrained into saving the republic.' This was a case of the end justifying what they knew to be illegitimate means. Most of them wanted merely to oblige their opponents to keep quiet, but the determination of most of the Girondin leaders to answer the Parisian coup with a national counter-coup made some kind of repressive action inevitable. This might be sufficient to justify the action of the

Montagnards in the eyes of historians, but it was not good enough for deputies who liked to believe that all their actions were governed by principle, or for Saint-Just himself, for whom every political decision was a choice between absolutes of right and wrong.

However moderate his – perhaps reluctant – conclusions, the shape of his argument anticipated his philippics of the following years.[2] Everything that had happened was the result of a Girondin plot. 'The conspiracy about which I have just spoken is exposed at last; it is not for me to confound the men; they are confounded already. It is not for me to tear the bloody truth out of their hearts by oratory. I have merely to give you a simple account of the recognized facts.' However dreadful the plot had been, with any luck it was the last. 'I have described the conspiracy. May fate decree that we have seen the final storms of liberty! Free men are born for justice; there is little to be gained from troubling the world. Justice consists in repressing those who do so.'

Most of the speech was an extraordinary mixture of fact, rumour and insinuation. From time to time he touched on the real situation. 'They drove you to repress them by the violence into which they threw you. You recognized the danger to the country and the impossibility of legislating if they were tolerated any longer.' 'You could not legislate with them and you were not allowed to legislate without them.' Speaking of the Girondins' attacks on the Commune in the previous summer and their exploitation of the September massacres, he said with some justification, 'One would have thought it was a matter, not of founding a republic, but of penalizing all those who had destroyed the monarchy.'

Those who, in time of revolution, want to stablize a provisional and anarchic government are surreptitiously preparing the return of tyranny. Since this provisional government can maintain itself only by the repression of the

---

[2] For the text see C. Vellay, *Oeuvres complètes de Saint-Just*, 2 vols (Paris, 1908), vol. II, pp. 1–31.

people and not by harmony, the social body is eventually subjected. Since there is no pattern of stable government on a basis of law, everything changes and degenerates, there is no longer a public interest and at last the need for peace drives men to put up with slavery.

That was acutely observed. It had been true of the Girondins and it was to be equally true of the Montagnards a year later.

That was not enough, however, to legitimize the forcible purge of an assembly that ought to have been able to look after itself. What was needed was something more dramatic. The real struggle had been nothing less than a conflict between right and wrong. 'Look at the history of France during the past year. All the vices sought out each other and joined forces. The poor man remained alone, disfigured by his indigence and his virtue.' There was more to this than the kind of rhetorical flourish that he could never resist. He was actually arguing, and he perhaps believed, that the Girondins were the embodiment of 'all the vices' – and therefore the natural leaders of the rich and the royalists. Of course they could not have been expected to advertise the fact. 'Since disguise and hypocrisy are the foundation of conspiracy, one must be very suspicious of the appearances behind which conspirators generally know how to conceal themselves.' Saint-Just, in other words, was privy to the secret intentions of men whose public professions did not admit of serious criticism.

Throughout his speech he referred to the Montagnards as 'the republican party'. Anyone who opposed them was therefore *ipso facto* an enemy of the republic. Naturally the proof that the Girondins had always been royalists had to be somewhat circumstantial since they had made a parade of their republicanism. Brissot was charged with supporting the monarchy on the eve of the insurrection of 10 August. He had, in fact, attacked those who wanted to risk an insurrection in Paris, but over the previous year or two he had been more critical of the monarchy than the author of the *Esprit de la révolution*. This, of course, merely indicated the depth of his deviousness. The secret intention of the Girondins was to preserve the monarchy whilst changing the dynasty, perhaps in favour of the duc d'Orléans. When Buzot had proposed to deport all the Bourbons (which included Orléans), his real intention had been to enlist the sympathy of the public on their behalf by appearing to persecute them. Against 'evidence' of this nature it was difficult to offer any kind of defence. Dumouriez, when he fled to the Austrians, had taken Orléans's son with him. 'How can one imagine that Brissot and the rest, who had made an agreement with Dumouriez, did not have the same objective when they followed the same line of conduct?' When accused of complicity with Dumouriez, the Girondins had laughed. 'Dissimulation smiles; innocence is distressed.' One of Saint-Just's weaknesses was his addiction to a policy of over-kill. After devoting much of his speech to the Girondins' plans to change the dynasty, it was rather inconsequential of him to try to involve them in another alleged plot to put the son of Louis XVI on the throne, with Marie Antoinette as regent.

Various other crimes were thrown in for good measure. Buzot and Gorsas were associating themselves with the anti-republican rebels in the Vendée. Barbaroux had tried to organize a march on the Convention on 14 January, at the time of the king's trial. Valazé and Pétion had presided over a meeting of forty deputies at which it was resolved to murder part of the assembly. The attitude of the Girondins towards the war was another example of their deviousness. Brissot and his allies had started it since they wanted a war against the whole of Europe, to divert attention from domestic policy and justify the strengthening of the government. In pursuit of this policy, Girondin ministers had concealed Prussian peace overtures in September 1792. Later in the year they pretended to fear war, in order to have a pretext for saving the life of the king. This concern for Louis XVI was a little odd if their objective was actually to change the dynasty. By the end of 1792 they were ready to sacrifice everything – if it really was a sacrifice – in pursuit of peace. Brissot warned that to execute the king would alienate Britain and Spain. 'Could the same need not be invoked later on to oblige you to keep the monarchy?' Since the monarchy had already been abolished, the answer to that seemed fairly obvious.

Ever since January the Girondins had been trying to start an insurrection in Paris. This had been about to erupt at the end of May, when, in response to the petitions of the people of Paris, 'who appeared sad', the assembly had finally saved the nation. 'You will end by understanding the danger from which you saved the people.' In other words, it had been the Convention that had saved Paris, not the other way round. This restored the self-respect of the deputies, provided they could forget that it did not correspond to the facts.

Without making an attempt to explain what this had got to do with the Girondins, Saint-Just asserted that General Dillon had been invited to put himself at the head of a royalist plot. Even he sounded a little tentative about this. 'Your committee had the impression that this plan was foiled by last month's insurrection.' He did not even accuse Dillon of having accepted the invitation. In case the deputies were sceptical about a plot that had never got off the ground, he described it in some rather implausible detail. Under its chiefs, who had all been arrested (although none of them was ever tried on this count), were twelve 'generals', each responsible for mobilizing four of the Paris Sections. 'The plan was told only to one man, who revealed it to five others, these five did the same, always dividing [*sic*] by five.' When everything was over and Louis XVII safely installed on the throne, all those involved were to be incorporated in the royal bodyguard and presented with a white ribbon and a medal showing an eagle overthrowing anarchy. Saint-Just assured the deputies that all this was confirmed by documents that the Committee of Public Safety would shortly publish. Unfortunately it never did.

It is futile, and perhaps misleading, to ask how far Saint-Just believed what he said. He probably did think that the paralysis of the Convention had been the fault of the Girondins. Since nothing in politics was ever accidental, but everything followed from principle, one had therefore to ask oneself why they had *wanted* to do it. The answer could only be that they were determined to prevent the Revolution from developing in the kind of republican way that Saint-Just himself had been trying to elaborate. If they were determined to obstruct the work of regeneration and the advent of *vertu* they must have been acting from motives of personal ambition, and they could therefore hope to enlist the support of the rich and vicious. They were consequently capable of every kind of turpitude, and, since it would have been self-defeating to have exposed their true intentions, they posed as revolutionaries and covered their tracks. The flimsy evidence of their plotting acquired a new credibility when one considered how such villains might be expected to behave. Saint-Just was not alone in this kind of thinking. Another deputy explained to the assembly, with reference to General Custine, 'One must not expect conspirators to leave behind material proof of their crimes. What we must do is gather up all the moral proofs.' It was, in other words, all in the mind of the accusers, which could take one a long way. Even so, Saint-Just could scarcely have believed that the Girondins intended to put *both* Orléans or his son *and* Louis XVII on the throne. It was already clear that he saw the business of accusation not as the construction of a logical case by the accumulation of reliable evidence of what people had actually done, but as the moral demolition of men whose guilt was a matter of conviction rather than of proof.

The conclusion to the speech – the action that the Committee of Public Safety invited the assembly to take – corresponded neither to Saint-Just's speech nor to the facts of the situation. In theory it was logical enough. The arrested Girondins were to be divided into three categories: nine were to be outlawed on the ground that they were stirring up rebellion in the provinces with a view to restoring the monarchy; five more, said to be still in Paris but accomplices of the nine, were to be sent for trial; Bertrand, a member of the Commission of Twelve who had opposed its policies, was singled out for praise; he and the remaining fourteen of those arrested were to resume their seats in the assembly. In fact, in addition to the nine 'traitors', nine others had fled, and all of them except Brissot were trying to foment revolt. Some of those whom Saint-Just had identified as leaders were not included amongst those who were proscribed or accused. In the case of Brissot, this was perhaps because the Convention had already voted to put him on trial. Valazé, however, who was said by

Saint-Just to have led a plot to murder some of the Montagnard deputies, was to be allowed to resume his seat in the assembly! Where the proposed punishment did not square with the actual behaviour of the men concerned, or with Saint-Just's accusations, it is reasonable to suspect occult protection, or failure to adjust his speech to the conclusions imposed by the committee. The moderation of his actual proposals should not blind us to the murderous implications of his argument.

What followed was perplexing. Saint-Just's speech should have been printed for circulation to the deputies before they voted on his proposals, but a week later this had not been done. Bertrand was duly recalled to the assembly, but no other action was taken, either to punish or to pardon. Desmoulins, the spoiled child of the Montagnards, attacked the Committee of Public Safety and denounced the charge against his friend, Dillon, as absurd. In a pamphlet, *Réponse de Camille Desmoulins à Arthur Dillon*, he let friendship get the better of discretion. 'After Legendre, the member of the Convention with the highest opinion of himself is Saint-Just. One can see from his carriage and behaviour that he regards his head as the cornerstone of the republic and that he carries it on his shoulders with respect, as though it were the Holy Sacrament.' Desmoulins went on to ridicule Saint-Just's poem, *Argant* (*sic*) as a production unknown to specialists in French literature. These were not insults that a man as touchy as Saint-Just was likely to forget.

The sequel was determined by events that had nothing to do with Saint-Just's charges. The revolt in the provinces was largely a fire of straw, but not in the major cities of the south, Lyon, Bordeaux and Marseille. Lyon in particular declared itself in open revolt and was subdued only after a regular siege. On 13 July Marat was murdered by Charlotte Corday – and was promptly canonized by the Montagnards, who had found him something of an embarrassment during his lifetime. Although Charlotte Corday acted on her own initiative, she had come from Caen, the seat of the rebellion in Normandy, and she had been in touch with one or two of the Girondins. The Montagnards, understandably if erroneously, believed her to have been acting as a Girondin agent. All this was bound to harden attitudes.

On 10 July radical changes were made to the membership of the Committee of Public Safety. Danton left, and most of the new members could be described as hard-liners. Saint-Just was re-elected but he came seventh out of nine, which suggested that his recent speech had not been an unqualified success. On the 15th Billaud-Varenne, one of the most radical of the Montagnards, delivered his own denunciation of the Girondins, repeating Saint-Just's allegations about their royalism and demanding the trial of thirty-five of them. On 28 July Barère, a political weathercock who had been re-elected to the committee like Saint-Just, now declared that the time had come to punish all traitors, and persuaded his colleagues to adopt Saint-Just's proposals – after almost three weeks. By this time the Girondin rump in the Convention had been reduced to silence and there was no opposition to the motion. Saint-Just had finally had his way, but the outcome could scarcely be described as a political triumph for him.

During the summer of 1793 everything went wrong for the revolutionaries. The French armies were pushed back on all fronts, and the Austrians began a methodical invasion of northern France. The situation in the Vendée was out of control. The rebels took Saumur, and panic swept up the Loire. A republican army managed to capture Marseille just before it could surrender to the fleet of Admiral Hood, but Toulon handed over to him almost half of the French fleet. Lyon was in revolt, and its defence had been entrusted to a royalist noble.

This succession of military disasters raised general feelings of suspicion amongst the revolutionaries that did not originate in paranoia, even if they tended to develop in that direction. The case of Toulon certainly suggested that the republic had more to fear from the treachery of conservative military leaders than from the possible incompetence of popular ones – and most of the army commanders were nobles who had made their way to the top under the monarchy. The discovery at Lille of the papers of an

English spy confirmed that the British government had established a network of agents in France. In the Vendée the various republican forces were commanded by generals who spent much of their time quarrelling with each other about strategy. The deputies attached to each of these forces tended to espouse the point of view of 'their' generals, and the military wrangling became politicized when the representatives, after their return to Paris, denounced each other to the Convention. After the expulsion of the Girondins from the assembly most of the local authorities had either taken their side or contemplated doing so. As the provincial protest collapsed they had to extricate themselves from their dangerous predicament, and one of the most promising ways of doing so was to denounce those who had 'misled' them. The old Committee of Public Safety, under Danton's leadership, had tried to win back the allegiance of the provinces in secret negotiations that did not always correspond to the implacability of republican virtue and could be made to look suspicious if leaked selectively and out of context. Deputies on mission to the armies clashed with the agents of the Ministry of War and everyone blamed failure on the incompetence – or was it something more than that? – of those who disagreed with him. Everyone in a position of any authority needed agents and subordinates whom he felt obliged to protect when they fell foul of rival clans. All this created a situation of incredible confusion in which it was possible, and sometimes plausible, to suspect ulterior motives behind every disagreement and to sniff treason in every defeat.

As if this were not enough, the Montagnards began to quarrel amongst themselves as soon as the adoption of the constitution and the collapse of the provincial revolt made it seem safe to do so. The irascible Marat, who had on the whole been content to play a journalistic role as the 'People's Friend', had frightened off any other pretenders to the leadership of the Parisian sans-culottes. His removal opened up a tempting succession. Jacques Roux, a priest whose championship of the poor had made him impatient with all the educated gentlemen in the Convention, irrespective of their political allegiance, was discredited and arrested as the result of a combined offensive of the Jacobin and Cordelier Clubs. That left the field clear for Hébert and his associates in the Cordelier Club. The most important of these was Vincent, an extremely violent young man of Saint-Just's age, who was second in command at the War Office. His influence over this vast bureaucratic empire allowed him to dispose of a good deal of patronage, both civil and military, all over the country. Vincent's protégé in the Vendée, Ronsin, was promoted from captain to general in the course of a single week. When Ronsin's superior officer, Biron, a former duke, criticized him for incompetence, the War Office leaked the complaints to Ronsin, and it was eventually Biron who was recalled to Paris and executed. Their control over the military establishment and their demagogic programme calculated to appeal to sans-culotte militants, made the Cordeliers dangerous men. Their leaders were people who had failed to get themselves elected to the Convention. They were in control of formidable forces but what they lacked – and aspired to – was political power. They frightened the assembly, where their support was negligible. Hébert tried and failed to replace the Minister of the Interior who resigned in mid-August. He and his supporters then campaigned for the partial implementation of the constitution.

In the autumn of 1793 and perhaps earlier, this involved situation was further complicated when a few of the deputies began to use their political influence in order to make money, either by associating themselves with war contracting or by blackmailing bankers and the East India Company with the threat of punitive legislation. Those whose most immediate concern was to line their pockets were not particular about the choice of their associates, and financial intrigues could bring together people who appeared to belong to opposite ends of the political spectrum. All this created an atmosphere of extraordinary suspicion and confusion. It is impossible now, as it was then, to get to the bottom of all the intrigues and to establish how many of the accusations that were flying in all directions had any basis in fact.[3] The historian can give it all up as an impossible job, but the men who were responsible

---

[3] The reader who would like to try is invited to begin with A. Mathiez, *La Conspiration de l'étranger* (Paris, 1918), ch. 1, before graduating to A. de Lestapis, *La 'Conspiration de Batz'* (Paris, 1969).

for the future of the republic had no such freedom. They were condemned to act, on a basis of evidence, rumour and intuition or guesswork that was unlikely to correspond with any precision to what was actually going on.

Throughout all the bickering and recrimination, one trend that can be isolated is the gradual emergence of the Committee of Public Safety as a war cabinet.[4] Robespierre joined it on 26 July. As he confessed, he knew nothing of military matters or of economics, and he was no organizer, but he had a shrewd eye for political tactics, he could usually deliver the support of his Jacobins, and he had a reputation for integrity that made it difficult to challenge those whom he guaranteed. In mid-August the committee was reinforced by the addition of two army officers, Carnot and Prieur de la Côte d'Or, who provided it with much-needed military expertise. Once the constitution was out of the way, Saint-Just had been doing his best to familiarize himself with military matters. His papers contain various notes on the state of the armies in late July and early August. One of these ('One bread ration consists of 24 oz. A two-ration loaf should weight 3 lb, which implies 58 oz of dough since bread loses 4 oz a ration during baking . . .') suggests that he was methodically learning his military logistics. It is said that Carnot offered to leave him in charge of military affairs, but that Saint-Just insisted on deferring to his colleague's greater experience. This is quite likely. The committee had to pull together to establish its collective authority, and all the evidence suggests that its members worked well together during the summer.

How exactly Saint-Just spent his time during August and September it is impossible to know. The Committee of Public Safety worked long hours, and most of its members who were in Paris spent a good deal of extra time defending its policies in the Convention, attending to their specialized bureaux or sitting on committees. Saint-Just was involved in none of these additional activities. On 9 August he presented a report to the Convention

[4] For a good account of the Committee of Public Safety, see R. R. Palmer, *Twelve who Ruled* (Princeton, 1941), reprinted as *The Year of the Terror* (Oxford, 1989).

on the provisioning of the armies. The deputies ordered it to be printed and then seem to have forgotten it. His role as a self-taught military specialist on the Committee of Public Safety was presumably taken over by the two professionals, Carnot and Prieur de la Côte d'Or. During all the sparring in the assembly, when Robespierre was continually on his feet, Saint-Just did not say a word. He does not seem to have attended the Jacobin Club. His signature was attached to decisions of the committee on most days, but rarely more than once or twice, and not at all between 24 August and 5 September, 9 and 17, or 21 and 27 September. He was reported to be preparing a report on the currency but he never delivered it. On 10 October he himself said that he had been instructed by his colleagues to make a statement about the colonies, but he had not done so when he left for the front a fortnight later. It is inconceivable that a man of his ability and energy should have been idle at such a time but his activities have left no traces.

It is unlikely that this had anything to do with the fact that Thérèse Thorin, his old friend and possible lover in Blérancourt, abandoned her husband and came to Paris at the end of July, where she took up residence close to the assembly and to Saint-Just's lodgings.[5] She divorced her husband, but not until July 1794, which suggests that she was not in any hurry. If she had hopes of marrying Saint-Just, she may have been discouraged by his apparent attachment to the sister of a fellow-deputy, Le Bas. She may also have felt that, since her ex-husband and her parents had been arrested as suspects, it would have been awkward for Saint-Just to marry her. In Blérancourt at least, they believed that he had arranged her flight to Paris. Saint-Just denied this in an impatient letter to his friend, Thuillier: 'Where the devil have you dreamed up what you told me about citizen Thorin? Please tell anyone who mentions it that I have nothing to do with all that.' The former deputy, Baudot, wrote many years later, 'When Saint-Just was in Paris he dined every day with his mistress, *chez* Gateau, his secretary.' Since he claimed that Gateau's own

---

[5] On this subject, see B. Vinot, *Saint-Just* (Paris, 1985), ch. 15.

mistress tipped him off that the Committee of Public Safety had its eye on him, he presumably knew what he was talking about, but he may not have been referring to Thérèse. She returned to the Aisne soon after Saint-Just's execution, which seems to suggest that she, at least, had been hoping for some sort of permanent relationship.

The Convention gradually got into the habit of referring more and more issues to the arbitration of the Committee of Public Safety. This did not please everyone. On 28 August Danton's friend, Delacroix, complained of the ineffectiveness of the 'government', and Billaud-Varenne proposed the creation of a new commission to supervise the ministers, which Robespierre opposed as a covert attack on the Committee of Public Safety. Another Montagnard, Chabot, complained that it seemed to be asleep. Early in September, when the first reports of the surrender of the fleet at Toulon coincided with popular agitation about food shortages, a crisis erupted. The Paris Commune diverted a workmen's demonstration into a march on the Convention. Robespierre had temporarily lost control of the Jacobins, who gave the movement their support. On 5 September a crowd of demonstrators invaded the assembly, where Billaud renewed his motion for the creation of a supervisory commission. Robespierre, who was in the chair, lost control of the meeting, and suggestions that the crowd's demands should be submitted to the Committee of Public Safety were angrily rejected. It looked like 2 June all over again. It was Danton who saved the day for the Montagnards with some inspired demagogy, pretending to welcome the demonstrators as allies. He preserved the integrity of the Convention, and with it the Committee of Public Safety, at the price of conceding the demands of the crowd. If Saint-Just was present, he said nothing. He was not the man for that kind of occasion. The Convention eventually committed itself to the arrest of suspects, the imposition of controls on prices and wages, and the creation of a 'revolutionary' army to suppress internal dissent and extract food from the recalcitrant peasants.[6] On the pretext that working men could not

[6] See the splendid account by Richard Cobb, *Les Armées révolutionnaires*, 2 vols (Paris, 1961 and 1963).

spare the time to attend the meetings of the Paris Sections, Danton carried a vote that attendance should henceforth be paid – but that these meetings should be restricted to two a week, which considerably weakened the political force of the Sections. Billaud-Varenne and Collot d'Herbois were added to the Committee of Public Safety, presumably to discourage them from sniping at it from outside, and they soon became loyal members of the revolutionary government.

Hébert and his allies had forced the government to accept their programme but they were no nearer to winning office for themselves. They continued to press for further radical measures, in the Jacobin Club, since they had few supporters in the assembly, and to denounce the restriction on the meetings of the Sections. In mid-September the Cordelier Club criticized the behaviour of representatives on mission and championed the agents of the ministers, which meant those of the War Office. Vincent demanded the recall of the deputies who were acting as political commissars with the armies, and the Commune petitioned for every field army to be accompanied by its own revolutionary tribunal. Hébert, in his newspaper, demanded the renewal of the Convention and the creation of the executive council provided for in the constitution. He kept up a steady barrage against the Committee of Public Safety. 'Within a month the counter-revolution will be an accomplished fact if we leave the Committee of Public Safety organized as it is today.' He accused it of trying to save Brissot. 'Montagnards, we shall never have a government so long as the committees usurp all the powers.' The demonstration of 5 September satisfied him for a time but he was soon back on the offensive. 'You promised people happiness when you erected that edifice [the constitution]. Woe on you if you fail to keep your word . . . Leave the ministers to get on with their job and don't let your committees meddle with the government of the republic.' He denounced the emergence of a new moderate party, with particular reference to 'Monsieur Barère de Vieuzac' who was a member of the committee.[7]

---

[7] *Le Père Duchesne*, nos 269, 272, 275 and 292.

On 24 and 25 September the committee, which had been arresting generals and criticizing deputies on mission, came under attack in the assembly itself. It was defended by some of its members, Billaud, Barère, Jeanbon Saint-André and Robespierre – but not by Saint-Just. Robespierre took the offensive, denouncing super-patriots in the clubs, and the assembly eventually gave the committee a vote of confidence. A fortnight later, on 10 October, Saint-Just rose to make a general report on the political situation.[8]

He began, as usual, with a statement of general principles, assuring the deputies that they were not to blame for anything and attributing the responsibility for everything that was going wrong to the government, which meant the ministers and their agents rather than the Committee of Public Safety. 'The laws are revolutionary; those who execute them are not.' It was understandable, in view of the political situation, that he should emphasize the need to repress all opposition, but his insistence on the legitimacy of force marked a further progress away from the utopian idyll of *De la Nature*. 'The republic will be founded only when the will of the sovereign [people] shall repress (*comprimer*) the monarchical minority and rule over it by right of conquest.' 'You have no restraint to observe when dealing with the enemies of the new order, and liberty must prevail at any price.

What was needed was to put an end to the provincial revolt, relieve the people, deal with the shortages of food and necessities, strengthen the armies and purge the state of the conspiracies that infested it. As always with Saint-Just, politics was a simple dichotomy between good and evil, and these objectives were all part of the same problem.

We cannot hope for prosperity so long as the last enemy of liberty still breathes. You must punish, not merely traitors, but the indifferent, whoever is passive in the republic and does nothing for it. Since the French people made known its will [presumably by accepting the constitution] whatever

[8] For the text, see C. Vellay, *Oeuvres complètes*, vol. II, pp. 75–89.

opposes it is outside the sovereign, and whatever is outside the sovereign is enemy.

This was an extension of the argument that he had used at the king's trial – when the assembly had refused to endorse it. By approving the constitution the French people had confirmed the right of the assembly to act in its name. Liberty meant obedience to this sovereign will. Failure to support the Convention – and the Committee of Public Safety so long as it enjoyed the confidence of the assembly – must therefore be punished in the name of liberty. Principles of peace and natural justice were excellent where 'the people' were concerned but 'the only thing in common between the people and its enemies is the sword.' Convinced, as always, that he was dealing with the virtuous majority in a manner appropriate to the social state, he had now arrived at a position where the salvation of the people depended on the extermination of its foes, whose self-identification with France's national enemies put them outside the harmonious community. The Committee of Public Safety did have to deal with foreign agents and with people who saw the Revolution primarily as a means for their own enrichment, but in Saint-Just's black-and-white world any critics of his own policies were liable to find themselves identified with the forces of evil.

After this fierce introduction Saint-Just accused the government of being full of time-servers, open to penetration by enemy agents and even of being in a state of war with the Convention. The generals belonged to the old order and were still looking for a chance to restore the monarchy. A good many of them *were* probably more at home in the pre-revolutionary world. Dumouriez had turned traitor and others were of dubious loyalty, but there was a difference between keeping an eye on them and branding them all as secret royalists, a difference that Saint-Just himself was to observe when he went to the front.

He then turned to economic policy, which he always saw as an integral part of the republican order. He denounced with good reason the massive corruption amongst army contractors, which he saw as a rejection of republican austerity. According to him,

133

three milliards of hot money were swilling around the country, buying situations and corrupting judges. The effect of price controls had been to increase the value of capital; rich speculators competed with government agents in the procurement of supplies for the army, forcing up prices, and – less plausibly – diverting labour from productive employment into their own service. Purchasers of Church property in 1790-1 had made a killing as a result of subsequent inflation, but he was quick to reassure his audience that all property, even theirs, was sacred. As usual on economic matters, his diagnosis was more convincing than his proposed treatment. Once again he demanded an end to the emission of paper money, which was the only way of financing the kind of war that the Committee of Public Safety was determined to fight. He saw that price controls alone could not prevent inflation if the government insisted on continually increasing the supply of currency, but all that he could suggest was the punitive taxation of the rich and the establishment of a special court to investigate all those who had handled public funds. Saint-Just did not like to lose an argument. He had hoped, and his colleagues on the committee had declined, to force suspects – many of whom were nobles – to work on the building of roads and canals. They were presumably still the prisoners of a sense of social propriety that had no place in his brave new world. Since he had lost the argument in the committee he could not propose the measure himself, but he invited the assembly to consider it. That was the last that was heard of that.

In the present circumstances there could be no question of applying the constitution, which lacked the 'violence' that was needed to repress the enemies of the republic. He still had the illusion that the government could be 'terrible towards itself' while remaining 'gentle and moderate' where the people were concerned. He followed this with some excellent advice, which he was soon to adopt himself, on the behaviour appropriate for deputies posted to supervise the armies. Taking up again what had been the main theme of his speeches during the winter, he then called for institutions and military laws appropriate to a republic. As usual, what interested him was principles, and he was inclined

134

to talk at random when discussing their practical application: at one point he demanded the adoption of shock tactics by the army and a little later on, worried by the high French casualties, insisted that it was necessary 'to make war with prudence.'

He concluded with another attack on the idleness and incompetence of a government where what should have been seen as public service was merely another job. In words that should still raise a cheer he castigated the vast amount of paper generated by the revolutionary government. 'I don't know how Rome and Egypt managed their affairs without these resources. They thought much and wrote little. The prolixity of the correspondence and instructions of the government is a sign of its inertia. *Il est impossible qu'on gouverne sans laconisme.*'

His proposals, accepted by the Convention, began by declaring that the government would remain 'revolutionary' for the duration of the war. This was more than an indefinite postponement of the constitution. It implied that the rule of law, the election of officials and the whole machinery of constitutional government could be suspended in the name of *salus populi*. The Committee of Public Safety was put in control of ministers, generals and local government. Henceforth it would correspond directly with the 600 districts, by-passing the eighty-five departments (which was unlikely to reduce paper-work!). Army commanders were to be nominated by the Committee of Public Safety and confirmed by the Convention. Saint-Just had failed to get these last two points adopted in the constitution but he did not give up easily. Each district was to make a census of its grain production and all surpluses were to be available for requisition. By March Paris was to have a year's reserves. This was wholly unrealistic, but it would cheer up the sans-culottes and convince them that the committee was on their side. The Convention was to set up a special court to investigate those who had handled public funds since the beginning of the Revolution. It never did.

These measures constituted a decisive turning-point in the process that turned the Committee of Public Safety into an effective war cabinet. Its powers had to be renewed every month but if it could win the war – and the military tide turned in favour of the republic in the autumn – it was reasonably safe. In political terms the main losers were the Cordeliers, whose power bases in the War Office, the army and the Paris Commune were now brought under the control of the committee. The assembly would welcome that and see the reinforced revolutionary government as protecting it from Parisian violence. The new dispensation, in other words, was a natural response to the political pressures of the summer. It meant, however, that for a man like Saint-Just the republic, as the embodiment of the general will, was to be identified, not with the French people or its representatives, but with the Committee of Public Safety, which represented the representatives.

It was probably a few days after his speech that Fabre d'Eglantine, one of Danton's less reputable friends, but a man who, at the time, enjoyed Robespierre's confidence, posed a series of questions to the Committee of General Security, or police committee, reinforced for the occasion by Robespierre and Saint-Just.[9] Each of these questions began with 'How is it that . . .', which allowed Fabre to make wide insinuations without having to prove anything in particular. His main target was a quartet of political adventurers, Proli, Desfieux, Dubuisson and Péreire, three of them foreigners, who were very active busybodies in and around the Jacobin Club. Unlike the Hébertists who disposed of a good deal of real power, Proli and the others operated at a lower level. At the time they were trying to organize a central committee of the Parisian popular societies, which was unlikely to win them friends, either in the Committee of Public Safety or in the Commune. If they were not actually in foreign pay – and the evidence for that is inconclusive – they certainly fitted the picture of men employed by France's foreign enemies to discredit the revolution by excess.[11] Fabre accused this quartet of having made

[9] For the text, see *Pièces trouvées dans les papiers de Robespierre et complices* (Paris, An III). Mathiez, *La Conspiration*, supplies valuable background material, despite his tendency to place all the participants in party pigeon-holes.

[10] For the proof that the British government was actually paying members of the Jacobin club to pose as extremists, see the letter to the Swiss banker, Perregaux, in Archives Nationales W.173.

the Montagnard deputy, Chabot, their tool and, more ominously, of having intimidated Hérault de Séchelles of the Committee of Public Safety. Hérault was of noble birth and, according to Fabre, Proli and his friends hoped, by a noisy campaign against nobles, in the Jacobin Club, to blackmail Hérault into giving away the secrets of the committee. He did not say that Hérault had complied but he accused him of maintaining 'a bureau of eighty spies'. The future was to reveal that Fabre was involved in financial intrigues of his own, and his attack on Hérault may merely have been caused by the latter's support for Proli against Fabre's own protégés in a squalid quarrel in the revolutionary underworld. Nevertheless Fabre's accusations made a lasting impression on Robespierre and Saint-Just.

On 16 October Saint-Just presented another report, on the subject of enemy aliens.[11] Faced with growing evidence, or apparent evidence, of British intervention in the affairs of the revolution, Barère had proposed, on the 8th, an embargo on all trade with England. Since the two countries had been at war since the beginning of the year, this might strike the modern reader as somewhat belated, but eighteenth-century wars were supposed to be the affair of governments rather than private individuals. Fabre d'Eglantine, supported by Robespierre, amended Barère's motion to include the arrest of all British civilians in France. This provoked the accusation that the Committee of Public Safety was trying to 'nationalize' the war by turning it against the British people, at a time when they were said to be beginning to dissociate themselves from their government's hostility to the Revolution. It was therefore proposed that the Covention should either repeal the law against the British or extend it to all enemy aliens.

Saint-Just began with his usual *tour d'horizon*, impugning the motives of the committee's critics. He was on firm ground when he claimed that the British were a special case since they had 'violated international law in regard to us, with unprecedented barbarity'. By imposing a food blockade and printing forged revolutionary currency, the British government had indeed

---

[11] For the text, see C. Vellay, *Oeuvres complètes*, vol. II, pp. 94–102.

violated eighteenth-century conventions and disgusted some of its own subjects. British warships had also seized a French frigate in a neutral port. None of the other powers resorted to measures of this kind, which the British government would probably not have used against a 'legitimate' ruler. Saint-Just was therefore able to present the proposal to intern all enemy aliens as an example of the way in which enemies of the Revolution were trying to exaggerate all its salutary measures in order to discredit them. 'Everything is being done to spread terror amongst the people themselves, when it should only be directed against their enemies, so that they will tire of the *heureuse effervescence* which alone has sustained liberty up to the present day and end up by joining forces with its enemies and returning to a policy of indulgence.' Such false 'extremists' formed one of the factions in the republic. Self-serving racketeers were another. This was getting rather away from enemy aliens. There *were* bandits in the Convention, and some of the more extreme terrorists were probably motivated by something more than ideological conviction, but if any criticism of the government's policies was to be treated as factious and men who saw themselves as super-patriots were to be accused of being secret advocates of indulgence, 'liberty', as defined by the Committee of Public Safety, looked like becoming a minority taste.

When he got round to economics, Saint-Just was much more down to earth. 'Your committee . . . looking at the universe, has eyes for the French people alone.' Trade with England was different from that with the rest of Europe since the British exported manufactured goods and luxuries. This depressed French industry, enriched rogues and provided the funds for the payment of British agents. Other countries sent France raw materials that were necessary for the war effort and beneficial to French industry. There were therefore good economic reasons for treating England as a special case.

He would not have been the man he was if he had not gone on to try to prove that his policies were 'really' in the interest of all decent people, even those in England. The French embargo was directed, not against the merchants, but against the British government, which relied on mercantile profits for taxation. If the merchants did suffer, the oppressed British people whom they exploited would be the first to rejoice. In the same vein, he went on to say, 'It is not against the English that you have passed the law for their arrest.' That again was the fault of their wicked government, and all they had to do was to overthrow it and France would be their friend. He reminded his colleagues that they had already pronounced Pitt to be 'the enemy of the human race'.

He threw in his usual mixture of aphorisms and generalizations. Anyone who criticized the severity of the French government was betraying his own inner corruption. The British were backing both moderation and extremism – which allowed the Committee of Public Safety to treat any criticism from Left or Right as evidence of foreign inspiration. 'You will conquer through force and not through the scruples that are being urged on you.' That could justify all kinds of things. Every normal human being had a residual loyalty to the land in which he was born. That was useful for throwing suspicion on foreigners, but Saint-Just did not stop to reflect that it ruled out any prospect of the French being hailed as liberators in the lands that they invaded.

Despite his previous argument that the call for the internment of all enemy aliens was actually intended to discredit the Revolution, he then adopted it in the name of the committee! Only the embargo on trade was restricted to England. Repression, in other words, was austere republicanism when practiced by the government, but suspect when urged on it from the floor of the assembly. Anyone who accused the committee of not being repressive enough was actually trying to moderate the Revolution by deliberately going too far and arousing sympathy for his pretended victims. That was what he had said about Buzot and the Bourbons.

By mid-October 1793 he had committed himself to a conception of politics that was suspicious, ideologically Manichean and intolerant of all criticism. A long interlude of service at the front then gave him a last chance to escape from his world of absolutes and abstractions by coming to terms with the realities of government.

8

The Military Commissar

Alsace, at the end of the eighteenth century, was quite unlike any other part of France. It had been annexed comparatively recently, during the previous century, and the monarchy had respected its local identity. A French province from the administrative point of view, socially, culturally and economically it remained part of a German world where nationality was a matter of feeling rather than political allegiance. Before the Revolution it was separated from the rest of France by a customs barrier, and its main trade routes were along and across the Rhine. The overwhelming mass of the population spoke German or Alsatian and could not understand French. In the one city of any importance, Strasbourg, the social and intellectual elite could also speak French, but they had often been educated in Germany. Protestantism had been tolerated by the monarchy in Alsace, but since it was not recognized in the rest of France, the Protestant pastors in Strasbourg had been to school and university abroad. This was also true of many Catholics. Schneider, who was to emerge as an extremist during the autumn of 1793, was an Austrian who had been professor of Greek at the university of Bonn before he was appointed episcopal vicar at Strasbourg. Even the bilingual leaders of Strasbourg society, whilst they might share in the national enthusiasm for the revolution, did so with a difference and retained a strong sense of their peculiar local identity. They felt somewhat apart from Frenchmen who came from what they called 'the interior'. Alsace was also unique in the importance of its Jewish population. The men of 1789 believed that part of their mission was to incorporate the Jews into French society by granting them full civic rights. Earlier discrimination had tended to confine them to commerce and banking, and their role as suppliers of capital had not always endeared them to their debtors. Class tensions in Alsace were therefore liable to be exacerbated by popular anti-semitism. As revolutionary governments became more radical, they became more suspicious of the affluent, and more inclined to identify themselves with urban artisans. Where Alsace was concerned this meant, for the most part, people who could barely understand French. The Jacobin Club at Strasbourg conducted its sessions in both French and German.

The impact of the Revolution on this idiosyncratic society was both complex and difficult for men from the 'interior' to appreciate. Alsace could not respond like the rest of the country to the new conception of France as an integrated national community. To the majority of the rural population, isolated by the linguistic barrier, the Revolution was an essentially alien movement. When the revolutionaries reorganized the Church they provoked a good deal of local hostility. In the Bas-Rhin 90 per cent of the clergy refused to take the oath to the new religious settlement and forfeited their livings. In the only other part of France where there was a similar general rejection of the Civil Constitution of the Clergy – the Vendée –the sequel had been armed revolt against the republic. As early as 1791 there were signs of serious disaffection in the rural areas of Alsace where the population was inclined to sympathize with royalism and with its cardinal-archbishop, Rohan, who declined to take the oath to the Civil Constitution, abandoned his palace in Strasbourg and withdrew to that part of his diocese that lay beyond the Rhine.

Strasbourg itself was rather more responsive to the new message. The Revolution was initially welcomed by the urban elite, which saw it as an essentially political movement. Such people at first dominated the local Jacobin Club which, like most such clubs in the rest of France, was well-heeled, well-mannered and moderate in its politics.[1] After the king's flight in 1791 things changed, and the club passed under the control of men of a more radical temper. They also tended to be less local. With the threat of war in 1791 and war itself a year later, Strasbourg acquired a new significance as a base on the frontier, and army officers – from the interior – assumed a new importance within the Jacobin Club. This probably accentuated a trend, also present in the Vendée, for urban radicalism and rural conservatism to exacerbate each other as fear reinforced conviction on both sides. The Strasbourg Jacobins were exceptional in calling for a republic in 1791 and demanding war as early as January 1792.

When the outbreak of war brought the overthrow of the monarchy Strasbourg went through a particularly stormy year. Alarmed at the way things were going, the moderates created their own club. When he heard of the Parisian insurrection of 10 August 1792 the mayor closed down the Jacobins. During the local elections that autumn the members of the Jacobin Club were eliminated from the municipal government and retained only three seats on the administration of the department. This situation was reversed by visiting Montagnard representatives on mission, who purged the administration and installed one of their local supporters as mayor, despite opposition from the Sections, or political wards, which reflected grass-roots opinion. When the representatives moved on, the Sections reasserted themselves, only to have their own nominees for municipal office dismissed by the department. As in other provincial cities in the spring of 1793, there was an essentially local conflict between urban radicals, who relied on support from visiting deputies from Paris, and the Sections, who resented this interference from outside. Such local particularism was especially strong in Alsace. Each side looked for support in high places, and since the protectors of the local radicals

---

[1] See H. Gough, 'Politics and Power: The Triumph of Jacobinism in Strasbourg, 1791–93', *Historical Journal*, 23 (1980).

were Montagnard deputies, their opponents tended to identify themselves with the Girondins. When, after the Parisian coup d'état of 2 June 1793, the Girondins tried to organize a national revolt against Paris, this raised understandable doubts about the loyalty of the disaffected local authorities.

The situation was particularly grave in Alsace, since German-speaking opponents of the Montagnards were thought likely to sympathize with the Austrian and Prussian armies immediately to the north of them in the Palatinate and just across the Rhine. Whether or not the local authorities were actually prepared to welcome the allied armies, suspicious Frenchmen, unfamiliar with local politics and unable to understand what the people around them were saying, were bound to see themselves as a kind of beleaguered garrison, defending a stronghold with a civilian population whose heart was not in the fight. In October 1793, before Saint-Just arrived, other representatives on mission purged the administration of the department yet again, set up a *comité de surveillance* drawn from all the local authorities and gave the criminal court 'revolutionary' powers, which allowed it to dispense with some judicial formalities and to judge without appeal.

What made the situation even more dangerous than that in the Vendée was the proximity of enemy troops. During the autumn of 1793 the Committee of Public Safety had managed to recover some ground in Belgium, but only by depleting the armies on the eastern front. In the face of pressure from the Austrian and Prussian forces, the gains made in the previous year were abandoned, France was invaded, her frontier fortresses taken or besieged, and by late October an Austrian army had penetrated almost as far as Strasbourg itself. Thirty or forty miles to the westward the Prussians threatened to outflank the Army of the Rhine and to invade Lorraine. In September the Committee of Public Safety undertook a wholesale purge of the army commanders, who were blamed for the unsuccessful campaigns of the summer. The Moselle Army, facing the Prussians, was entrusted to Hoche who, at twenty-five, was even younger than Saint-Just. Pichegru, who was given command of the Rhine Army, was regarded as an experienced veteran. He was thirty-two. Both generals were men of humble origin who had risen through the ranks. They owed everything to the Revolution, they had proved their ability and they were ambitious to make a name for themselves, but they had no experience of high command and they were in charge of troops demoralized by defeat and facing a winter campaign for which they were desperately short of equipment and supplies. The War Minister, when he decided to make Pichegru senior to Hoche, told him that he was to assume supreme command if the two armies linked up. Unfortunately he did not tell this to Hoche, but this was of no immediate consequence whilst the French armies faced different opponents on separate fronts.

In mid-October the Committee of Public Safety decided to send Saint-Just and Le Bas of the Committee of General Security to the Rhine Army. There was not exactly a shortage of political commissars on the eastern front, where there were already four attached to each of the two French armies of the Rhine and Moselle. Two more were despatched to the Rhine Army only ten days before Saint-Just and Le Bas. The latter were perhaps in a special position since – unlike all the others – they sat on the two most powerful committees of the assembly but this, in itself, gave them no officially superior status. Their powers were defined as 'extraordinary' but since those of their colleagues were 'unlimited' this scarcely clarified the situation. Quite apart from this hierarchical problem, the plethora of deputies in a military area threatened to repeat what had happened in the Vendée, where the representatives on mission had endorsed the professional rivalries of 'their' generals.

Philippe Le Bas was a few years older than Saint-Just, but not yet thirty. For a Montagnard, he was an unusually modest man. He wrote to his father that it was not his practice to intervene in debates when others had already made his points for him, and he had not thought it worth his while to publish his speech on the appropriate punishment for Louis XVI. He was, however, no nonentity and, unlike Saint-Just, he had already been on one mission to the front. A native of the Pas-de-Calais, he knew the

Robespierres. He was one of the little circle that gathered at the house of Duplay, where Robespierre lived, and a few weeks before setting out for Alsace he had married Duplay's youngest daughter, Elisabeth.[2] The question naturally arises of how far Saint-Just was personally responsible for the decisions that went out over the names of himself and Le Bas, and it is insoluble. Perhaps it does not matter very much, since the two men seem to have thought along very similar lines. Le Bas wrote to his wife, towards the beginning of their mission, 'I like and respect him more and more every day . . . The most perfect agreement and constant harmony have prevailed between us.' In July 1794 he was virtually to commit suicide when he insisted on taking his place alongside the proscribed Saint-Just. When he and another deputy had been sent to the Army of the North during the summer, they inaugurated their mission with a proclamation denouncing absenteeism and blaming indiscipline on the officers. They arrested generals and sent officers before the revolutionary tribunal. This set the pattern for what was to happen in Alsace, although the language of the proclamations there had a new crispness that came unmistakably from Saint-Just. When Le Bas wrote to the Committee of Public Safety or to Robespierre, Saint-Just sometimes added a postscript. It is reasonable to assume that they acted in concert, although Saint-Just probably played the leading part. When they returned to Alsace in December, after a brief visit to Paris, accompanied by Le Bas's wife and sister, it was Saint-Just, rather than Elisabeth's husband, who dictated the terms on which the women would be allowed to go. To avoid a wearisome repetition of 'Saint-Just and Le Bas', I intend to follow the practice of most historians, when describing the mission to Alsace, of referring to the former alone, but the reader should bear in mind that both men were involved.

The essential object of the mission was to reverse the military situation, save Strasbourg and drive the Austrians and Prussians out of France before winter put an end to campaigning.[3] This

---

[2] See Stéphane-Pol, *Autour de Robespierre: le conventionnel Le Bas* (Paris, n.d.).

[3] On the mission as a whole, the indispensable source is J. P. Gross, *Saint-Just, sa politique et ses missions* (Paris, 1976).

meant that the first objective of the two deputies was to pull the Rhine Army together by restoring discipline and reviving its morale. Their initial proclamation promised precisely that.

> We have arrived and we swear in the name of the army that the enemy will be conquered. If there are amongst you traitors or men indifferent to the people's cause, we bring the sword that shall strike them. Soldiers! We have come to avenge you and to give you leaders who will conduct you to victory. We are resolved to seek out merit, to reward and promote it and to track down every crime, whoever may have committed it.

This may have gone down well with the troops but it probably made rather a different impression on the other deputies in the area by its assumption that everything had to be done from scratch and that it would be done by the two newcomers.

Saint-Just appreciated that morale-building was something of an exercise in public relations. This gave him a good opportunity to indulge his penchant for epigrammatic language and flamboyant gesture. Periodic proclamations assured the army of victory and hurled defiance at the enemy. He replied to a Prussian request for a parley, 'All that the Republic accepts from its enemies and sends back to them is lead.' Fine words did not blind him to the need for the buttering of parsnips. His interventions to ensure the well-being of the soldiers suggested that the deputies were thinking primarily of the rank and file and were not inclined to equate the army with its staff officers. As we shall see, he took extraordinary measures to ensure that the troops had boots, shirts and cloaks for the winter campaign. The wounded were to be given comfortable beds in the houses of the more prosperous citizens of Strasbourg. Such general measures were reinforced by well publicized examples of both reward and punishment. Individual soldiers were given horses and arms to reward distinguished conduct. When some of them expressed apprehension about what was happening to their farms in their absence, Saint-Just wrote to the local authorities of the men concerned requesting them to make sure that the land was cultivated at the public expense. When the unfortunate Méquignet, however, requested permission to leave the army and return to Poitiers to look after his fortune of 40,000 livres, Saint-Just had him publicly cashiered and imprisoned for the duration of the war.[4] He intended to generate the impression that nothing could escape his notice, that merit would always be sure of its reward, and its opposite of punishment. His order to Dièche, the general in command of the town garrison, 'Send the gunner who brought this to the clothing store and arrest the clerk who said that he had no time to serve him', was enough to raise a cheer in any army.

Although he did not follow his own advice to representatives at the front to sleep under canvas, Saint-Just did not spare himself. He was on the move all the time, and when the French armies took the offensive he was in the thick of things, proving himself to be as fearless as any of the troops. This was convincingly attested by the deputy, Baudot, who was attached to the Moselle Army. 'I too have been with the armies and seen him in action – and I never saw anything like it. My testimony cannot be suspected for I certainly have no liking for him.'[5]

Saint-Just's determination to show his solicitude for the troops was not prompted by any concern for his popularity. He made it clear to all involved, generals, administrators, local Jacobins, private soldiers – and to his colleagues from the Convention – that he considered himself to be in charge and that his will was law. This was how he envisaged 'revolutionary' action: the suspension of time-wasting formalities in favour of instantaneous action directed by the man in command. As he wrote to Robespierre, 'People make too many laws and too few examples.'

In an attempt to restore some discipline to the defeated army, all ranks were confined to camp and officers told that they would be held responsible if their men succumbed to the temptations of

---

[4] A. Soboul, 'Sur la mission de Saint-Just à l'armée du Rhin', *Annales historiques de la révolution française*, 136–7 (1954), pp. 221–2. This article reprints decrees and proclamations, in Saint-Just's hand, relating to the first part of his mission to the Rhine Army.

[5] M. A. Baudot, *Notes historiques sur la Convention nationale, le Directoire, l'Empire et l'exil des votants* (Geneva, 1974), p. 166.

nearby Strasbourg. Dièche was ordered to tell the man in charge of the military hospital that he had twenty-four hours in which to stop admitting malingerers. Three days later the same director, the senior surgeon and chief medical officer all had half of their salary stopped for a month to punish them for the insanitary conditions in their hospital. Any officer found in Strasbourg was to be disciplined, as the unfortunate captain who asked Saint-Just the way to the theatre discovered to his cost. Soldiers trying to enter the city hidden in carts and wagons were to be shot.

As Le Bas explained in a letter to his wife, he and Saint-Just were trying to give the impression that they had eyes everywhere and that any infraction of their rules would be promptly discovered and punished. 'At the moment when he is least expecting it, a general finds us paying him a visit and demanding an account of his conduct.' They followed their usual practice of seizing on specific examples and giving them maximum publicity. A lieutenant was told to explain why one private had been passed over and another, without the requisite period of service, promoted corporal in his place. This sort of thing probably kept everyone in authority on his toes, but it must have meant that the men in command had to devote a good deal of their time to matters of administrative detail. The commander-in-chief, Pichegru, received four requests in a day for information about such matters as the disposal of twenty-three horses. Dièche was reprimanded for failing to reply to five similar enquiries. How far this led to obsession with minutiae and reluctance to assume responsibility on the part of those in command it is impossible to say.

In accordance with the principles of 'revolutionary' action, the powers of the military court were strengthened, and its jurisdiction extended to civilians. Saint-Just preferred this tribunal to the civilian court that his fellow-representatives had elevated to revolutionary status. What he wanted was swift and dramatic action that would impress and intimidate. This meant making examples. Faced with complaints about the quality of the bread baked for the army, he ordered the military prosecutor to hold an inquiry and to 'make an example on the spot'. There was an obvious danger here that frightened subordinates would demonstrate their zeal by finding scapegoats and paying more attention to the number of their victims than to their guilt. One general was dismissed and then reinstated the next day when it was discovered that he had been blamed for something done by someone else. Saint-Just sent Pichegru's chief of staff before the revolutionary tribunal and then reinstated him when Pichegru complained. He was prepared to listen to other people and to change his mind when challenged by men he trusted, but someone had to have the courage to confront him and he himself was perhaps more concerned with the effect of his 'examples' than with the guilt of those he accused. The military court had ten men shot with the maximum publicity, in front of the army: one general, two colonels, one captain, three NCOs, one private, a man from the army administration and a war contractor. Saint-Just was not a terrorist like those of his colleagues in other areas who engaged in mass executions, but the man who had once been unable to forgive Rousseau for his acceptance of the death penalty had no inhibitions about enforcing it in the name of the Revolution.

Saint-Just saw one of his main functions as ensuring that the troops got the supplies and equipment they needed if they were to take the offensive. His direct line to Carnot allowed him to dispel the latter's comfortable illusion that there were 100,000 men available for action in Alsace, and to persuade the Committee of Public Safety to send reinforcements to the eastern front. Taking a comprehensive view of his 'extraordinary' powers, he threatened the administrators of eight neighbouring departments with the revolutionary tribunal if they did not immediately comply with requisitions of food imposed on them in August. During the autumn of 1793 other representatives on mission, encouraged by the revolutionary government to act on their own initiative, often imposed requisitions and taxes on their own authority but none of them acted on the same scale as Saint-Just. The richer citizens of Strasbourg were ordered to raise 9,000,000 livres and to supply 5,000 boots and 15,000 shirts, besides providing 2,000 beds for wounded soldiers. Although his area of responsibility was officially confined to the Rhine Army, he imposed another levy of 5,000,000 livres on Nancy without consulting his colleagues in

Lorraine. The money was initially described as a voluntary subscription, then it became a forced loan, and it was eventually made clear that none of it would be repaid. Of Strasbourg's nine million, six were allocated to the army, one for improving the fortifications of the town, and the remaining two for the relief of the civilian population. At Nancy the army was to get 90 per cent of the money raised. True to his preoccupation with inflation, Saint-Just claimed that he was going to reduce prices by restricting the amount of capital in circulation, but since he proposed to spend the money as soon as he had raised it, this did not look very realistic.

On the whole, Saint-Just and Le Bas left strategy to the generals, confining their own activity to providing the armies with the resources, both moral and material, that they needed for victory. Saint-Just seems to have envisaged the main French offensive as coming from 'his' Rhine Army, with Hoche and the Moselle Army in support. Carnot, however, preferred an outflanking movement by Hoche, aiming at the Rhine, in order to threaten the communications of the Austrian forces before Strasbourg. A general offensive began on 11 November. Pichegru made little headway and it was Hoche who drove the enemy back. Ignoring his instructions to advance eastwards and take the Austrians in the rear, he headed north-east, apparently making for the Palatinate, only to be bloodily repulsed at Kaiserslautern. He then fell back, abandoning some of the territory that he had just gained. In early December Saint-Just and Le Bas made a hurried visit to Paris, presumably to discuss the situation with Carnot. Rather surprisingly, none of them seemed disposed to blame Hoche, even though he had refused to communicate his plans to Saint-Just on grounds of military secrecy. Later that month the French armies resumed the attack. This time Hoche headed eastwards, the Austrians were outflanked, the allied armies driven out of France and the republican armies advanced into Germany. Understandably enough, since it was the Moselle Army that had played the greater part in the victory, the deputies attached to that army, Baudot and Lacoste, put Hoche in supreme command. Hoche naturally accepted this, since he was unaware that the War Minister had reserved the post for Pichegru. The latter offered his resignation, and the disagreement cannot have improved relations between Baudot and Lacoste on the one hand and Saint-Just and Le Bas on the other. One should not make too much of this, however. What mattered was the victory.

What one makes of Saint-Just's contribution to the success of the French armies is likely to be determined by one's sympathy or antipathy towards the man himself, since the verdict rests on intuition rather than on proof. Some of his achievements were more impressive on paper than in actual fact. Despite his threats, much of the extraordinary taxation was never paid, most of the money raised was never spent, and the residue was taken over by the Treasury in the spring of 1794. The assessments seem to have been arbitrary, even by revolutionary standards: a Turkheim banker had his contribution reduced on appeal from 160,000 to 30,000 livres. In other words, the effect of the forced 'loan' was moral rather than material, although that was probably not how it appeared to the major contributors. The requisition of boots and clothing, on the other hand, was much more effective, bringing in 17,000 boots and over 20,000 shirts in Strasbourg alone. The effect of this on an ill-equipped army, fighting in winter weather, must have been very considerable. Saint-Just's admirers have presented him as the saviour of Alsace, but it is worth remembering that the main military contribution came from Hoche and the Moselle Army. Although his mission was officially to the Rhine Army, Saint-Just had also helped to provide Hoche with reinforcements of men and supplies. He had stood by him after the check at Kaiserslautern and he is entitled to some of the credit for Hoche's success. It would be going too far, however, to regard the French victory as the direct consequence of Saint-Just's 'revolutionary' initiatives in Strasbourg. His incessant interference in the management of Pichegru's army may have had something to do with its comparatively modest performance. These are matters that historians are free to debate at leisure. From the point of view of the Committee of Public Safety, what mattered was that French troops, who had looked like losing Strasbourg in October, had driven the enemy out of France by the end of the year. When it came to allocating the credit for this very satisfactory state of affairs, the committee would have a natural tendency to attribute the main share to its own men, Carnot and Saint-Just. It had sent Saint-Just out to do a job and it looked as though he had done it very well indeed.

Where military matters were concerned – and they were what counted most – it is not difficult to argue that his eventual success was itself the justification for the means that he chose to employ. In civilian politics such clear-cut results were unobtainable. The deputies in Alsace were the prisoners of a situation that they had not created and could not entirely control. They may have convinced themselves that they had found the correct solution to their problems, but whatever they did was liable to create as many difficulties as it resolved. There *were* counter-revolutionaries and enemy agents about, who had to be detected and eliminated, besides loyal republicans who disagreed with each other about what should be done, and it was not always possible to distinguish the one from the other. Underlying everything else were tensions between Alsatians and the men from the interior. Whatever path Saint-Just tried to hack through this jungle, it was probably impossible for anyone, especially for an outsider, to avoid losing his bearings and interpreting the tangled situation in terms of what he wanted to believe.

From the start Saint-Just tended to rely on the army – in other words, on men from the interior – to implement his policies. He neglected the local criminal court in favour of the military tribunal, even where civilians were concerned. He tended to disregard the various agencies of local government – department, district and municipality – and to use as his intermediary the military governor of Strasbourg, Dièche, who was not a local man. To begin with, like the other representatives on mission, he turned for advice about local politics to the Jacobin Club, inviting it to let him have its views on the competence and reliability of Dièche, the administrators of the department and the staff officers of the National Guard at Strasbourg. Unlike his colleagues, Mallarmé and Lacoste, who liked to give their republican rhetoric an airing in the club, Saint-Just and Le Bas do not appear to have attended its meetings. They kept their distance and communicated with it by letter. Although they asked the club for its opinion, they did not pay much attention to it: the club denounced Dièche as drunken and incapable, but this did not shake the deputies' confidence in him.

What seems to have turned Saint-Just against the local men was the – probably false – report of a plot by all the administrative bodies to betray Strasbourg to the Austrians. Before one is in too much of a hurry to condemn his credulity one has to remember that the nephew of the Austrian commander-in-chief was picked up in the city and fourteen local people were arrested at a meeting with the Austrian chief of intelligence, who escaped. The deputies might well write to the Committee of Public Safety, 'We have earned the right to be suspicious.' What followed was probably a mistake, but they were in no position to take risks. They purged the entire administration at all levels. All but three members of the department were arrested, together with the district and the entire municipality, apart from the mayor. Men who had been presidents or secretaries of the Sections at the time of the coup d'état against the Girondins were also imprisoned. Two of Saint-Just's colleagues, Guyardin and Milhaud, arrested the staff officers of the National Guard, while Dièche seized its commanding officer. This was to make a clean sweep of men who may have belonged to a particular faction but were also seen by the Alsatians as their own people. The purge extended beyond Strasbourg itself, to include the municipal officers of Neuf-Brisach and Saverne and the departmental administration of the Meurthe, who were scarcely within the jurisdiction of men who had been sent to the Rhine Army. Saint-Just complained to the *comité de surveillance* at Strasbourg that there were 'thousands' of suspects at large in the city and it had arrested none of them.

This was too much even for Dièche and Monet, the mayor of Strasbourg, even though neither was a local man. When each of them protested Monet was put firmly in his place: 'We are not here to fraternize with the authorities but to judge them.' He took the hint, henceforth did what he was told and became one of Saint-Just's trusted agents. The Jacobin Club seems to have been less willing to accept the elimination of people who owed their offices to local election, and there was little further contact between the club and the deputies until they purged it in December. From his own point of view, Saint-Just behaved with revolutionary rectitude. He did not send men for trial unless he believed that there was credible evidence against them. He regarded the dismissal of the local officials as a necessary precaution and, in accordance with the Law of Suspects, such men were merely to be detained and not put on trial. He gave orders that, once safely transferred to the interior, they were to be humanely treated, and it was not his fault if they were actually held incommunicado. What he did was understandable enough, in the critical circumstances, but it was bound to alienate local opinion which, in turn, reinforced his suspicions of all Alsatians.

These feelings were shared by Gateau, whom he had summoned to help him. In a letter to their mutual friend, Daubigny, Gateau denounced the 'fanaticism, indolence and Germanic stupidity' of the local population. This had become the general opinion of the men from the interior. Monet who, although mayor of Strasbourg, came from Savoy, agreed that Alsace could be regenerated only by people from other parts of France. Dièche – from the Rouergue – concurred that 'heads more German than French' needed 'vigour and terror'. Baudot and Lacoste went even further. When, at the end of the year, there was a mass exodus from northern Alsace of the frightened civilian population, fleeing with the retreating allied armies, they made the helpful suggestion that the government should seize this opportunity to colonize the area with men from other parts of France. 'The only thing to do is to guillotine a quarter of the inhabitants of these parts and keep only those who have taken an active part in the Revolution.' By comparison with some of his colleagues, Saint-Just was not merely a moderate but a humanitarian. Nevertheless he noted in his diary that it would be a good idea to change the names of all the towns and villages in Alsace and call them after French soldiers. He invited the Alsaciennes to abandon their famous costume and head-dress, as a symbol of both Germanism and Catholicism. At the end of his mission he set aside 600,000 livres from the 2,000,000 previously allocated to the poor, for the establishment of a French-language school in every village. Like a good deal else that he did, this was a gesture rather than a policy: francophone teachers were hard to find and not a single school was actually opened.

In conformity with his poor view of the local population, Saint-Just therefore ordered the Strasbourg Jacobins to write to the clubs in seven neighbouring departments, inviting them to send missionaries to Alsace to regenerate the local population. About fifty militants responded to the call, and the process of selection ensured that they would not be men of a modest or self-effacing stamp. Their leader was Schneider, the former professor of Greek at Bonn and episcopal vicar at Strasbourg, who was currently acting as public prosecutor to the revolutionary tribunal. This was the old civilian court, not the military tribunal favoured by Saint-Just, who does not seem to have had much direct contact with Schneider. Calling themselves the *Propagande*, Schneider's men roved over the Bas-Rhin, decked out in uniforms that they created for themselves, trailing their cavalry sabres and accompanied by a military escort. Saint-Just seems to have put paid to attempts to raise a local 'revolutionary' army, but that was probably because he did not trust the Alsatians. Schneider's band was a revolutionary army in all but name. It sent suspects for trial before the revolutionary tribunal, imposed special taxes on the rich, requisitioned supplies and inflicted heavy penalties on traders who disregarded price controls. One unfortunate was fined 3,000 livres for charging too much for a couple of lettuces. By the standards of the time, Schneider's men were not particularly bloody, but they were still responsible for the execution of thirty-one men. As befitted extremists in the autumn of 1793, they took an active part in the assault on religion that swept the country in November. On the 20th Schneider himself was one of those who abjured the priesthood at the Festival of Reason in Strasbourg cathedral. Dechristianization was not universally popular with the local radicals, especially when it came to destroying the monuments to 'superstition' in their own cathedral.

Saint-Just was not directly involved in any of these activities, but he must have been well aware of what was going on and he allowed it to happen. He was not the kind of man to tolerate activities of which he disapproved. He himself signed an order for the destruction of the statues outside the cathedral, and there is no convincing evidence to suggest that he dissociated himself from the attack on religion. Schneider's style was different from his own but Saint-Just had been responsible for the creation of the *Propagande*, and its activities were very similar to what he himself was doing.

Early in December Saint-Just and Le Bas paid their brief visit to Paris, where they must have been surprised by the change in the political climate.[6] The Committee of Public Safety had come to realize the danger of anarchy as a result of the do-it-yourself enthusiasm of local extremists, whose excesses threatened to produce chaos and to provoke revolt. A law voted on 4 December put the machinery of the Terror under the control of the two governing committees. Representatives on mission were henceforth prohibited from raising taxes of their own, and local revolutionary armies were dissolved. Robespierre had already declared war on dechristianization. This was not merely a matter of saying that the extremists were going too far. In the feverish atmosphere of 1793, whatever was unorthodox was suspected of being intentionally counter-revolutionary, and orthodoxy was coming to be defined as acceptance of the policies of the Committee of Public Safety. For Robespierre dechristianization, which had been actively promoted by Proli and his quartet, was not merely vulgar and offensive to his deep-rooted deism. He saw it as an attempt by foreigners and enemy agents to divide the country and set the revolutionaries at each other's throats, under the disguise of innocent revolutionary enthusiasm. Saint-Just had been away from Paris politics for a long time. What was going on – or what was believed to be going on – was not something that one could discover from reading the newspapers. When Robespierre presumably briefed him about what was 'really' happening he was in no position to check this from his own observations, and he

---

[6] See below, pp. 161–70.

himself was, in any case, equally prone to sniff counter-revolution in every whiff of dissent.

He returned to Alsace in a new frame of mind. The histrionic Schneider, Austrian priest turned dechristianizer, corresponded very well to the kind of man whom Robespierre regarded as the latest and most dangerous enemy of the Revolution. Schneider himself provided Saint-Just with the pretext he needed, by making a flamboyant entry into Strasbourg with a coach and six, accompanied by his new wife, a wealthy heiress, said by Schneider's enemies to be the latest of his requisitions. Within twenty-four hours of his return to Alsace, Saint-Just had him arrested, exposed on the scaffold alongside the guillotine and sent off to Paris for trial by the revolutionary tribunal. Saint-Just was later to denounce him as a counter-revolutionary, and he was executed in the spring of 1794. The other members of the *Propagande* could consider themselves lucky to be sent back to their homes without being prosecuted.

This initiated the third phase in Saint-Just's Alsatian policy. He had begun by trying to work with the local people but come to distrust them. Then he imported missionaries from the interior, only to come to the conclusion that they were no more reliable. All that remained was to enforce the government's policies by men who could be relied on to carry out orders. That meant, in the first instance, Dièche and Monet. The department was purged once again, and also the Jacobin Club. Henceforth it transacted its business in French only, which must have cut it off from the local artisans. The new *comité de surveillance* did not include a single local man. The revolutionary tribunal began prosecuting Schneider's agents as enthusiastically as it had formerly disposed of their victims. Saint-Just himself was later to complain, in a famous phrase, that the Revolution was 'frozen'. He never understood that this was the inevitable result of a situation in which safety was to be sought only in blind obedience to whatever happened to be the orthodoxy of the moment.

He was able to dispose of the local population more or less as he wished, but he did not have the same authority over the other deputies who were in Alsace on missions similar to his own. How he got on with them would affect future relations in the assembly when they had all returned to Paris. From the start he made it clear to the Committee of Public Safety that he considered the others to be in the way, urging his colleagues to recall them and arguing that two, or at most four, were enough in Strasbourg. The committee duly reduced the numbers to four with each army but also dispatched one of its members, Hérault de Séchelles, to Alsace on a mission of his own. On arrival Hérault suggested opening up a correspondence with Saint-Just and Le Bas. The latter commented, rather oddly, in a letter to Robespierre, 'We are astonished.' He went on to complain that the representatives on mission who had failed to prevent the advance of the Austrians ought to have been recalled. Saint-Just added a cryptic postscript: 'Confidence has no value any longer when one shares it with the corrupt.' This is usually taken to be a reference to Hérault, who had been denounced by Fabre d'Eglantine, in Saint-Just's presence, but it could have been aimed at the other deputies as well. Whatever it meant, it was scarcely a prelude to good relations.

From the start Saint-Just and Le Bas considered themselves to be in a class apart. 'In accordance with the nature of our mission we considered it our duty to act in isolation.' That was not how the others saw it, and they resented Saint-Just's assumption that his membership of the Committee of Public Safety endowed him with superior status. One must not make too much of this. The others did occasionally correspond with Saint-Just and he was prepared, on occasion, to take their advice. When Milhaud and Guyardin assured him that a *procureur-général* of Saverne whom he had dismissed was an excellent citizen, Saint-Just reinstated him. There was, however, bound to be friction when deputies with ill-defined powers and areas of jurisdiction got in each other's way, especially when two of them behaved as though they thought themselves to be speaking in the name of the revolutionary government. Saint-Just had no inhibitions about dispatching orders to areas far from Strasbourg. When he purged the administrators at Nancy, Faure, who was on mission there, reinstated some of them. Baudot and Lacoste, who had not had a chance to learn about the changed atmosphere in Paris, were understandably shocked by Saint-Just's abrupt turning against Schneider, which he did not bother to explain to them. They complained about Schneider's 'persecution' and protested again when Saint-Just went on to purge the administration of the department without consulting them.

These discontents surfaced briefly in the assembly on 29 December, just before Saint-Just's return to Paris. Hérault complained that he was being criticized for his extremism in Alsace. He knew that he had been denounced for his contacts with Proli, who was now wanted as an alleged counter-revolutionary, and demanded an opportunity to clear his name. Hérault was followed by Mallarmé, who had been recalled from Alsace, and Simon. Mallarmé claimed that Saint-Just and Le Bas had been mistaken when they ordered the trial of the administrators of the Meurthe, who had been appointed by the deputies Milhaud and Soubrany. According to Mallarmé the men concerned had been falsely denounced by rogues whom they were about to expose. Simon followed this up by saying that Saint-Just and Le Bas had made the same mistake at Strasbourg. There too they had been taken in by false accusations against worthy officials who had been appointed by other deputies. The assembly referred both matters to the two governing committees, who could have had no idea of the merits of these charges and counter-charges. Neither Mallarmé nor Simon questioned Saint-Just's motives, but that was only moderately reassuring. By the end of 1793 to suggest that a man had made a mistake was the first step towards implying that it was done for a purpose. Like over-zealous psychiatrists, the deputies were inclined to ask themselves why the patient had chosen to allow himself to become ill.

Saint-Just's mission to the Rhine Army can therefore be rated a military success. That was what mattered most at the time. On the basis of *post hoc ergo propter hoc* he deserved the credit for the reversal of the military situation. His colleagues on the committee would not forget that, at a time when it was under fire and owed its survival to its military achievements. He had shown himself to be a man of energy and courage. When confronted with logistic problems he could get things done by methods whose success legitimized whatever was arbitrary or unorthodox. This was what he understood by 'revolutionary' government. Where politics was concerned the situation was different and he could not hope for the same kind of results. Revolutionary government aspired to enlist the spontaneous enthusiasm of the population as a whole for policies with which 'the people' could identify. That was not going to happen in Alsace. Saint-Just had perhaps better reasons than most unsuccessful politicians for believing that it was not his fault. In many respects Alsace *was* foreign. It was also an exposed frontier outpost where the government could not afford to take any risks. If purging administrators meant forfeiting local support, that was a price that had to be paid. He was perhaps more at fault in giving his tacit approval to Schneider and his band, in the belief that Alsace could be regenerated by a different kind of popular movement, imposed from the outside. His subsequent volte-face suggested that safety was to be found only in obedience.

If regeneration seemed as far off as ever, that was because unworthy agents had betrayed 'the people'. But perhaps Alsatians were not really 'people' in the same way as the French. Until they had been re-educated – in French – they would have to be ruled by men who knew what was best for them, men like Dièche and Monet, who could be relied on to do what they were told. If Saint-Just came to the conclusion that this was the lesson of his mission to the Rhine Army, that would be in accordance with what we know of his temperament, his convictions and the position in which he found himself. He had probably not yet asked himself the awkward question of what to do if the situation in Alsace were to be repeated in the rest of France. Perhaps Frenchmen were not the real people either, until they had been re-educated.

9

Preparing for Combat

Towards the end of 1793 the Montagnard deputy, Levasseur, like Saint-Just, returned to Paris after a long absence at the front and was shocked to discover what had happened to the Convention during his absence. 'I found it so transformed that my head swam and I could scarcely recognize my colleagues . . . instead of the old Mountain that had been so compact and united, a swarm of rival factions that dared not fight each other in the open . . . were carrying on an underground war that was perhaps more dangerous than open combat on the floor of the assembly.'[1]

To some extent this was a matter of the rivalry and competition for office that are to be expected in any political body, but it had been given a new edge by the concessions made to the extremists during the autumn. The law of suspects, passed in September, gave *comités révolutionnaires* all over the country the right to arrest people and keep them in gaol indefinitely without trial. This put a deadly weapon into the hands of militants, some of them with doubtful revolutionary credentials, who were free to indulge their political principles or fantasies and to gratify their personal

[1] R. Levasseur, *Mémoires*, 4 vols (Paris, 1829–31), vol. II, p. 288.

rivalries. The gaols filled with 'suspects' of every kind, some of them the victims of gang warfare between competing revolutionary factions. The small fry, when they fell foul of hostile bands, appealed for protection to sympathetic deputies in the assembly, who found themselves at loggerheads with each other because of the petty quarrels of their clients. Proli and his friends tried to take advantage of the new situation by setting up a central committee to co-ordinate the activities of the *comités révolutionnaires* of the Paris Sections. This went down badly with the Commune, which asserted its own right of control over the new body, only to be called to order by the Committees of Public Safety and General Security.

As had happened in Alsace, disagreements about strategy were responsible for the emergence of rival partnerships between generals and the representatives on mission attached to their forces. This was particularly acute in the Vendée, where the Cordeliers Boulanger and Rossignol, the protégés of the War Minister, Bouchotte, and his deputy, Vincent, were in conflict with the duc de Biron, Danton's friend Westermann and Fabre d'Eglantine's brother. Incensed by all the military blunders; the deputy Philippeaux, when he returned to Paris, denounced the Cordeliers and accused the government of deliberately prolonging the war.

The Cordelier Club had become the headquarters of men who had been disappointed in their hopes of election to the Convention: Hébert, Ronsin and Vincent. They enjoyed a good deal of influence and power, but they were impatient for more. They resented the fact that the centralization of revolutionary government under the committees of the Convention reduced their own authority. They enjoyed some sympathy in the Jacobin Club, which was always well disposed towards anything that looked like radicalism, and the opinion of the Jacobins counted for a good deal in the Convention.

Within the assembly itself the growing power of the Committee of Public Safety created resentment, especially from representatives on mission who were recalled as a mark of disfavour. Some of the former leaders of the Revolution were beginning to argue that the time had come to seek peace and to wind down the Terror. Danton, to whom such people tended to look as their natural leader, returned from virtual retirement at Arcis-sur-Aube at the end of November and joined Robespierre in attacking dechristianization.[2]

The assault on religion had attracted support from a variety of people in search of a popular cause but it had been particularly associated with the extremists.[3] When Robespierre condemned it the basis therefore existed for an informal alliance between him and the moderates, which set the political tone during the first half of December. It reached its high-water mark when Fabre d'Eglantine obtained the arrest of Vincent and Ronsin on the 17th. Four days later the tide turned with the return of Collot d'Herbois of the Committee of Public Safety, who, with Ronsin, had presided over mass executions at Lyon. Collot, to save himself from Ronsin's fate, turned on the moderates. Confronted by this danger of a split within the Montagnards, Robespierre drew back, and by the end of the year he, Collot and Danton formed a kind of neutral triumvirate, whilst their friends and political allies continued to denounce each other at the Jacobin Club.

Cutting across these conflicts and infecting the wounds that they inflicted was the influence of corruption. After successfully blackmailing bankers, the racketeers turned on the East India Company and persuaded the assembly to vote its liquidation. Fabre d'Eglantine, commended by Robespierre for his vigilance, objected that the terms of the proposed Bill would allow the directors of the company to carry away their assets, and persuaded the assembly itself to take charge of the liquidation. On 14 November Chabot, a former radical turned moderate, who was being attacked by Hébert in the Jacobins, revealed that the text that had actually been published, without anyone's noticing it

---

[2] For a rather fuller summary of the politics of the period, see N. Hampson, *The Life and Opinions of Maximilien Robespierre* (London, 1974), ch. 7.

[3] I have preferred the conveniently vague expressions 'moderates' and 'radicals' or 'extremists' to the customary 'Dantonists' and 'Hébertists' to avoid giving the impression that the two men controlled organized parties.

disregarded Fabre's amendment.[4] He probably did not know that Fabre himself was involved in the fraud. The other corrupt deputies were minor men whose political reputations were already compromised. Fabre, however, was a friend of Danton who enjoyed the confidence of Robespierre. Fabre's reputation for sharp-eyed integrity was such that he was actually invited to assist the two members of the Committee of General Security who had been ordered to investigate the fraud in which Fabre himself was involved. This was the safest place for him to be, but he could not be sure of continuing to pull the wool over people's eyes, and one can see why he in particular was impatient to put an end to the Terror. The revelation of Fabre's guilt, early in January, had far-reaching political implications. Danton abandoned his neutrality in order to defend his friend, and Robespierre, incensed at having been made to look a fool, began to take a more serious view of the faction-fighting within the assembly.

There was another dimension to the divisions within the revolutionaries. The British Government, in addition to the usual spies who supplied it with military information, maintained agents within the Jacobin Club who passed themselves off as extremists. Fabre, in October, had insinuated that Proli and his band were such foreign agents who had bamboozled Chabot and Hérault de Séchelles into working for them. Chabot in turn, perhaps in the hope of getting Hébert off his back, insisted that behind the corruption was a counter-revolutionary plot, controlled by the baron de Batz and ultimately by Pitt, to destroy the Convention by buying those deputies who were for sale and setting the others against each other by a campaign of defamation. He hinted that Hébert was one of Batz's agents in this plot. Chabot was a singularly unreliable witness, but his allegations could not simply be brushed aside since he was the man who had revealed the actual fraud connected with the liquidation of the East India Company. The two governing committees, whatever their initial scepticism, eventually came to believe in the existence of the

---

[4] See N. Hampson, 'François Chabot and his Plot', *Transactions of the Royal Historical Society* (1976).

Batz plot, or at least to behave as though they did. They may have been wrong but they were not merely paranoid. Chabot insisted that corruption and counter-revolution were two aspects of the same foreign plot and that they provided the secret key to the political conflicts amongst the revolutionaries. In this poisoned atmosphere it became common practice for everyone to denounce his opponents as foreign agents, about whom he knew more than he was prepared to reveal at the moment – presumably in the hope that if the others had any guilty secrets they might be frightened into silence.

This was the political climate that Levasseur found so distasteful. Even the least inquisitive reader is likely to want to know what was really going on and how many of the accusations were actually true, but there is no way of satisfying his curiosity. There is, of course, plenty of evidence about who denounced whom, but very little to show whether or not the accusations were true, or were believed by those who made them. Hébert and Danton's friend Desmoulins, in their different ways, were brilliant journalists, and the polemic between the *Père Duchesne* and the *Vieux Cordelier* (a newspaper that Desmoulins created in December) still makes lively reading, but it does not tell us very much about what was actually going on. The records of the two governing committees are full of administrative decisions but were not intended to reveal to the nation the divisions within a supposedly united movement. Private sources of information are scanty, for this was not a time when prudent men were tempted to put pen to paper or to keep such compromising material as might come their way. There are also memoirs, written by the survivors when the dust had settled, but since the main protagonists exterminated each other, those who were in a position to say what they knew tended not to know very much. Sometimes the problem arises from an *embarras de richesses*: from his retreat in Italy the comte d'Antraigues supplied the crowned heads of Europe with intelligence of affairs in France, some of it claiming to come from a secretary of the Committee of Public Safety. When the committee intercepted one of these bulletins it was sufficiently impressed by its accuracy to believe that Hérault was leaking the information. This flattered d'Antraigues whose reports were often untrue or implausible, as when he kept insisting that Robespierre and Saint-Just were at odds with each other.

In this situation none of the courses open to the historian is very tempting. If he believes everything, his account of events is liable to read like the description of a session on the dodgems, with the different cars careering around in no particular direction, bouncing off each other and following no rational courses.[5] To believe as little as possible is to make fewer mistakes . . . and even fewer discoveries.[6] To accept some of the evidence and reject the rest is liable to mean endorsing what agrees with one's initial assumptions.[7] There is a sense in which the historian's helplessness does not matter very much: if he and his readers are wandering around in a fog, so were the revolutionaries. They had good grounds for assuming ulterior motives behind some of the protestations of single-minded devotion to the Revolution and no means of distinguishing what was true from what some people wanted others to believe. Perhaps the safest way of proceeding is to concentrate on what was said at the time, which at least offers an indication of what the speakers wanted people to think that they thought.

The most sensible assessment of the situation as a whole comes from Levasseur, even if it was a case of emotion being recollected in tranquillity and scarcely agreed with what he said at the time:

> Within practically all the newly-formed parties the majority was acting in good faith. Within practically all of them one could also find signs of perverted plans and perfidious intentions . . . All sensible people had understood the need to strengthen the revolutionary government . . . Once this power was organized, however, men who had hoped to be part of it and found themselves excluded soon showed their discontent. They understood that, in theory, what was

[5] See, for example, A. Ollivier, *Saint-Just ou la force des choses* (Paris, 1954), pp. 357–437.

[6] E.g. A. Mathiez, *La Conspiration de l'étranger* (Paris, 1918), ch. 8, and Hampson, 'Chabot'.

[7] E.g. Mathiez, *La Conspiration*, ch. 7, and Hampson, *Robespierre*, pp. 192–223.

needed was united and powerful leadership, but they felt offended as soon as it was imposed on them . . . Clearly it was a big step from this to conspiracies against the republic. To overthrow the existing government was not the same thing as to attack the republic, but it ought to be done openly, by political means, within the Convention.[8]

If one can believe Levasseur, all the Montagnards were agreed on the need to wind up the Revolution. 'They all wanted to return to clemency and to a legal order, but each of them wanted to take a different road.' Having, like the sorcerer's apprentice, conjured up the forces of popular anarchy in order to defeat their domestic and foreign enemies, they were to some extent the prisoners of their own auxiliaries. To turn against the sans-culottes would be to endanger the Revolution before its victory was secure. As Levasseur saw it, Robespierre and Danton could have co-operated to steer the republic safely into port but for the intransigence of Saint-Just, who was the real leader of the revolutionary government.

Considering only the goal he intended to reach, he did not concern himself much with the means that he would have to use; the safest always seemed to him to be the best. To establish the republic of which he had dreamed for a long time, he would have sacrificed his own head, but also those of a hundred thousand others . . . Robespierre had some of the vanity that comes from egoism; Saint-Just was full of the pride born of firm convictions . . . with his habit of regarding all dissidents as criminals and treating them merely as obstacles to be overcome, he was ready to sacrifice anyone with influence who used it to oppose his views.'[9]

For a long time Robespierre had kept a remarkably cool head in this bewildering situation. Convinced, like Levasseur, that the real enemies of the Revolution were dangerous only when they

[8] Levasseur, *Mémoires*, vol. II pp. 291–3.
[9] Ibid. pp. 324–5.

deceived the leaders into fighting each other, he tried hard to separate the sheep from the goats. Dechristianization seemed to him a clear case of counter-revolutionaries trying to provoke popular resistance whilst posing as extremists. This led him towards the moderates. When they tried to change the membership of the Committee of Public Safety on 12 December, he probably began to have his doubts, and by the end of the year he was distancing himself from both factions, though still reluctant to believe that their leaders were more than misled.

In a speech on the political situation that he made on Christmas Day Robespierre adopted a point of view that was very close to Saint-Just's. The natural state of a republic – which corresponded more or less to Saint-Just's 'civil state' – was one of civil liberty and consensus. This goal could be attained only by the forcible defeat of those who were determined, for reasons which they themselves knew to be selfish, to frustrate it. As he put it, echoing Saint-Just, 'The Revolution is the war of liberty against its enemies.' During this violent phase public liberty took precedence over civil liberty. The republic existed for the benefit of its citizens but 'to the enemies of the people it owes only death.' This repeated the argument of his younger colleague in the case of the king's trial, reiterated in his speech of the previous autumn on revolutionary government, but Robespierre was more concerned to open the eyes of the misled, whilst Saint-Just thought primarily of exterminating those who were deceiving them in order to sabotage the Revolution.

Robespierre was badly shaken by the revelation of Fabre's corruption in January 1794, which led him to wonder whether the leaders of the factions were really unaware of the ends for which they were being used. The text has survived of a speech that he never delivered, presumably because it was censored by his colleagues, which probably dates from this period. In this he argued that the two factions were working together to destroy the Revolution. Hébert was now classed amongst the guilty, presumably as a result of Chabot's denunciation. Danton and Robespierre's friend Desmoulins were still given the benefit of the doubt, as men who were genuinely misled by the real culprits. Robespierre took some risks in order to defend Desmoulins, but Danton was equally determined to stand by *his* friend, Fabre, despite the overwhelming evidence against him.

In a desperate attempt to postpone the inevitable, Robespierre used his moral authority over the Jacobins to divert them from their penchant for faction fighting into an examination of the 'crimes of the British government'. This kept them occupied for about a fortnight, but the subject was not inexhaustible and when they looked like returning to more exciting business the Committee of Public Safety seems to have imposed silence on both sides, Robespierre then made a final effort to persuade his colleagues to concentrate on higher things. On 5 February he tried to define the ideological goals of the Revolution and to indicate the means necessary to achieve them. For him, as for Saint-Just, the objective was 'the peaceful enjoyment of liberty and equality'. This would 'fulfil the wishes of nature and accomplish the destiny of mankind'. Since the ideal state of his hopes was defined in essentially moral terms, moral vices were as dangerous as political ones, but he reassured his audience that 'We do not intend to cast the republic in a Spartan mould.' A few weeks later Saint-Just was to have different views about that. More optimistic than his colleague, Robespierre believed that the French people had already regenerated itself by five years of revolution. Its very success, however, in laying the foundations of a new moral order had united against it both the corrupt and the ambitious. To defeat this coalition and create a pacific society in which *vertu* would prevail without coercion required 'the despotism of liberty against tyranny'. Only republicans could be citizens in a republic and their opponents had to be treated as 'foreigners, or rather, as enemies'. *Vertu* and its opposite divided the righteous from the unregenerate, and the two were to be identified by moral conviction rather than by the kind of formal proofs appropriate to civil courts. He believed that the attack on the Committee of Public Safety had been defeated, but the factions were still in being and he implied that any criticism of the policies of the government would be interpreted as an attack on the Revolution itself.

Both Robespierre and Saint-Just had a foot in two contrasting worlds. Their objective was an ideal society that had been made possible by the Revolution for the first time in human history. The majesty of the goal justified whatever sacrifices were necessary to attain it. At the same time, as members of a government struggling to maintain itself in office and to defeat its opponents, they had perforce to operate in a world of party politics that was singularly vicious in its hatreds. Robespierre, at this stage, was more preoccupied with the vision than with the faction fighting, and his personal sympathies towards some of his opponents inclined him towards charitable verdicts. Saint-Just was made of sterner stuff. He was more disposed towards radical policies and he had more in common with the extremists than with the moderates – provided that they knew their place. The unfortunate Schneider could testify to what happened when they got above themselves. He had no sympathy for Danton, and Desmoulins suspected that Saint-Just had not forgotten his unfortunate jibe about carrying his head like the Holy Sacrament. Now that the Revolution had thrown up a government that was both virtuous and effective, any falling away from the path that led to the ideal state must be due to the corruption or ambition of its enemies – or perhaps to vices that had been bred into the people themselves by the vicious habits of the monarchy. Hitherto the two men had been able to keep their two worlds apart, or at least to assume that the Montagnards were free from the vices that infected royalists and Girondins. By 1794 they were being driven to different conclusions. The revolutionary government was in pure hands – their own, as it happened – and if the millennium did not seem to be getting any nearer this must be due to the selfishness and self-indulgence of people who, quite consciously, put their own interests before those of the community. The government had encouraged these false friends, under the mistaken impression that they were not aware of the purposes for which they were being used, but the time was coming when such indulgence would have to stop.

After his return from Alsace Saint-Just immersed himself in administration. It is a reasonable guess that he also tried to catch up on what had been happening to the Montagnards during his absence and that he was briefed by Robespierre, a man whose views were very similar to his own, but he made no speeches; if he wrote any letters they have not survived and we have no clue to his thoughts.

On 27 January 1794 he was on the road again, once more with Le Bas, on a brief mission to the Army of the North. This was a very different business from his recent mission to Alsace. There was no military crisis; fighting was at a standstill for the winter, and his orders were merely to report on the state of the French bases at Lille, Maubeuge and Bouchain. He was granted the 'unlimited powers of a representative of the people', which put him on the same footing as his colleagues in the field. This time he claimed no special status and he co-operated with the others.

Despite this self-restraint, his mission was distinguished by his usual dramatic gestures. On the way out he and Les Bas were made to descend from their coach by zealous policemen who wanted to make quite sure of their identity. Treating this as an insult to the dignity of the Convention, Saint-Just ordered the arrest of the local *comité de surveillance*. Its members were released after a few days, but one cannot help wondering what Saint-Just would have made of the incident if it had involved a deputy whom he disliked. Despite the law of 4 December 1793 which had provided revolutionary government with a kind of constitution, he still considered himself free to act as he thought best. Quite illegally, he ordered the demolition of the houses of men convicted of selling above the controlled prices. This was praised by Collot in the Jacobin Club in Paris but it had no practical effect since local officials insisted on conforming to the law. Even more arbitrary was his order for the confiscation of the property of a man accused of being a counter-revolutionary, who had not yet been tried. This was an early instance of his attitude towards suspects. The fact of their arrest seemed to him a presumption of their guilt and their trial was a matter of confirming the decision of the authorities rather than a serious investigation of whether or not they were guilty of specific charges.

Far wider in its effects was his order on 4 February for the arrest of all nobles in the Pas-de-Calais, the Nord, the Somme and the

Aisne. As usual, he did not concern himself with details of definition. It was assumed by the local authorities that the order applied to whole families, and most of those actually arrested were women. Le Bon, a particularly paranoid deputy who was to terrorize Arras – with the approval of the Committee of Public Safety – arrested the agents and tenant farmers of the nobility for good measure. Even Le Bas's father was denounced as an 'aristocrat', though this mistake was naturally soon rectified. As usual, Saint-Just was more concerned with the striking gesture than with what actually happened. Many of the minor nobles were farmers or textile manufacturers. Their imprisonment meant unemployment and a fall in food production. When the local population protested at the arrest of these 'fathers of the people' Le Bon gave way to his righteous indignation: 'It is indecent, after four years of revolutionary labour, to see whole communes regretting their masters in return for a morsel of bread.' Saint-Just, to do him justice, specified on 19 February that his order applied only to the nobles themselves, but after his return to Paris he made no attempt to restrain Le Bon.

Saint-Just and Le Bas ordered one or two spectacular acts of compensation when they heard of individuals who had suffered from the arbitrary actions of local authorities. He was always ready to believe the worst of the administration and he presumably felt that while he was around innocence could be sure of protection, but if he saw himself as an Apollo amongst mortals, a good many local people must have thought of him as Lucifer.

By the middle of February he was back in Paris. During the spring of 1794 the economic policy of the government was evolving in a new direction. In the previous autumn, when the radicals had been on the offensive, bankers, merchants and manufacturers had been viewed with suspicion, and foreigners with hostility. This had not been good for the economy or for the importing of essential war materials. The government now felt strong enough to make the necessary adjustments. The importing of necessities and war materials was to be encouraged, which implied giving more scope to bankers and merchants. A new system of price and wage controls was introduced in the hope of converting what had been a matter of local improvisation into a planned national policy. Wholesalers and retailers were now guaranteed limited profits, which raised prices to consumers. If everyone played by the rules – and in actual practice it was impossible to eliminate the black market – the ratio between wages and prices was now no more favourable, and where some goods were concerned it was considerably less favourable, than it had been in 1790. The emphasis of government policy had shifted from doing something for the consumer to enforcing a moral economy in which every man should be guaranteed a modest livelihood. That was the intention, but an eighteenth-century government, unused to running the economy, was not always aware of the practical implications of its policies. Its benevolent intentions were not evident to dockyard workers who found their wages twice reduced in the space of a few months. Wages in the national arms factories in Paris were paid at the low official rate, which had not yet been enforced on private enterprise. When the aggrieved workers went on strike they were accused of sabotaging the war effort and threatened with the revolutionary tribunal. The government, in other words, shared Le Bon's impatience with those who forgot about the regeneration of humanity in their preoccupation with 'a morsel of bread'.

Republican morality was the order of the day. A circular of 17 January which reads as though it was written by Robespierre or Saint-Just, told local authorities how they were to implement the law of 4 December 1793 on revolutionary government. 'Reason is already triumphant throughout the political sphere and as for morality, its reign is not far distant.' What was needed to bring these things to pass was not so much a trained intelligence as a pure and upright heart. This was very edifying, but it all depended on how – and by whom – purity was to be defined.

Ever since the moderate offensive in December 1793 the question of what to do about the tens of thousands of arrested suspects had been on the agenda. Desmoulins proposed a 'committee of clemency' to liberate those who should never have been arrested. Robespierre persuaded the assembly to accept this, under the less compromising title of a 'committee of justice', but the governing committee do not seem to have been very happy about it, and Billaud-Varenne, who said that it should never have been proposed in the first place, persuaded the Convention to drop the idea. On 22 February the two committees were instructed to present a report on the question of what to do about the political prisoners. When they entrusted this to Saint-Just it was clear that there would be no revival of any committee of clemency. He was probably closer, at this time, to the viewpoint of Billaud-Varenne and Collot d'Herbois than to Robespierre, and Robespierre himself had hardened his attitude since the exposure of Fabre's corruption.

When Saint-Just delivered his report on 26 February it took the usual shape of an attempt to see a specific problem in terms of general principles.[10] He began by telling his colleagues that, as in the case of Louis XVI, the issue was not judicial but political. 'You are not concerned with the civic aspect but with public safety, which is the prime consideration for us all. We must be just all the same, but in terms of the public interest rather than the private interest . . . You have not to decide what refers to this individual or that, but what concerns the republic.' The detention of suspects was a public necessity. Since French society, even now, was not founded on the laws of nature, many of its members were still motivated by self-interest and avarice. Since 'Monarchy is not so much a king as crime, and the essence of a republic is *vertu*', it followed that, if the republic were to survive, it would have to purify itself. This called for the creation of 'republican institutions', something that was to preoccupy him more and more during the coming months. Their function was to *comprimer les moeurs*, which was also becoming rather an obsession with him. In the meantime, anyone who wanted to examine the cases of the suspects in the name of 'weakness and false sentimentality' was ignoring the public good, and anyone who proposed pardoning crime could only be motivated by a secret ambition to restore the monarchy. This was the policy of France's foreign enemies. Those

---

[10] See C. Vellay, *Oeuvres complètes de Saint-Just*, 2 vols (Paris, 1908), vol. II, pp. 228–41 and 247–8.

who proposed it were therefore playing the enemy's game. From this it was only a small step to regarding them as foreign agents.

What constituted a republic was not merely *vertu* but also 'the total destruction of whatever is opposed to it'. This led him to justify the moderation of the republicans by some wild abuse of the monarchy – he was never very good on statistics. Louis XVI was alleged to have slaughtered 8,000 people in 1788, and under the monarchy there had been 400,000 in gaol and 3,000 broken on the wheel every year. Even if these figures had not been demonstrably absurd, the excesses of the monarchy would not seem to have justified their imitation by the republic, but Saint-Just went on to argue that the end justified the means and that it was legitimate for France to employ, in the defence of liberty, methods that were inexcusable when used in support of tyranny.

Those who criticized the severity of the government were 'men who want to destroy the scaffold because they are afraid of mounting it'. This was part of his open attack on the moderates, who were blamed for all of France's ills, such as corruption and food shortages, and even accused of wanting to open the prisons in order to mobilize forces for a coup d'état. If only all the royalists had been rounded up a year earlier there would have been no civil war. This had always been Marat's argument, that massacring some people now would do away with the need to murder more in the future, and Saint-Just went on to praise that sinister advocate of slaughter, as he was to do in all his subsequent speeches. His admiration for Marat was something new, and it boded no good for his opponents. He went on to argue that the government had been on the right lines in the previous autumn (when he himself had been helping to formulate policy in Paris) but that it had lost its way (during his absence in Alsace). 'The dynamism of the revolutionary government, which had established the dictatorship of justice, has collapsed.' All the trouble came from the moderates. 'The popular societies are absolutely calm.' This was an interesting observation at a time when the Cordelier Club was beginning to play with the idea of a new insurrection.

Saint-Just then suddenly took off on a different tangent, arguing that the course of the Revolution was leading people to perceive new truths to which they had previously been blind. The corrupt were often wealthy people whose money gave them economic power over their dependants. If this was to be prevented, 'The man who has shown himself to be the enemy of his country cannot be allowed to own property in it . . . The property of *patriotes* is sacred but the goods of conspirators are at the disposal of all the wretched.' The government was now republican but civil society was still aristocratic. Whatever this implied, it certainly suggested that it was the duty of the government to raise society to its own level.

After his usual diatribe against the abuse of power by civil servants, Saint-Just persuaded the assembly to vote that the Committee of General Security should be entrusted with the work of identifying and liberating imprisoned *patriotes*. Those who were considered to be enemies of the people were to have their property confiscated and were to be detained until the end of the war, when they would be deported. A week later he introduced a second Bill ordering all communes to send a list of their poor to the Committee of General Security. *Comités de surveillance* were to submit the names of all of their political prisoners, with an account of their conduct since 1789, and the Committee of Public Safety was to submit a report on how to make the wealth of the 'enemies of the revolution' available for the relief of the poor.

The question of how one should interpret these '*ventôse*' (March) decrees has raised a good deal of historical controversy, much of it reflecting the ideas of the twentieth century rather than those of Saint-Just. The new laws have been described as primarily intended to effect a redistribution of wealth, even as the first gleams of a socialist dawn. Mathiez saw them as a hint to the Cordeliers that Saint-Just was on their side. More cynically, recent historians sympathetic to Saint-Just and the Montagnards have seen them as a somewhat Machiavellian attempt to buy popular support while the government dealt with its radical opponents. That seems a little hard on Saint-Just and it is contrary to the whole tenor of his speech. A dispassionate examination of what he said, in the context of his career as a whole, suggests another interpretation.

In some respects he was expressing in terms of practical policy the ideas about the nature of the Revolution that Robespierre had elaborated on 5 February, but whereas Robespierre had insisted on the existence of a dual threat from both moderates and extremists, Saint-Just directed the whole of his fire against the former. He was not the kind of man to try to buy anyone's support, and he certainly gave no sign that he was contemplating action against anyone except the moderates. Collot, who was working hard to keep the Cordeliers and the Jacobins united, praised the speech as a prelude to the liberation of arrested *extremists*.

If one looks at what Saint-Just actually said, the main thrust of the speech is punitive. The Revolution had degenerated since the previous autumn, and the siren voices of 'indulgence' had encouraged the growth of both faction and corruption. Since the republic was synonymous with *vertu* its survival required the extermination of the vicious, and if this involved destroying some of the innocent by mistake, this was a necessary price to pay for the attainment of the great revolutionary goal. There was more to it than that, Hitherto 'suspects' as their name implied, were people who were believed to be unreliable, although there was not enough evidence for even a revolutionary court to convict them of anything. In each of his speeches Saint-Just described the political prisoners as either *patriotes* or 'enemies of the people.' By implication at least, this eliminated the category of 'suspect' altogether, and enemies of the people would be lucky if they suffered nothing worse than deportation.

This was to be confirmed by what happened later. On 12 March Saint-Just proposed the creation of six commissions to try the people in gaol and decide what should be done with them. This seems to have aroused some opposition within the governing committees, and only two of the commissions were eventually to function. By 11 May reports on 40,000 suspects had already reached the government, and there could be no possibility of giving serious consideration to the veracity of the charges against so many people. The two commissions ordered 300 of the first 450 cases they considered to be sent for trial by the revolutionary tribunal. After 10 June the only sentence that this court could impose was death, and trial had been reduced to a grim judicial farce. If the *ventôse* decrees had been fully implemented they would therefore have resulted in the death of tens of thousands of political prisoners. That may not have been Saint-Just's intention at the time, but he was not a man who worried much about the consequences of his actions and he never modified his policy. Indeed, it was in the hope of conciliating him, on 22 July, that the governing committees agreed to set up the remaining four commissions. It is difficult not to believe that, so far as he was concerned, the main object of the new law was to purge the republic of vast numbers of political undesirables.

The distribution of confiscated property to the poor was a secondary consideration, as it had been at Strasbourg. Saint-Just's concern for the poor was genuine but abstract. Obsessed by his Spartan ideal of frugal self-sufficiency, he was not interested in developing the economy with a view to reducing unemployment or increasing the standard of living. He was a man of gestures, and this was one of them. One could contemplate giving away confiscated land to those who had none, but it would not have done much good to the urban artisan, and how did one redistribute a brewery or an export business? The most that could have been done was to sell it to some worthy *patriote*, who could be relied on not to abuse his economic patronage, and distribute the proceeds to the poor in the form of alms. This would have amounted to rather less than a social revolution. What actually happened was that the poor suspected that the intention of the government was to identify those incapable of supporting themselves, so that they could be shipped off to the colonies. They were therefore reluctant to allow their names to go forward, and the revolutionary dictatorship collapsed before any property was actually transferred. It was the story of Strasbourg all over again.

The *ventôse* speeches bring us back to the question of the relationship between Saint-Just and Robespierre. As we have seen, their theoretical conception of the Revolution and how it must be preserved was virtually the same. Ideas that occurred to one of them were promptly assimilated by the other. Saint-Just had taken no interest in religion before his mission to Alsace, where he had done nothing to check dechristianization. When Robespierre became convinced that the attack on religion was intended to provoke popular resistance to the revolutionary government, it became a regular feature of Saint-Just's denunciation of the schemers and the corrupt.

Where the application of these principles was concerned the two men held similar but not identical views. This was partly a matter of temperament. Robespierre, in his speech on 5 February, devoted a fair amount of time to the beatific contemplation of the sunlit future before resigning himself to the bloody business of attaining it. Saint-Just gave utopia half a sentence – 'We want to establish an order of things in which a universal tendency towards the good prevails' – before he added 'and the factions find themselves suddenly hurled on to the scaffold.' He was more pessimistic as well as more punitive. 'Since human self-interest is invincible, the freedom of a people can scarcely be established except by the sword.' Robespierre seemed to think that once a limited number of the wicked had been eliminated the virtuous masses would inherit the earth. Ever since the previous year Saint-Just had set out to 'make the people what one wants them to be', and he was increasingly insistent on the need to *comprimer les moeurs* and to reshape society by means of republican institutions. This aligned him with Billaud-Varenne, who wanted to 'recreate the people in order to restore it to democracy'. Robespierre disclaimed any intention of creating a new Sparta, which Saint-Just was soon to define as his objective.

When it came to party politics the differences were more obvious. Robespierre, after flirting with the moderates, had eventually declared war on both factions, but for a long time he tried to contain the feuding by political means, and even when this failed he was still inclined to limit the damage and to try to convince himself that his opponents were merely foolish or misled. In December 1793 he risked his reputation in the Jacobin Club to defend Danton and Desmoulins, and even in January 1794 he forced the club, very much against its will, to rescind a vote for the expulsion of Desmoulins. For a long time he seemed reluctant to believe that Chabot had been a participant in the plot that he denounced. Saint-Just was convinced that the Revolution had retrogressed since the radical phase of the previous autumn. His old friend Daubigny, when he was trying to rehabilitate himself by denouncing Saint-Just after his death, said that he was always denouncing Danton and Philippeaux as traitors, although he did not believe it. That has to be treated with scepticism, although it is not implausible. Of one thing one could be fairly certain: Saint-Just would never be deflected from his course by any considerations of personal friendship. He was also becoming increasingly impressed by the sanguinary ideas of Marat, a man whom Robespierre had always viewed with some suspicion and distaste. In February 1794 both men were agreed on denouncing as counter-revolutionary any criticism of the government, and both believed that the campaign of the moderates had produced a revival of what they called aristocracy. Robespierre, however, thought that this had failed, and he assured the deputies that there were no traitors in the assembly. Saint-Just did not share his optimism, and both in his conduct on mission and in his *ventôse* speeches, he was nearer to the policies of Billaud and Collot and to the kind of attitudes that prevailed in the Cordelier Club.

10

❧

The Inquisitor

From the middle of February 1794 until well into March the Committee of Public Safety was in some danger of losing control over the political situation. Two of its members were absent in Brittany and the west coast ports. Hérault's reputation had been fatally damaged by Fabre's insinuations, which were still believed despite the exposure of Fabre himself, and by the mistaken suspicion that he was leaking information to foreign agents. He was still nominally a member of the committee but he was excluded from its deliberations. Billaud-Varenne was away at Saint-Malo from 19 February until 10 March, helping to organize an attack on the Channel Islands that was eventually cancelled, and Robespierre and Couthon were ill. On at least two previous occasions, before the insurrection of 10 August 1792 and the overthrow of the Girondins, Robespierre had been out of action for short periods. It is tempting, in the absence of any medical information, to assume that these were nervous illnesses induced by his awareness of an impending crisis. In the past such attacks had lasted for only a few days but in 1794 he was absent from the Jacobin Club and the Assembly from 10 February until 13 March and there is a case for arguing that he never recovered his grip over himself and revolutionary politics. Of the remaining six members three, Carnot, Prieur de la Côte d'Or and Lindet were specialists who immersed themselves in their departmental work. That left only Barère, Collot d'Herbois and Saint-Just. Barère was a useful factotum but a political lightweight who would always support what he believed to be the winning side. The only member of the committee with much influence over the Jacobin Club, which Saint-Just rarely attended, was Collot.

This was too good an opportunity for the extremists to miss. Vincent and Ronsin had been released from gaol at the beginning of February and were soon denouncing the moderates, hinting that the government had run out of steam and calling for a new insurrection. Saint-Just had a good deal of sympathy with their point of view although he had no intention of looking for advice or support from outsiders. If one can believe Tissot, who was an assiduous attender of debates in the Jacobin Club and the assembly, in late February the Committee of Public Safety summoned Hébert, Vincent and Ronsin to ask them to 'elaborate their plans for reform' and offered Vincent an important post in charge of the administration of the Army of the North presumably in the hope of getting him out of Paris.[1] Torn between their ambitions and their fears, the Cordeliers played with the idea of a new revolution. On 2 March Ronsin called for an insurrection but was silenced by Hébert. Two days later Hébert himself attacked the moderates, although he steered clear of Danton and suggested that Desmoulins was merely misled. Rather more rashly he also criticized Amar of the Committee of General Security and Carnot's brother. The Cordeliers put a black veil over the declaration of the rights of man, as a signal that they were oppressed. On the following day Momoro, one of their leading members, persuaded the Marat Section to declare for an insurrection, but the Paris Commune, guided by its leading official, Chaumette, refused its support. This produced a warning speech from Barère in the assembly, promising action against both factions and the submission in the near future of Amar's long-delayed report on

---

[1] P. F. Tissot, *Histoire de la révolution française*, 6 vols (Paris, 1839), vol. V, pp. 105–6.

Chabot and his plot. Collot, on behalf of the Jacobins, visited the Cordeliers on the 7th and persuaded them to affirm the solidarity of the two clubs and to remove the black veil. Two days later they resumed their talk of insurrection, although without Hébert's support.

It is not difficult to understand the hopes and fears of the Cordeliers. What is less clear is the attitude of the government. The extremists' demand for more radical policies and for the elimination of the moderates coincided with Saint-Just's own views. Collot was doing all he could to preserve good relations and, if he chose, he could easily make his peace with the would-be insurgents. Saint-Just was less likely to tolerate independent action from any one outside the government. The Montagnards, however, were the prisoners of their dual conception of politics. On the practical level, an effective government, with more power than any of its revolutionary predecessors, was facing a possible attack from Paris, which had succeeded in imposing its will on the assembly in every previous confrontation. That called for a careful assessment of the odds and a policy of either appeasement or repression. In theoretical terms the Montagnards could not appeal for support against an illegal appeal to force, since they owed their domination of the assembly to precisely such a coup, on 2 June 1793. *La sainte insurrection* – provided that it succeeded – was a manifestation of the will of the sovereign people. If it failed it was an impious attempt by a counter-revolutionary faction to dictate to the people's representatives. A good revolutionary knew how to combine the two points of view. What was difficult was to predict who was going to win and to hedge one's bets in the meantime.

It was perhaps the indecision of the Cordeliers, the refusal of the Commune to support them and their failure to win the support of the Sections, that persuaded the government to strike. By the second week of March, Robespierre, Couthon and Billaud were back in the Committee of Public Safety. The committee had plenty of evidence than an insurrection had been discussed, if not exactly planned, but since the right to revolt against oppression was guaranteed by the 1793 constitution, whether or not that was a criminal offence depended on one's views of the behaviour of the government. On 12 March Saint-Just rose to make a speech to the assembly on the political factions. Aware of the threat from the Cordeliers but not of the government's attitude, the deputies must have listened to him with more interest and apprehension than usual.[2]

As always, he began with some general principles which indicated the direction in which his political ideas were evolving. There was a natural identity between the interests of a free government and a free people. Whereas Robespierre had argued that it was for the government to devote itself to the people, who had only to be themselves, Saint-Just insisted that there were obligations on both sides. If the government must serve the people, *they* had to be just and *vertueux*. The first of these conditions had been met and there was nothing wrong with the government. Its duty was therefore to keep the people up to scratch, and any sign of opposition was evidence of popular corruption which it was the government's duty to eradicate. In the past it had been legitimate for the people to demand their liberty when they were oppressed, but now that liberty had triumphed any agitation could come only from those who put their own interests before those of the community. The fact that he dared to make this bold claim was itself the proof of his own probity.

Since morality and revolutionary politics were two sides of the same coin, royalism, treason and financial corruption were also different aspects of the same disease. All kinds of opposition were manifestations of the same plot, which originated with the foreign enemy. The conspirators dissimulated and tried to pass themselves off as good revolutionaries, so that it was impossible to detect them by looking at the policies that they pretended to advocate. One could sometimes identify them by their tendency to adopt different views at different times. No one was likely to risk reminding the author of the *Esprit de la révolution* and the sometime patron of Schneider that he had done the same thing

---

[2] For the text see C. Vellay, *Oeuvres complètes de Saint-Just*, 2 vols (Paris, 1908), vol. II, pp. 256–80.

himself. In fact, it was less difficult than one might have imagined to spot a counter-revolutionary, since any attempt to create a party was a sign of disaffection.

Since his speech was intended to prepare the ground for future action, Saint-Just could not put his opponents on their guard by indicating who they were. 'The interest of the people and that of justice does not allow me to tell you more.' Those who listened to his speech may well have got the impression that his target was the moderates, which perhaps corresponded to his own inclination. If the present situation was troubled, this was the consequence of 'that parricidal indulgence that I recently condemned'. There was to be no more of that. 'No more pity, no weakness towards the guilty . . . Henceforth the government will pardon no more crimes.' He then repeated his recent argument that the republic was entitled to use in the defence of liberty methods that were illegitimate when employed by monarchies.

Going further than Robespierre, he offered the relatively well-heeled deputies 'the happiness of Sparta and of Athens in its finest days . . . a plough, a field, a cottage protected from the Exchequer and a family protected from the lust of brigands.' He himself would not have had much idea of what to do with a plough, a field or a family. He praised the inhabitants of the Corrèze and the Haute-Vienne for living mainly on chestnuts, and those of the Puy-de-Dôme for making do with bread and vegetables, and he had a special word of condemnation for the sons of artisans who tried to raise themselves by means of the Revolution. Those of his admirers who have tried to present him as the humble servant of the peasant and the artisan do not seem to have read him very carefully. He no doubt saw himself as the protector of 'the poor', provided that they knew their place, and he was always ready to take up their cause against their and his political opponents, but, like Rousseau, he was not thinking of ways to improve the standard of living of working people but of the kind of subsistence agriculture that he believed to have prevailed in the classical world. This was as remote from his audience as it was from his own experience.

Four categories of people were singled out for specific condemnation: members of the administration (as always), the idle rich, grumblers and people who were trying to make a career out of the Revolution. To have suggested that he himself had used it to gratify his passion for fame would have been to reveal that one did not know the difference between disinterested public service and careerism – or that one pretended ignorance, for reasons that might be worth investigation.

What his audience, who had heard a good deal of this before, were impatient to know on 26 February was where the blow was going to fall, and that he could not tell them. He produced a list of the accusations that were going to be made against the Cordeliers, of being royalists and foreign agents, of creating a food shortage in Paris in order to goad the sans-culottes into action, of smuggling arms into the capital and planning to open the prisons to mobilize forces for a coup d'état, but these were charges that could be made against anyone. If the accusations of starving Paris and pretending to be extremists seemed to be directed against the radicals, his denunciation of Chabot's accomplices and of those who were trying to save him pointed in the opposite direction. His final proposals, which the assembly hastened to adopt, amounted to a general programme of intensified punitive vigilance that did not appear to have any specific target, and the deputies were no doubt reassured by article 3, which imposed the death penalty on anyone usurping the power or challenging the security and dignity of the assembly. Article 7 provided for the creation of six commissions to investigate suspects in implementation of the *ventôse* law.

Saint-Just's point of view was not wholly unreasonable. The Committee of Public Safety was making a success of what mattered most of all, winning the war, and its critics often *were* self-interested or corrupt. The leaders of the Cordeliers were violent men, intent on personal power, who were perhaps capable of organizing an insurrection but certainly not of governing a country. Some of the moderates were corrupt, in the everyday sense of the word, and more concerned with saving their necks, or those of their friends, than with the future of the Revolution. The members of the Committee of Public Safety, in contrast, were disinterested, in the financial sense at least, and certainly efficient.

They were ruthless and cruel and Collot, in particular, had the massacres of Lyon of his mind, if not on his conscience. One could argue that, having satisfied their own ambitions, they succumbed to the temptation to identify the national interest with their retention of power. They tended to see things the opposite way round, but the fact that they were genuinely concerned with the defence of the Revolution put them in a different category from their opponents.

The real charges against Saint-Just are rather different. He had talked himself into a fantasy world of false absolutes, in which the *vertu* of the government contrasted with the turpitude of all those who were less than enthusiastic in their acceptance of its policies. He took for granted the purity, not merely of the government but of its innumerable agents. In actual fact the prisons were overflowing with people of every kind: counter-revolutionaries, harmless people who thought that things had been better in the past, nobles of every persuasion, speculators, the rich and anyone who had incurred the jealousy or enmity of a swarm of informers, policemen and fanatics. The law of suspects left these people at the mercy of whoever happened to exercise local authority: the reasonable and the disinterested, the drunken and violent, the vicious, the corrupt and those with scores to settle.[3] Those who are inclined to dismiss such a version of the state of affairs as counter-revolutionary propaganda or the uncritical repetition of the self-interested complaints of the guilty, might like to consider Robespierre's views on the subject. On 26 July he was to denounce those agents of the revolutionary government who had 'plunged *patriotes* into dungeons and spread terror through all conditions of men . . . declared war on peaceful citizens, inflated incurable religious prejudices or matters of no importance into crimes, so that they could find guilt everywhere and make the revolution a threat to the people itself'.

If Saint-Just was not aware of this he ought to have been, and it made nonsense of his Manichean division of France into the

[3] For an account of the activities of Héron, the chief police official of the two committees, see G. Lenôtre, *Vieilles Maisons, vieux papiers*, 6th series (Paris, 1930), ch. 2, 'Le Farouche Amar'.

virtuous and the corrupt/ambitious/royalists/enemy agents. If he did understand the actual situation and merely pretended that a man could not feather his own nest without being one of Pitt's agents, or aspire to overthrow the Committee of Public Safety without wanting to restore the monarchy, he was as dangerous as he was unscrupulous, inventing accusations that he did not believe in order to dispose of possible rivals. The question of how far he did believe what he said – and there are infinite degrees of semi-belief – and how far he said whatever suited his tactical purpose, was perhaps of more concern to his own conscience than it is to us. He had to act as though he believed it, and he was now committed to a murderous impasse of his own making. 'No more pity and weakness towards the guilty' was the banner under which he would have to live and die. If all opponents were to be regarded as royalists and foreign agents they would have to be slaughtered as soon as identified, and if the safety of the republic took precedence over justice to individuals no one could be given the benefit of any doubt. This applied both to the assembly and to the country at large. Since all opposition was to be regarded as counter-revolutionary and the petty bureaucrats in the revolutionary administration were eager to demonstrate their vigilance, the Terror looked like going on for ever.

On the night after Saint-Just's speech the leading Cordeliers were arrested. The choice of victims suggested tactical calculation rather than ideological fanaticism. To guard against a hostile reaction in Paris, the mayor, Pache, and Chaumette, the *procureur* of the Commune, were spared – for the time being. One or two bankers and a food control inspector were thrown in to provide popular targets for sans-culotte hatred. When the Girondins had been condemned in the autumn their trial had been covered at length in the leading newspaper, the *Moniteur*, which now promised its readers a similar treat. Its next reference to the Cordeliers was its report of their execution, which suggested that, despite its concern to protect the sovereign people from its enemies, the government did not intend that they should learn much about the process. From its own point of view the trial went well. The accused were discredited, the sans-culottes did not stir and all the men in the dock were found guilty and executed, with the exception of the police informer who had been planted amongst them.

Most of the deputies probably slept more soundly for the elimination of the Cordeliers, none of whom sat in the assembly.[4] Vincent and Ronsin in particular were violent men, much given to talk of purging the Convention, and few of the back-bench deputies could have relished the thought of another 2 June. On 17 March Saint-Just was on his feet again – throughout the month he spoke in the assembly only in order to proscribe – and this time two deputies were involved, but the circumstances were unusual and the government seemed to have a reasonable case. The law of 12 March had included in the category of traitors anyone who sheltered an *émigré*, and also prescribed that arrested conspirators were to be held incommunicado. If Saint-Just is to be believed, an *émigré* was caught in Hérault's apartment, and Hérault and Simon – the man who had criticized Saint-Just's activities in Alsace – despite the protests of the Section authorities, insisted on visiting him, presumably to advise him on what to say and what to conceal. If one accepted this account – which Simon denied – the case looked clear enough. Saint-Just did not strengthen it by repeating Fabre's charges against Hérault and implying that Simon's support for Schneider was proof of his guilt. The two men were charged, not merely with violating the law of 12 March, but with 'complicity in the plot', whatever that meant.

In the speech that paved the way for the arrest of the Cordeliers Saint-Just had announced the government's intention to punish the corrupt, which presumably referred to the men who had been arrested in connection with the East India Company scandal. Their guilt seems well established, and the safest course would have been to send them before an ordinary criminal court. Their conviction would then have put them out of the way for a long time and their acquittal would not have involved any political crisis. That, however, would have been contrary to Saint-Just's insistence that every kind of political intrigue or financial

---

[4] The German Baron Clootz had been expelled from the Convention as a foreigner.

racketeering was part of the same counter-revolutionary plot. It was therefore decided that Chabot, Fabre and the rest of them should go before the revolutionary tribunal. This posed no serious problems for Fouquier-Tinville, the public prosecutor. He had a good case and a massive dossier of evidence. On 26 March he gave orders for the trial of 'Chabot etc.'[5] An undated memorandum listed the witnesses who were to appear in the trial of 'Chabot, Basire, Fabre d'Eglantine, Delaunay d'Angers and others', which was fixed for 2 April.[6] Everything seemed to be under control when the entire situation was transformed by the arrest of Danton, Desmoulins, Delacroix and Philippeaux on the night of 30–1 March. This turned a straightforward criminal trial into a major political crisis, and it gave Fouquier only two days in which to prepare an indictment, without any proper evidence to support it.

Why the governing committees decided to take this desperate gamble is a question that has received surprisingly little attention from historians, who have usually been content with vague remarks about Robespierre's jealousy of his rival or the committees' determination, after eliminating the extremists, to strike a balancing blow against the moderates. The first of these reasons looks like the opposite of the truth, and the second, although it may have been in the back of people's minds, is not much of an explanation and needs to be examined more closely in the light of the evidence. On 20 March Bourdon de l'Oise, perhaps the most persistent critic of the government, persuaded the assembly to order the arrest of Héron, the committees' chief policeman. Robespierre and Couthon got this reversed, and Couthon told the deputies that the Hébertist faction had not been the only one, threatening 'one of these days' to name the moderates. Danton did not take an active part in the sniping at the government, and Bourdon, who had been doing so for a long time, came to no harm. On 21 March Tallien won the applause of the Jacobin Club for a denunciation of the moderates but Robespierre dissuaded the club from having it

[5] Archives Nationales, W.342.
[6] Archives Nationales, W.173.

printed, on the ground that they had been frightened off and were no longer dangerous. On the next day Barère told the assembly that the corrupt would be destroyed, but he hinted that the moderates should recognize that they could not win, and should rally round the government. All this suggests that no decision had yet been taken and that members of the Committee of Public Safety hoped to dispose of the financial speculators without involving Danton.

Billaud-Varenne was to claim later – without any denial by Robespierre – that when he first proposed proscribing Danton, Robespierre angrily accused him of wanting to destroy the best *patriotes*. Taschereau-Fargues, a friend of Robespierre at the time, wrote later that Billaud and Collot hated Danton because he would not sacrifice the Ministers of the Interior and of Foreign Affairs to make way for their own nominees.[7] Tissot thought that Danton's enemies were Billaud and Saint-Just, and that Robespierre was reluctant to sacrifice him, but 'it was easy to frighten him.' There were meetings between Robespierre and Danton, one of them arranged by Daubigny, who wrote that Danton complained that Billaud and Saint-Just were intriguing against him.[8] The Committee of Public Safety was obviously divided – Lindet refused to sign the order for the arrests – and it seems highly likely that Danton's enemies would not have prevailed without the support of Saint-Just. The most likely explanation of their eventual decision to kill Danton was that they dared not leave him alive. If they were not to discredit themselves they had to act against Chabot and Fabre, which meant persuading the assembly to lift their parliamentary immunity. Danton had many faults, but abandoning his friends was not one of them. If he took the field against the government in order to save Fabre, he was only too likely to carry the Convention with him and to overturn the Committee of Public Safety. This was probably what 'frightened' Robespierre.

The committees were under no illusion about the risk that they

[7] P. A. Taschereau-Fargues, *A Maximilien Robespierre aux enfers* (Paris, An III), p. 17.
[8] Villain Daubigny, *Principaux Evénements pour et contre la Révolution* (Paris, An III), p. 49 n. 1.

were running. This was the first time that the government had proposed purging leading Montagnards. Desmoulins was a popular man, the only deputy whom even his opponents usually referred to by his Christian name, and Danton, if not exactly regarded as a model of integrity, was nevertheless a revolutionary titan who have saved the deputies from Paris on 5 September 1793. Since his return from Arcis-sur-Aube he had not been very active, but he was a formidable orator and if he had to fight for his life he was quite capable of uniting the deputies in his own and their defence. Committed Montagnards were in a minority in the Convention, where most of the deputies were likely to welcome any call for clemency and a return to normal government. If Danton could be brought down no one was safe.

What followed gave some indication of the extent to which the two committees were living on their nerves. Saint-Just must have seemed the natural choice for the delivery of the speech of proscription; by now he was something of a specialist in the art. With extraordinary arrogance, he insisted on denouncing Danton to his face. Robespierre initially supported him but according to Taschereau, 'since fear was an irresistible argument where he was concerned' he was persuaded to change his mind. Vadier of the Committee of General Security told Robespierre that he could risk being guillotined if he wanted but Vadier himself had no intention of taking that kind of gamble, and Danton must first be arrested and then denounced *in absentia*. Saint-Just then threw his hat in the fire and stormed out. 'A' and 'V' (presumably Amar and Vadier) ran after him and were just in time to stop him throwing the only copy of his speech after it.[9] It was one of the few occasions when Saint-Just failed to get his own way, and he had to content himself with leaving his speech unchanged and apostrophizing the absent Danton.

Saint-Just drafted a hasty report, only half a dozen sentences of which have survived.[10] He submitted this to Robespierre, who

[9] Taschereau-Fargues, *A Maximilien Robespierre*, pp. 16–17. He claims to have had his information directly from Vadier.

[10] See A. Mathiez, 'Les notes de Robespierre contre les Dantonistes' in *Robespierre terroriste* (Paris, 1921), reprinted in *Etudes sur Robespierre* (Paris, 1958).

began by making a few marginal corrections but, warming to his task, enlarged these into a whole dossier of 'evidence' against the man whom he had so recently described as the best of *patriotes*. He must have been very frightened indeed. These formed the basis of Saint-Just's report. He often quoted Robespierre verbatim, although he made one or two alterations that suggested hard-headed calculation rather than republican *vertu*. He ignored Robespierre's miserable attempt to suggest that Desmoulins had not been very guilty, and added one or two charges of his own. He suppressed Robespierre's accusation that Danton had supported the Bill for the abolition of slavery merely in order to destroy the French colonies. Robespierre had also been a little too blunt in his reference to what happened on 2 June. 'During the disgraceful procession at the Tuileries, Hérault, Lacroix [Delacroix] and Danton wanted to have Hanriot arrested and later made a criminal offence out of his action to free himself from the oppression that would have meant the triumph of tyranny.' Remembering that most of the audience had taken part in the 'procession' and might have other views about who had tyrannized whom, Saint-Just amended this to 'You made a crime out of his action to escape from your oppression', which kept everything nicely vague. He did not hesitate to twist Robespierre's text when it looked as though it might have the wrong effect. Robespierre had written, 'When Desmoulins' father expressed his satisfaction [with the *Vieux Cordelier*] and embraced him tenderly, Fabre, who was present, was moved to tears and Desmoulins, astonished, had no further doubts about Fabre having a kind heart and therefore being a *patriote*.' This emerged as 'When Desmoulins was reading to someone an article of his in which he called for a committee of clemency towards the aristocracy and said that the Convention was the Court of Tiberius, Fabre began to weep. Crocodiles also shed tears.'

Danton and his colleagues were arrested during the night of 30–1 March. Things almost went wrong when the Convention met on the following day and Danton's friend Legendre, to widespread murmurs of support, demanded that they be given a hearing. It was Robespierre who saved the day by terrifying Legendre and reducing the deputies to cowed silence. Saint-Just was no good at that sort of thing. When he entered shortly afterwards he had a captive audience in more senses than one.[11]

What followed was perhaps the most rambling and implausible of all his speeches, but he had had to compose it in a hurry and he had nothing that would have passed for evidence in any normal court. He began by praising his own bravery in sending people to their death. 'It needs some courage to speak to you of severity after so much severity.' There was some truth in this since the committees knew that they were risking their necks whether they tried Danton or not, but that was not quite what Saint-Just wanted his audience to believe. It was not true that the revolutionaries were destroying each other since 'Not one genuine *patriote* will perish at the hands of justice.' This would be the last purge. 'You will have no more examples to give and you will enjoy peace . . . only *patriotes* will be left. When the factions have been abolished, endow the republic with gentle *moeurs*. Re-establish esteem and respect for the individual in civil society . . . Liberty is calling you back to nature.'

After the reassurance came the threats. 'The days of crime are past. Woe to anyone who champions it! Politics wears no more masks. Let all that is criminal perish. One does not make a republic with one's gloves on but with savage rigour, with inflexible rigour towards all traitors.' This sounded like a curious way to enjoy peace. Yet again he brought out the argument that all the trouble was due to mistaken leniency in the past. He borrowed from Robespierre the accusation that Danton had not liked Marat, but the six other references to Marat as a touchstone of revolutionary orthodoxy were his own. He threw in the argument, to which he was becoming increasingly attached, that it was for the government to reform the people and not vice versa. 'Conspiracies teach governments to keep watch on *moeurs* and to preserve the purity of the principles on which legislation is based.' He followed this by the ritual denunciation of the agents of the administration and condemnation of those who were in too much

---

[11] Vellay, *Oeuvres complètes*, vol. II, pp. 305–32.

of a hurry to shake off their 'honourable obscurity'. What mattered was morality rather than intelligence, and a good republican was a good hater. 'Danton, are you not criminally responsible for not having hated the enemies of the people enough?' It was perhaps the most justified of all his charges.

This was no doubt all very uplifting, but it did not get him anywhere in particular, and he had said most of it before. Then he came to the actual charges. He argued that all the accused had been members of a single royalist plot directed by the foreign powers, and especially by England, which went back to 1789. Orleanists, Mirabeau, Lafayette, the Girondins and the Cordeliers had all been involved together. They had admittedly *appeared* to be each other's bitter enemies, but Saint-Just, who never concerned himself much about detail, did not explain whether this was a sham fight or whether the British government had employed the singularly devious strategy of setting its agents to destroy each other. It was, of course, naïve to pay any attention to what the conspirators had said for public consumption. When the Girondins had proposed to banish Orléans, that had really been a subtle move to allow them to bring him back in triumph after they had discredited the Montagnards. If evidence could mean either what it said or the exact opposite, it was rather difficult to defend oneself. Danton had shared in the responsibility for the war against England, which was rather odd since he was a British agent and the war was destined to overthrow the British monarchy.

Some of the accusations related to inoffensive actions or ones that any normal person would have regarded as meritorious, and some were absurd. Danton had saved the life of the constitutional monarchist, Duport, in the summer of 1792, which presumably meant that Saint-Just would have preferred him to have been slaughtered in the September massacres. He had tried to prevent a breach between the Girondins and the Montagnards. During the previous year he had called for an increase in the size of the army when he should have been denouncing its generals, and he had persuaded Parisians to volunteer for the front so that aristocrats could seize the unguarded capital in their absence.

All evidence was grist to the mill, however suspect the source. The accusations against Hérault, who had been included in the plot, presumably as the most convenient way of getting rid of him, came from his fellow-conspirator, Fabre, and from enemy agents. It was also foreign spies who reported that Danton had had contacts with the imprisoned royal family. Saint-Just devoted most of his time to Danton, association with whom was enough to condemn the rest. 'Whoever is the friend of a man who negotiated with the Court is guilty of baseness. One's judgement may be deceived but the mistakes of conscience are crimes.' Desmoulins had edited the *Vieux Cordelier*; Delacroix, besides being corrupt, had wanted to implement the 1793 constitution, which would have meant new elections; Philippeaux had attacked the Committee of Public Safety; Dumouriez, who had eventually become a traitor, had once praised the military talent of Fabre's brother. If that did not prove that Fabre himself was a traitor there was something wrong with revolutionary justice.

Few historians today are likely to share the admiration of Mathiez for this joint production of Robespierre and Saint-Just, which he considered a tribute to Robespierre's courage and intelligence. 'He invented nothing. He forged no calumny against the Dantonists but subjected their policies to reasoned criticism.'[12] It would take very little time or ingenuity to construct a similar case against the two accusers. Each of them in his time had expressed reservations about Marat. Robespierre had called Mirabeau an illustrious man, and as recently as December 1793 he had gone to great lengths to defend those notorious British agents, Danton and Desmoulins. Saint-Just had praised both Danton and Mirabeau, and written that Desmoulins was feared only by those who deserved his denunciations. In their audacity, as Saint-Just might have put it, neither man had bothered to conceal his royalism. Robespierre had been lyrical in his praise of 'a prince worthy to cherish and protect liberty', admittedly before the Revolution began, and Saint-Just had described the tigress Marie Antoinette as 'more deceived than deceiving'. There was not a

---

[12] Mathiez, *Etudes sur Robespierre*, pp. 154–5.

man, even including Marat, who had not changed his opinions during the course of the Revolution, and all were vulnerable to the charge of having once backed men who turned out to be losers.

This is not to suggest that Danton and his associates were martyred innocents. During the early years of the Revolution Danton had taken money from anyone who would give it to him. He and Delacroix had lined their pockets in Belgium, and he had always tried to keep in with all sides. Fabre's conduct would have earned him a lengthy gaol sentence in any country. Desmoulins had given the Girondins the same sort of treatment that he was now receiving. All those who were arrested on 31 March had criticized the Committee of Public Safety and tried to change both its membership and its policies. One could make out a good case for saying that they had been mistaken in trying to relax the Terror before the republic had established its military superiority over the combined forces of its opponents. None of this proved that they were royalists or foreign agents, which were the charges on which they were tried.

What was perhaps even more sinister, from the point of view of the deputies, was the fact that none of the evidence was new. Apart from Fabre's participation in the East India Company swindle, Robespierre had known it all when he had defended Danton and Desmoulins. If anything had emerged since then to persuade him that he had been duped by them as well as by Fabre, he would certainly have revealed it to Saint-Just. The committees, in other words, had been familiar for a long time with the 'plot' that they now claimed to have discovered. The deputies must have been uneasily aware that the same sort of case could be fabricated against any of them. If the committees could do it to Danton they could do it to anyone.

They had not yet done it to Danton. The debate in the assembly was one thing and the trial was another. It aroused the sleeping lion and terrified the government, which must have congratulated itself on not allowing him to defend himself in the Convention. So far as one can gather, for the information was heavily censored, he won over the dense audience at his trial, and while the court officials could be relied on to do whatever the government told

them, it would scarcely be practicable to arrest the jury if it
delivered the wrong verdict. Amar, Vadier, Voulland and David
of the Committee of General Security were in constant attendance,
having private conversations with the jurors. Fouquier-Tinville, if
one can trust Daubigny, went to the Committee of Public Safety
with a list of witnesses whom the accused proposed to call. Billaud
and Saint-Just said there could be no question of this, and when
Fouquier pointed out that it was their legal right they sent him
packing.[13] He and Herman, the president of the court, sent a
desperate letter to the committee:

> The accused are denouncing to the people what they say is
> the rejection of their demand to call their witnesses . . . their
> repeated demands are disturbing the session and they are
> proclaiming that, short of a decree, they will not be silent
> until their witnesses have been heard. We invite you to
> prescribe formally what we should do about this request
> since judicial procedure offers us no grounds for rejecting it.

They knew what was needed but it was for someone else to take
the responsibility.

Saint-Just stepped into the breach. The convenient denunciation
by a police informer of yet another plot allowed him to silence
Danton and to tidy things up at the same time.[14] This was no
occasion for scruples, and when he addressed the assembly the
message from Fouquier and Herman that the accused were
demanding their legal rights became 'the revolt of the guilty'. This
naturally confirmed their culpability. 'What innocent man ever
revolted against the law?' He could not have been expected to
concede that they were protesting in the name of the law, but this
was going a little far. He did not explain how this 'revolt' was
connected to the alleged plot by General Dillon and Desmoulins's
wife to murder the revolutionary tribunal. What mattered was the
general effect. Even by his own not very demanding standards, he

---

[13] One such list of witnesses is to be found in Archives Nationales W.342.
[14] Vellay, *Oeuvres complètes*, vol. II, pp. 356–8.

protested too much. 'Your committees are not concerned about
their lives but about their honour . . . The wretches! They confess
their crimes by their resistance to the law.' This did the trick. The
docile assembly voted that the trial should continue in the absence
of the accused, if they caused any more trouble. Fouquier was able
to control the remainder of the proceedings, which he stopped, as
he was entitled to, after three days, and he got his verdict, but it
had been a close-run thing. On 13 April the new prison plot
allowed the committees to dispose at one stroke of Dillon, Simon,
Chaumette, the former archbishop of Paris and the widows of
both Hébert and Desmoulins. It looked more like a tidying up of
loose ends than the destruction of a conspiracy. If Robespierre and
Saint-Just still believed in their republican *vertu*, they must have
been believing sort of people.

Within a couple of days of this trial Saint-Just was in action
again, delivering his last report to the assembly.[15] It marked a
further retreat into the world of fantasy and paranoia. His object
was to explain why the extermination of all the conspirators had
not solved France's problems. By this time he had convinced
himself, or hoped to convince his audience, that everything that
went wrong was the product of a counter-revolutionary plot
against republican morality.

He began by examining the state of the economy, which had
always been one of his preoccupations. An intelligent and
perceptive analysis of the dislocation of relations between town
and country and between the different parts of France led him to
the implausible diagnosis that scarcity had been the deliberate
work of conspirators who were intent on undermining the
republic. 'If you establish the reign of distributive justice, within a
month the face of the republic will be transformed and plenty will
return again.' The contrast between his outlook now and his lucid
and level-headed speech of 29 November 1792 indicates the extent
of his descent into make-believe and fanaticism. Like everything
else, economic sabotage went back to the beginning of the

---

[15] Ibid., pp. 367–90. Mathiez has demonstrated that Saint-Just's alleged report on
relations with the neutral powers was invented by d'Antraigues. A. Mathiez, *La
Conspiration de l'étranger* (Paris, 1918), ch. 8.

revolution. From 1789 onwards the Finance Minister, Necker, had been in collusion with Orléans, the pretender to the throne. The Constituent Assembly, which Saint-Just had once admired so much, had deliberately ruined France's colonies in order to create scarcity, force up prices and discredit the revolutionary paper money. At the same time that he accused those who had bought Church lands of converting their wealth into liquid assets for the purpose of speculation in colonial produce, he reassured his audience that the government was not thinking of economic levelling. Its intention was to 'confirm all rights and reassure the purchasers'. What was needed was not a transfer of wealth but a new attitude towards property.

In a properly conducted republic there would be no conflicts of economic interest. 'It is not merely a matter of the unity of the government but of the unity of all the interests and relationships between citizens.' Any sign of economic conflict was therefore evidence that conspirators were involved. To prevent them from working on the material interests of the citizens it was necessary to 'create a public conscience'. 'The word is not *intelligence* but *conscience*.' If only this could be achieved all problems would solve themselves. 'All things under the sun are beginning anew.' 'Let us go and settle on river banks, nurse our children and bring them up to be disinterested and intrepid.' If the absurdity of this bachelor of twenty-six posing as an Old Testament patriarch struck any of his audience, they knew better than to let it show. The Convention must therefore 'draft civil institutions, of which no one has thought; without them there is no lasting liberty.'

This was looking towards the future. The immediate need was for practical measures, and if his goal was a matter of nebulous fantasy, to steps towards it that he proposed were only too likely to take practical shape. As he kept telling the deputies, everything that was going wrong was their fault for having been so indulgent in the past. 'The people would have been happy now if we had had no scruples about striking down whatever was opposed to the Revolution.' This was not cruelty but kindness since the only ones to suffer would be the oppressors of the people. 'Marat was gentle at home and frightened only traitors.' When he came to his customary strictures about the application of revolutionary policies, the arrogant administrators were now joined by the police and the judges. The former were corrupt and oppressive, and the latter negligent and lax in their pursuit of counter-revolutionaries. This implied either that traitors had penetrated the entire revolutionary establishment or that, in addition to the *vertueux* and the corrupt there was a whole world of ordinary people who would distort the benevolent wisdom of the Legislator in accordance with their own indolence, self-importance and prejudice. The trouble, of course, did not arise from an excess of severity. The agents of the administration – in which category he included judges – gave themselves airs and behaved as though they were elected representatives. They were inclined to spare those who could make it worth their while instead of straining every nerve to rid the republic of its enemies. Time and again he returned to the need to extend the hunt for the agents of the conspirators throughout the whole of France. 'Woe to those who defend the conspirators. They merely confirm the judgement that condemned them and reveal their own complicity. Purge the country of its declared enemies.' In one passage he implied that what he had in mind was the deportation of suspects, which again suggested that the intention behind the *ventôse* law had been mainly punitive, since he made no reference to any redistribution of property in favour of the poor. Whatever the problem, the solution was always to punish more people more severely.

He concluded by proposing a series of measures that were to shape the policy of the government during the coming weeks. Henceforth all 'conspirators' were to be tried in Paris. This would demand an expansion of the revolutionary tribunal and perhaps an acceleration of its procedures. The two committees were to intensify their efforts to track down the accomplices of those who had already been executed. The popular commissions that were to implement the *ventôse* law were to be in operation by 4 May. They were to deport anyone of independent means, apart from the sick and the elderly, who 'complained of the Revolution'. The Committee of Public Safety was empowered to investigate and where necessary to punish all agents of the administration. Nobles and enemy aliens, with specific exceptions, were to be expelled from Paris, the ports and fortress towns. They were debarred from membership of popular societies and *comités révolutionnaires* and were not to attend meetings of their Sections. A commission was to be created to draft 'civil institutions fit to preserve *moeurs* and the spirit of liberty'. If anyone had believed Saint-Just on 31 March when he assured the deputies that if only they would agree to proscribe Danton and the others, 'You will have no more examples to give and you will enjoy peace', he knew better now.

II

Things Fall Apart

Towards the end of April 1794 everything seemed to be going Saint-Just's way. The Committee of Public Safety and the Convention had endorsed his plans for the eradication of dissent and for tight central control over the administration. On the positive side, it looked as though he might soon be able to implement his conception of national regeneration. On 22 April Couthon persuaded the committee that one of its members should draft a code of 'social institutions' for presentation to the assembly. This had become an increasingly insistent leitmotiv of Saint-Just's during the previous months, and it was perhaps about this time that he began putting his ideas on paper.[1] As always, the protection of the sheep was inseparable from the extermination of the wolves, and in mid-May the first two commissions were created to examine the imprisoned suspects. The malpractices of public officials had been one of his preoccupations for a long time, and in order to implement the recommendations of his speech of 14 April a police bureau was established, responsible to the Committee of Public Safety rather than to that of General Security, to control and punish the agents of the government.

[1] For the result, see the Epilogue, below.

His work was interrupted when he was sent once more on a mission to the army, to deal with the military threat that had developed on the Belgian front. The spring campaign opened with an offensive by the allied armies, which were concentrated in the centre, with the main French forces on their east and west flanks. Carnot was impatient to invade Holland by a march northwards along the coast, using the French troops on the east of the front in a containing role. Pichegru had been transferred from Alsace and put in command of the entire northern front, but it was difficult for him to co-ordinate strategy when his troops were widely dispersed and operating in two separate sectors. On 29 April Saint-Just left Paris to join the French forces on the eastern sector of the front. The fact that he identified himself with the fortunes of the troops on the French right when Carnot intended to reserve the main offensive for those on the left was to have unfortunate consequences. As usual, Saint-Just took Le Bas with him, but the relationship between the two men was not what it had been in the heroic days in Alsace. Le Bas now found him 'a strange man' with whom it was impossible to communicate. The main reason for this was almost certainly Saint-Just's failure to return the affection of Le Bas's sister, Henriette, who had accompanied them during the Alsatian campaign. The scanty evidence suggests that Henriette and her brother had mistaken Saint-Just's intentions and that both were hurt when he made it clear that she could expect nothing from him. It would be a mistake to make too much of this. Nothing suggests that Saint-Just had encouraged Henriette, and Le Bas was still sufficiently devoted to him to sacrifice his life by supporting him in July.

Saint-Just seems to have had some success in unifying the administration and supply arrangements of the scattered French forces, but not in obtaining the adoption of a concerted strategy. He insisted on going over to the offensive at once, without waiting for the arrival of the 40,000 men whom Jourdan was bringing from the Rhine Army, but three French attacks all failed, and an assault on Charleroi was repulsed. In early June Saint-Just was temporarily recalled to Paris for political reasons, which gave him and Carnot a chance to discuss strategy. The Committee of

Public Safety ordered all the representatives on mission on the Belgian front to subordinate their personal inclinations to the common purpose. 'We should deplore any personal considerations that disturbed the harmony which must prevail between the operations on the left and right flanks, without which we can hope for no success.' This may have been intended as a shot across Saint-Just's bows, in which case it does not seem to have had much effect. He probably assumed that it applied to the others.

The military situation was transformed by the arrival of Jourdan's forces, which tilted the balance of numbers in favour of the French. Carnot ordered the greater part of them to be transferred to the western flank, and it was presumably Saint-Just who was responsible for detaining all of them in the eastern sector. This made possible the capture of Charleroi, which surrendered unconditionally after Saint-Just rejected all the garrison's attempts to negotiate terms. On 26 June the French forces on the right flank then won a decisive victory at the hard-fought battle of Fleurus. For some hours the outcome hung in the balance, and the result may have owed something to Saint-Just's draconian measures to enforce discipline after the earlier reverses. During the siege of Charleroi he had sent a court martial into the trenches to enforce his order that anyone who broke ranks would be shot. Although the French troops were too exhausted to pursue their defeated enemies after Fleurus, the allies evacuated Belgium, which Saint-Just naturally regarded as the vindication of his strategy.

Levasseur, in his memoirs, records an interesting meeting with Saint-Just when the two of them were with the northern armies. This at least serves as an indication of the need for caution when dealing with the subsequent recollections of people who claimed to be describing events of which they had personal knowledge. According to Levasseur, he had taunted Saint-Just, in public, for his reluctance to get involved in the fighting. This sounds improbable, in view of Baudot's tribute to his personal courage. On the following day, in Levasseur's tent, Saint-Just accidentally discharged a musket, which would have exposed him to the suspicion of murder if Levasseur had been hit. This may have brought a rapprochement between the two men. Levasseur complained of the law (of 10 June) which deprived those who were tried by the revolutionary tribunal of the right to be represented by counsel. Saint-Just replied that, after a few more punishments, clemency would be the order of the day. Levasseur then suggested that the Committee of Public Safety had left things rather late. 'Another party may get in first and use the same tactics to overthrow you.' Saint-Just flared up at once: 'Only a republican like you could speak to me like that without appearing suspicious.'[2]

It is a good story, unfortunately too good to be true. Levasseur and Saint-Just did meet in June, but Levasseur, in a footnote, ascribes the incident quoted above to 'the time of the *Vieux Cordelier*', in other words, to the winter of 1793–4, when the two men were hundreds of miles apart. The reference to a possible campaign in favour of clemency would fit the earlier period, but there were no signs of the emergence of any moderate party at the time of the passage of the law of 10 June. How much Levasseur remembered and how much he invented, consciously or otherwise, it is impossible to guess.

There are much stronger grounds for thinking that clemency was very far from Saint-Just's mind. Whilst the allied troops were still on the offensive and there were fears of disaffection in France, on his own initiative he ordered his colleague, Le Bon, to set up in Cambrai a section of the revolutionary tribunal that Le Bon had created in Arras, and told him to remain in Cambrai until given permission to leave. The flimsy pretext that he was not creating a new court – which would have violated the law – but merely detaching a section of an existing one would have provoked him to scathing irony if it had been advanced by anyone else. Saint-Just, moreover, had no right to usurp the authority of the Committee of Public Safety by giving orders to Le Bon. He knew enough about the man to have been able to predict what would happen next. Le Bon wrote to him, 'I will make everyone tremble', and the Cambrai court imposed 152 death sentences within seven weeks. Le Bon claimed to be acting against the rich in particular, but he himself admitted that most of those actually

[2] R. Levasseur, *Mémoires*, 4 vols (Paris, 1829–31), vol. II, pp. 241–3.

206

executed were comparatively poor. Saint-Just may not have intended this, but he was responsible for the fact that it happened, and if he did not know what was going on he ought to have done. When Le Bon was summoned to Paris to justify his activities, Le Bas defended him in a letter to Robespierre.

Whilst Saint-Just was away at the front the revolutionary regime was beginning to break up as a result of its internal tensions. To understand why everything exploded so dramatically at the end of July one has to examine the political situation as a whole. After the elimination of the Girondins the Convention consisted of two loose agglomerations of deputies. The majority, whom the more ardent revolutionaries described contemptuously as the Marais, or swamp, belonged to no party. Outraged by the Parisian coup d'état of 2 June 1793, insulted by the Montagnards and threatened by the Hébertists, they had kept their heads below the parapet and tolerated the revolutionary dictatorship in the hope that it would protect them from foreign invasion and Parisian violence, but they had no particular attachment to any of the revolutionary factions. With the overthrow of Hébert and the victory of the revolutionary armies, neither of the factors that had guaranteed their subservience to the government applied any longer. The other group, which consisted of the more obscure members of those who regarded themselves as Montagnards, was known as the Plain. These men had committed themselves to the revolutionary cause. Most of them were regicides who had everything to fear from a royalist restoration. They had given hostages to fortune, and their allegiance was not merely to France but to the Revolution. This did not guarantee their support for any particular government. Many of them had admired Danton and sympathized with the moderates who were inclined to regard him as their leader. Others, whilst on mission in the provinces, had committed themselves to policies of dechristianization or indiscriminate terrorism that the government had subsequently disavowed. A few had misused their power to their personal advantage. They and others were apprehensive about being denounced by rival factions in Paris or in the provinces where they had ruled as proconsuls. Like the Marais, they had tolerated the growing power of the Committee of Public Safety in the hope that it would keep Paris under control and preserve France from foreign invasion. As spring turned into summer, the growing concentration of power in the hands of the committee coincided with the disappearance of the need for it in the eyes of the Plain. It would be a mistake to regard these people as necessarily moderate or inclined to clemency. Some were, but others had practised extreme terrorism in their time. What they all shared was apprehension about the attitude of an increasingly autocratic government that equated deviation with treason and defined orthodoxy in terms of its current and changing attitudes. Those representatives on mission who regarded their recall as a sign of disapproval were particularly anxious about their standing with leaders whose paranoia seemed to increase in proportion to their power. There were no great issues of principle dividing the Plain from the government, and the two would have been able to coexist if their fears of each other had not engendered suspicions which led to defensive manoeuvres that seemed to substantiate the rumours of factions and purges, of which they were the consequence rather than the cause. The Plain began by being on its guard against revolutionary government as a whole, in other words, the two ruling committees. Only gradually did the deputies realize that they could hope to work on tensions between the two committees and within the Committee of Public Safety itself.

The Committee of General Security occupied a somewhat anomalous position. Officially entrusted with the defence of the Revolution against its political enemies, it saw its powers being gradually eroded by the encroachments of the Committee of Public Safety. The two commissions to examine suspects were to report to the latter. The police bureau created to supervise the agents of the government was also an agency of the Committee of Public Safety. So long as Saint-Just was in charge of the bureau this does not seem to have been a serious issue since he co-operated with his colleagues on the police committee. Robespierre, who took his place while he was at the front, was much more inclined to treat the bureau as his private empire. It was, after all, the first administrative function that he had held during the Revolution and was not the man to be unduly concerned about anyone else's feelings.

All these factors meant that the increasingly despotic power of the Committee of Public Safety was a source of resentment to everyone else. In the short run this might not have mattered if the members of the committee had remained united, since no one dared to challenge them. They were, however, becoming increasingly suspicious of each other. To some extent this may have been the simple product of overwork and excessive hours in each other's company. As in the case of the Plain, their suspicions hardened into self-fulfilling prophecies. There was a marked tendency for the leading men to staff the revolutionary institutions that they controlled with their clients, not political allies but men of humbler rank on whose personal devotion they could rely.[3] This was not entirely new – Saint-Just had taken Thuillier and Gateau with him on all his missions – but it became more pronounced as the leaders realized that the only way they could ensure that the machinery of revolutionary government would not be used against them was to keep it under their personal control. The more successful they were, the more they alarmed their colleagues and potential rivals. One man's defensive precautions were another man's threat.

The destruction of the radicals had been followed by a partition of their spheres of influence. On the whole Carnot was able to take over the War Office. Robespierre inherited the Paris Commune – both the new mayor and the *agent national* (government agent) were his personal followers – and the revolutionary tribunal.[4] Saint-Just put some of his own men in the police bureau and took a personal interest in the commissions that were to investigate suspects.

There is no convincing evidence to suggest that the members of the Committee of Public Safety were in serious disagreement

---

[3] J. P. Gross, *Saint-Just, sa politique et ses missions* (Paris, 1976), pp. 340–1, supplies the names of some of the clients of Saint-Just, Robespierre and Le Bas who were promoted in this way.

[4] See Archives Nationales F[7] 4436 for a long list of the jurors whom he vetoed.

about major issues of policy. None of them seems to have been in favour of an immediate relaxation of the Terror. When the official in charge of the administration of revolutionary 'justice' proposed 'to purge the prisons at one blow and sweep the soil of liberty clean of this detritus, this refuse of humanity', the committee's 'approved' was signed by Robespierre, Billaud and Barère.[5] As late as 11 July Robespierre complained that 'national justice' was not being exercised 'with the force and activity demanded by the interests of a great people' and that it was being directed against the wrong targets. He ascribed this to a plot against the Committee of Public Safety as a whole. By the summer of 1794, who was right and who wrong had come to depend on the arbitrary fiat of those in authority. Robespierre was determined to make an example of some of the Montagnards. He probably had in mind no more than half a dozen, but self-interested rumour multiplied the figure by ten. If one can believe Carnot's son, after the proscription of Danton had almost gone wrong, the Committee of Public Safety had made a policy decision not to risk another purge of deputies. This was something that Robespierre refused to accept. His particular enemy was Fouché. Suspect as a dechristianizer, he was implicated in the merciless repression at Lyon and had alienated the local Jacobins, who had succeeded in enlisting Robespierre's sympathies. Fouché had remained at Lyon up to April 1794, but until the end of 1793 he had been accompanied by Robespierre's colleague on the Committee of Public Safety, Collot, and Collot presumably regarded any attack on Fouché as a possible threat to himself.

Saint-Just is unlikely to have had any objection to an intensification of the Terror – to which he had contributed more than anyone else – but there is no evidence to suggest that he agreed with Robespierre and his faithful Couthon about the desirability of risking another purge of deputies. His own enemy was Carnot, with whom he quarrelled twice in April, before he went to the front. The questions at issue seem to have been technical matters of army administration and the defence of clients in the War

[5] Archives Nationales F[7] 4436.

Office. Prieur de la Côte d'Or supported Carnot, and on one occasion at least Robespierre is said to have sided with Saint-Just. Prieur's subsequent claim that Saint-Just said that he could have Carnot executed, and that Carnot replied by proposing to send Robespierre (but not, apparently, Saint-Just) before the revolutionary tribunal, sounds very improbable.[6] Billaud-Varenne, in a speech in which he referred to 'that scoundrel Pericles', said that victory must prepare the way for peace, and the French must not become a people of warriors. The first of these remarks is generally assumed to have been aimed in Robespierre's direction, and the second may have had Saint-Just in mind. It seems fairly clear that Robespierre and Couthon were detaching themselves from the majority of their colleagues. Saint-Just would never be content with anyone else's direction of the armed forces, and his dislike of Carnot was exacerbated by the business of the 28,000 troops that Carnot tried to detach from the eastern army, but this does not mean that Robespierre, Couthon and Saint-Just formed a triumvirate, united in opposition to the rest of the committee.

As the tense months went by there was a general expectation that the intolerable stresses would explode in some sort of bloody crisis, but it was impossible for anyone to predict what form it would take or who would find themselves allied to whom. Any attack on members of the revolutionary government from the floor of the Convention would be likely to unite the two committees in self-defence, and anyone who hinted at his true feelings in his search for allies was liable to find that, if the balance of forces shifted, he had merely compromised himself before informers.

Towards the end of May Saint-Just returned from the front on a brief visit to Paris. According to the subsequent testimony of Billaud, 'Robespierre recalled Saint-Just from the Army of the North, announcing that he was bringing him back to denounce a faction that was alleged to exist in the Convention. The dictator's accomplice was so intimidated by the reception he received [in the Committee of Public Safety] that he had to disown Robespierre's

[6] *Mémoires sur Carnot par son fils* (Paris, 1861), pp. 524–5.

démarche and return to the front at once.'[7] Unfortunately, when
Billaud, Carnot and the other survivors of the July crisis described
what had happened, their main concern was not to be as useful as
possible to future historians but to protect their reputations, their
liberty and their lives, by presenting themselves as the intended
victims of a Robespierrist triumvirate. To take their evidence at
face value would be rather like basing a biography of Trotsky on
the evidence of Stalin. If Billaud was really surprised by the
sudden appearance of Saint-Just in Paris, he must have had a very
bad memory, since he himself was one of those who wrote urging
him to return on the ground that 'the committee needs to
concentrate the energy and ability of all its members [to confront]
the most desperate danger.' Such a decision would not have been
taken lightly, with the French armies poised for a general
offensive. This raises the question of what the committee believed
to constitute the 'desperate danger'.

The most likely explanation concerns the real or imagined
activities of the baron de Batz. After his denunciation by Chabot
in the previous November, the governing committees had seemed
for a long time determined to ignore Batz. His name had been
kept out of the trial of the Hébertists, and when Lulier, the chief
administrative official of the Paris department, had been added to
those accused with Danton, as an agent of Batz, he was the only
man to be acquitted. On 22 April this policy was suddenly
reversed by the Committee of General Security for reasons that
are still obscure. The police committee then ordered the public
prosecutor, Fouquier-Tinville.

> to redouble your efforts to discover the infamous Batz.
> Remember in all your interrogations that he has agents
> everywhere, even in the prisons, and that this Catiline has
> been the constant heart of all the plots against Liberty and the
> Republic . . . Neglect no hints and spare no promises,
> financial or otherwise. You may request the freedom of any

---

[7] In the draft of a speech, reproduced in G. Walter, *La Conjuration du 9 thermidor* (Paris, 1974), p. 469.

prisoner who promises to reveal him or to hand him over, dead or alive.[8]

The committee was not usually so lavish with its offers of pardon. Soon afterwards it ordered the arrest of all the suspected members of the Batz network who had been left at liberty, presumably in the hope that their surveillance might lead the police to Batz himself. Fouquier-Tinville took the committee at its word and offered a free pardon to Batz's secretary, Devaux, in an unsuccessful attempt to persuade him to reveal his master's whereabouts.[9]

On 22 May a drop-out called Admiral or Admirat, after failing to get into Robespierre's lodgings and hanging about the Convention and the offices of the Committee of Public Safety, returned to the appartments where both he and Collot lived.[10] When Collot came home, Admiral attacked him on the stairs but one of his pistols misfired and the other missed. He does not seem to have been a very effective counter-revolutionary and his motives remain obscure, but it emerged at his interrogation that his acquaintances included some of the suspected members of Batz's network and he seems to have known something of Batz himself.[11] On the following day a girl called Cécile Renault tried to get access to Robespierre in order, as she put it, to see what a tyrant looked like. She was armed with two small knives. Cécile was possibly inoffensive, probably retarded, and certainly acting on her own initiative, but it was understandable if members of the Committee of Public Safety began to feel rather exposed. Two days later they sent for Saint-Just and on 26 May secured the passage of an infamous law that no British or Hanoverian prisoners were to be taken. Batz, of course, was said to be the agent of Pitt.

[8] Archives Nationales W.389.

[9] Ibid.

[10] This, at least, was what he told Fouquier-Tinville (Archives Nationales W.389). According to the traditional story he fell asleep in the Strangers' Gallery of the Convention and did not wake up until all the deputies had gone home.

[11] His interrogation by the president of the revolutionary tribunal on 28 May is in Archives Nationales W.389.

If these events provide a possible explanation for the return of Saint-Just, it is difficult to account for the sequel. In view of his performances against the Girondins, the extremists and the moderates, and his speech of 15 April, he was the obvious man to introduce the law of 10 June for the reorganization of the revolutionary tribunal, and to present the report on the Batz conspiracy four days later. Instead he returned to the front on 10 June, and it was Lacoste of the Committee of General Security – with whom Saint-Just had not got on very well in Alsace – who delivered the speech on the Batz plot. For once the committees had got hold of what looked like a genuine counter-revolutionary plot, and one would have expected Saint-Just to have been in his element showing how it fitted in with all his previous denunciations. It is possible, although not very likely, that he wanted to dissociate himself from the law of 10 June, but why the committee, after bringing him back, failed to use him remains obscure.

In retrospect the law of 10 June (22 *prairial* in the revolutionary calendar) appeared so abominable that everyone blamed it on someone else. The members of the Committee of Public Safety who survived the July crisis insisted that it had been invented by Robespierre and Couthon behind their backs. The faithful Gateau, writing several years later, said that Saint-Just wept when he read it, although, in his next sentence, he talks of Saint-Just's cult of Robespierre. All this is not very convincing. During its stormy passage through the assembly the Bill was defended not merely by Robespierre but also by Billaud and Barère, and it seems inconceivable that it could have been drafted whilst Saint-Just was in Paris without his being aware of its contents. It began by creating a new category of 'enemies of the people', defined in terms so vague that it would encompass all the former suspects together with anyone else whom the government wanted out of the way: all those who spread despondency, circulated false news, misled public opinion, depraved morals or abused public office. This corresponded fairly closely to Saint-Just's own catalogue of the deadly revolutionary sins. When trying these people, the revolutionary tribunal would henceforth be allowed to impose only one penalty: death. The defence was allowed neither counsel nor the right to call witnesses, and the jury could terminate a trial as soon as it felt confident of its verdict.

This was to turn the revolutionary tribunal into what the twentieth century was to call a people's court. Given the reasoning of the revolutionaries it was logical enough. As Saint-Just had argued in his denunciation of Danton, the mere fact of accusation by a body that enjoyed the confidence of the elected representatives of the people constituted a presumption of guilt. The object of a trial was therefore essentially to ratify what already amounted to a verdict, and to safeguard against mistakes. The judgement was a matter of conviction, in both senses of the term. Earlier in the year Robespierre had insisted that what mattered was whether a man was a good revolutionary or an enemy, rather than whether he had actually done this or that. If he was an enemy, his technical innocence on the specific charge that had allowed him to be apprehended was neither here nor there. Once the court had identified him as an enemy of the people its duty was clear. It did not take long for one good *patriote* to recognize another . . . or his opposite. One can see why Robespierre was so keen on personally vetting the composition of the jury.

What worried the Plain was not so much the ferocity of the law as the provision that *anyone* could be sent for trial by the Convention, the public prosecutor or the Committee of Public Safety. This seemed to do away with parliamentary immunity. The Committee of General Security had its own reasons for objecting to the first draft of the Bill, but when it was added to the list of those allowed to proscribe it appeared to be satisfied. The Marais was probably not much concerned since its members could consider themselves to be fairly safe in their anonymous nullity. Those whom self-preservation armed with the courage of desperation were all Montagnards, and it took the combined efforts of Robespierre, Billaud and Barère to silence them. Typical of the debate was the moment when Bourdon de l'Oise, believing himself to be under personal attack, denied ever having belonged to any faction, to which Robespierre replied, 'I did not name Bourdon. If the cap fits let him wear it.'

The deputies seem to have been right in believing that

Robespierre's intention was to use the law at once against members of the Convention. They might have felt reassured if they had known of the furious row in the Committee of Public Safety while the Bill was still going through the assembly. As usual, all the evidence comes from interested parties, but it looks as though the rest of the committee united against Robespierre and Couthon. In other words, their objection was not to the law itself but to the way in which Robespierre proposed to use it, which might have threatened their own safety if he had driven the Convention to revolt. Saint-Just was not involved since he was out of Paris.

The law of 10 June led to an enormous increase in the number of death sentences and inaugurated the so-called 'Great Terror'. In the course of the next seven weeks 1,400 people were executed. If this had not necessarily been the intention of the authors of the law, it can scarcely have surprised them and they did nothing to stop it. This intensification of the Terror had its part to play in contributing to the disintegration of the revolutionary government. The Committee of General Security, although it had succeeded in asserting its claim to share in the right to proscribe, was suspicious of Robespierre's intentions and alienated by his packing the jury of the revolutionary tribunal with his own followers, and by the way in which he was running the police bureau during the absence of Saint-Just. After his battles of 11 June in connection with the new Bill, both in the Convention and in the Committee of Public Safety, Robespierre virtually boycotted both bodies, restricting his activity to managing the police bureau. When Saint-Just finally returned from the front, he does not seem to have supported Robespierre's campaign for a purge of the assembly but he played his part in the intensification of the Terror. He alone drafted an order for the simultaneous trial of over 150 people in connection with a nebulous prison plot, and it was the embarrassed Fouquier-Tinville who insisted on dividing them into three separate batches, tried on consecutive days. It did not make any difference to the verdict, but it looked better. This new ferocity of revolutionary 'justice' gave a more bloody edge to Saint-Just's plans for dealing with the suspects, who were now only too likely to find themselves executed rather than deported. This did not deter him from demanding the creation of the full complement of six commissions, of which only two were as yet functioning.

In extraordinary contrast to this massive bloodletting, this was the period when Robespierre tried, on his own authority, to consecrate the French nation to the kind of emotional deism to which he himself turned with increasing enthusiasm, perhaps as a consolation for his political disillusionment. On 5 May, while Saint-Just was away, Robespierre delivered his last major speech, on the subject of the relationship between religion and republican morality. His colleagues on the Committee of Public Safety had presumably entrusted him with some sort of report on the state of the nation, but they must have been as surprised as the rest of the assembly by the form it took. This amounted to the inauguration of a new state religion, modelled on the penultimate chapter of Rousseau's *Social Contract*, to be celebrated by great national festivals. For Robespierre this was a matter of passionate conviction, an expression of the essential meaning of the Revolution, rather than a device to rally support. His speech struck a note that was very different from Saint-Just's neo-classical philippics: 'This delightful land in which we live, the favoured child of nature, was created to be the realm of liberty and happiness; this proud and sensitive people was truly born for *vertu* and glory . . .' A month later, on 6 June, during Saint-Just's brief stay in Paris, the capital was treated to the first of the great religious festivals. Robespierre himself, as the current president of the assembly, marched at the head of the procession, in a sky-blue coat that he had had made for the occasion. Behind him walked the other deputies, near enough for him to overhear their ribald comments on what was for him a great religious experience. To them he seemed to be adding the role of Moses to that of grand inquisitor.

A week later Vadier, a Voltairean cynic on the Committee of General Security, entertained the Convention with an account of the extravagances of Cathérine Théot, an elderly religious visionary whose disciples included one or two of Robespierre's associates. Vadier implied that the 'Mother of God' was up to no political good, but his main purpose was presumably to make

Robespierre look ridiculous. The Committee of Public Safety raised no objections when Robespierre took the investigation of the Théot 'plot' out of the hands of the rival committee and succeeded in burying it, but he must have felt more isolated than ever amongst a pack of unbelievers, and it was perhaps this as much as his battle to carry the law of 10 June that induced him to absent himself from both the assembly and the Committee of Public Safety.

Where the spiritual significance of the Revolution was concerned, Saint-Just and Robespierre pursued parallel rather than identical courses. For both of them it was a kind of moral Armageddon. Victory over foreign enemies and domestic counter-revolutionaries, which most of the deputies saw as ends, were no more than the means that would make possible the moral regeneration of the country, without which the Revolution was merely another episode in the bloody chronicle of French history. It was presumably as a result of Robespierre's influence that Saint-Just had come to include deism amongst the necessary attributes of the good revolutionary. In the revised version of *De la nature* which he had abandoned after three chapters, the second was devoted to 'the principle of the divinity' and the first ended 'O supreme being, receive in thy bosom an ingenuous soul that comes from thee and aspires to raise itself to thee.' One has nevertheless the impression that religion was for him not the intense inner experience that it was for Robespierre. After writing that 'the principle of divinity was innocence and love', he added and then deleted, 'I am well aware that all this is only a dream but a dream is always the sentiment of a truth that exists no more.' In contrast to Robespierre, Saint-Just's cult of Stoicism and Sparta had no need of even a vaguely Christian underpinning. His prescription for the ideal future was to *comprimer les moeurs* rather than to liberate the emotions. He shared Robespierre's contempt for materialists and his belief that 'the only basis for civil society is morality', but his own vision of the ideal future was based on a transformation of men's principles rather than of their beliefs, on social institutions rather than communal worship.

When Saint-Just returned to Paris for the last time towards the end of June, he found, like Levasseur six months earlier, that the political situation had changed during his absence. Carnot, Prieur de la Côte d'Or and Lindet were still immersed in their departmental work, but Couthon was often absent and Robespierre had withdrawn in sullen resentment from both the assembly and the committee. Before he left, Saint-Just had perhaps felt that he had been in a position to shape the policies of the government. During his absence the leadership of the committee had passed to Billaud and Collot, and Saint-Just resented it. He disapproved of their attempt, together with Barère, to prise the control of Paris and of the revolutionary tribunal from the grip of Robespierre's men. He was to concede that he had no personal grounds for complaint: 'I was left in peace as a citizen with no pretensions who went his own way', and he implied that his colleagues on the committee regarded him as one of them, rather than as Robespierre's ally. On the other hand, he had a new grievance against Carnot over the latter's attempt to divert 28,000 of Jourdan's troops to the left flank of the French army. This gave rise to another quarrel in the committee. Since all the evidence about this comes from the protagonists on one side it has to be treated with caution. Prieur claimed to recall Saint-Just proposing that France should be governed by 'patriotic reputations', which may have referred to the institution of official censors on the Roman model. The story that Saint-Just proposed making Robespierre a dictator, in the Roman sense of a man temporarily entrusted with ultra-legal powers, sounds rather unlikely and Robespierre himself implied on 1 July that it was a slander invented by some of his colleagues on the committee.

Throughout most of July Saint-Just seems to have concentrated on his repressive work in the police bureau while Robespierre brooded and occasionally alarmed and confused the Jacobin Club by his allusions to plots and enemies, sometimes associating himself with the Committee of Public Safety and sometimes making veiled criticism of his colleagues and of the Committee of General Security. This sort of thing could not continue indefinitely, but no one cared to make the first move in what everyone knew would be a life and death conflict. On 22 July all the members of the Committee of Public Safety with the exception of Robespierre met in an attempt to patch up their differences, and Robespierre himself agreed to come to a second meeting on the next day. What happened has to be inferred from the subsequent revelations of the interested parties. Barère's story that Saint-Just, supported by Couthon and by Le Bas and David from the Committee of General Security, suggested making Robespierre dictator sounds very unlikely. If anything of the sort had happened it would have provided deadly ammunition for Robespierre's enemies when the crisis broke. Robespierre may well have come to the meeting with a list of deputies whom he wanted to proscribe, as Saint-Just more or less hinted. Robespierre did not give up easily. Everyone else seems to have got something from the ensuing compromise. Despite Billaud's assurance to Robespierre that they were all his friends, he was not allowed to get at the deputies. Saint-Just obtained the creation of the remaining four commissions to deal with the suspects arrested in the provinces, and the Committee of General Security was appeased by being given control over the police bureau. Saint-Just was then entrusted with a report to the Convention on the restored unity of the government. He accepted this on the condition, or so he was to claim, that he was allowed to respect the assembly and its members, which suggests that he disagreed with Robespierre about the need for a new purge. He deferred with some resentment to the demand of Billaud and Collot that he say nothing about the Supreme Being. Ruhl, of the Committee of General Security, who claimed, rather implausibly, to have known nothing of the disagreement between the two committees, said that Saint-Just opened the meeting on the 23rd by praising Robespierre and insisting on the need to organize republican government. Most of the rest of the meeting seems to have consisted, according to Ruhl, of a wrangle between Robespierre and his opponents in which Saint-Just was not involved.

All this suggests the elaboration of a compromise that Saint-Just himself was prepared to accept. Barère's speech to the Convention announcing the restored unity of the government spread panic amongst those who had been inciting the Committee of General

Security against Robespierre or the Committee of Public Safety, and now feared that the harmony of the governing committees would be sealed with their own blood. Voulland, of the Committee of General Security, writing to his constituents, at first denied any disagreement and then told them that Robespierre had been misled but that all differences were being resolved. Robespierre, unlike Saint-Just, had won no concessions. In his fevered imagination all those who disagreed with him were enemies of the people, and anyone who refused to proscribe them was no better. He was not prepared to call off his campaign against erring Montagnards – Couthon revived it in the Jacobin Club on the 24th – and if he chose to break the truce Saint-Just would be faced with a difficult choice. Personal sentiment inclined him towards Robespierre and he had no time for Billaud, Collot and Carnot. At the same time he had accepted the compromise, and if Robespierre chose to endanger the revolutionary government by breaking it, Saint-Just was under no obligation to support him.

Things came to a head on 26 July when Robespierre made a rambling and repetitive speech to the Convention, that was a strang mixture of paranoia and self-pity. Speaking for much of the time in the first person singular, he detailed 'the persecutions of which I am the object', presenting himself as the innocent victim of foreign enemies and domestic counter-revolutionaries. The whole fate of the Revolution seemed to him to be identified with his person. Any criticism of him was proof of counter-revolutionary intentions and he was the main, if not the only target for the attacks of royalists and the corrupt. The only enemies whom he specifically named were Cambon, Ramel and Mallarmé of the finance committee. When Cambon angrily defended himself, Robespierre at once retreated and admitted that he might have been mistaken, which scarcely inspired confidence in his reliability as an exposer of plots. More obliquely, he criticized the agents of the Committee of General Security and complained that the armies, finance and administration were controlled by 'those who are hounding me'. Not content with forcing him to absent himself from the Committee of Public Safety, they were now intent on his life. This presumably referred to Billaud, Collot and Carnot, as well as to the men on the finance committee. Barère was criticized for making too much of a fuss over French victories, without being accused of participation in the 'plot'. Robespierre concluded by demanding the purge of both governing committees and the subordination of the police committee to the Committee of Public Safety.

For so accomplished a politician it was an extraordinarily misdirected effort. He attacked all or most of the members of the three most powerful committees of the assembly without appealing for support to any constituency in particular. At one point he seemed to despair of the Montagnards and turn for support to the Marais. He might have got it if he had offered them any prospect of bringing the Terror to an end but, obsessed by factions and conspiracies, he went out of his way to defend its worst excesses. He complained of the failure to shoot British prisoners, and defended the law of 10 June on the ground that 'the penal law must involve a certain vagueness' because of the dissimulation and hypocrisy of the enemy. The safeguard of *patriotes* was not to be found in 'the slowness or feebleness of national justice but in the principles and integrity of those who exercise it'. That was not going to reassure anyone.

Nevertheless, so great was Robespierre's hold over the assembly that Lecointre who, a month or two before, had been talking of assassinating him, proposed the printing of his speech, and Barère seconded him. It was Cambon who, realizing that a soft answer would turn away no wrath where he himself was concerned, stood up to Robespierre and told him that he alone was dividing the government. This encouraged Bourdon de l'Oise, supported by Billaud, to propose referring Robespierre's proposals to the two committees. That sounded vaguely businesslike, although not to Robespierre who shouted that it was making the accused the judges of their accuser. In the end the decision to print the speech – which implied a measure of approval by the assembly – was reversed and the session closed inconclusively.

Robespierre had presumably not consulted Saint-Just about his speech and the latter cannot have appreciated this unilateral repudiation of a compromise that was supposed to be the subject of his next report. Robespierre, by his own impulsive action, had risked the survival of the revolutionary government and the lives of everybody concerned. Nevertheless, if Saint-Just had to choose, he would find it hard to resist the pull of past friendship, common enemies and the sense that he and Robespierre stood for similar things: Robespierre, in his speech, had referred three times to the need for those republican institutions that meant so much to Saint-Just. But he might not have to enlist under someone else's colours in a war that he did not want to fight. Robespierre's hysteria had burst the bubble of his infallibility, and one did not have to endorse his ramblings about plots and enemies. It might still be possible to revive the compromise of 23 July in one form or another. If so, he was the only man to do it, and he might yet emerge as the arbiter of the situation.

That evening Robespierre repeated his speech to an audience of admirers in the Jacobin Club. When he had finished, Billaud and Collot proposed discussing the speech rather than the plot that Robespierre claimed to have revealed. This incensed Robespierre's followers, and after some angry exchanges Billaud and Collot were thrown out. In no very amiable mood they returned to the Committee of Public Safety where they found Saint-Just working on the report that he hoped to present the following day. It was supposed to be about the restored harmony of the government. Some historians have suggested that he wrote grimly on, in order to immobilize his hostile colleagues by the mere fact of his presence. This is not very plausible since they could either have thrown him out or met elsewhere. They probably did not know where he stood, and he too may not have been very sure. The Paris Commune was already talking of starting an insurrection to defend Robespierre, and at about two o'clock in the morning Saint-Just joined with Barère, Collot and four members of the Committee of General Security in ordering Hanriot, the commander-in-chief of the National Guard, to report to them, presumably in the hope of neutralizing him.[12] This is all the more

---

[12] Quoted in Walter, *La Conjuration*, pp. 481–2. According to B. Vinot, *Saint-Just* (Paris, 1985), p. 316, who does not quote his source, Saint-Just did foil an attempt by Billaud to arrest the mayor and *agent national* of Paris.

surprising if, as Barère was to claim, he, Collot and Lacoste had attacked Saint-Just after Collot's humiliation by the Jacobins. According to Tissot, it was Collot alone who attacked Saint-Just, when the other members of the committees were still trying to detach him from Robespierre. This accords with the remark in Saint-Just's speech that what persuaded him to expose the divisions in the government before the assembly was the behaviour of one man. Saint-Just reassured his colleagues by promising to show them his report before presenting it to the assembly. Towards five o'clock on the morning of the 27th, however, he slipped away, and about midday he sent them a message to the effect that one of them had wounded his feelings and that he was therefore going directly to the assembly.

When he rose to speak the deputies presumably took it for granted that he would support Robespierre, and he was shouted down by a pre-arranged chorus of catcalls. From that moment until his death he seems to have wrapped himself in Stoic resignation to his fate. Unlike Robespierre, who struggled desperately to get a hearing, he allowed events to take their course. After a couple of hours of denunciation an obscure deputy secured a vote for Robespierre's arrest. His brother insisted on joining him. Fréron, supported by Lacoste, then moved the arrest of Couthon and Saint-Just, on the ground that they had conspired with Robespierre to form a ruling triumvirate. Le Bas, like Augustin Robespierre, insisted on joining the proscribed men. About six-thirty all of them were sent off to gaol.[13]

If the deputies had listened to Saint-Just they might perhaps have revised their views about the triumvirate. Whether from discretion or mental confusion – and it must have been hard to compose a speech in the circumstances of the previous night – he was evasive about whether he was accusing his opponents of anything worse than ambition, but nowhere did he indulge in Robespierre's wild fantasies about counter-revolutionary plots. He began by asserting his own independence: 'I belong to no

---

[13] The most detailed account of the events of 9 thermidor (27 July) is to be found in P. Sainte-Claire Deville, *La Commune de l'An II* (Paris, 1946), pp. 189–357.

faction. I will fight them all.' What had happened was that the absence of some members of the Committee of Public Safety and the immersion of others in administration had encouraged the remaining two or three (in other words, Billaud, Collot and Barère) to try to concentrate power in their own hands. They had entrusted him with the report in order to neutralize him, which was one way of saying that they had hoped to win him over. Their target was Robespierre, whom they had succeeded in provoking. Saint-Just was somewhat evasive about Robespierre's own intentions, which he presumably had to infer, like everyone else, from his speech. He said that Robespierre had always shown 'restraint' in the Committee of Public Safety when discussing a purge of deputies, which presumably implied that he had not wanted to execute very many. He had not expressed himself very clearly, but his isolation and bitterness were some excuse for that. Saint-Just then put Robespierre rather firmly in his place. 'He had no ground for complaint and he had not in fact complained about the committees, for the committees seem to me [*sic*] to be still worthy of your esteem, and the mishaps that I have described are due to the isolation and excessive power of one or two isolated individuals.' This was not what Robespierre had said at all, and Saint-Just was, in effect, throwing him a lifebelt on condition that he accepted Saint-Just's own view of the situation. He criticized Billaud and Collot for their lack of 'modesty' and for getting above themselves. His high opinion of the virtue of modesty did not prevent him from drawing attention to his own contribution to the revolutionary cause. He criticized Barère for giving the government all the credit for military victories: 'Battles are won only by those who take part in them.' Carnot too came in for some rough handling. His strategy had been 'senseless'. Nevertheless, 'The members [of the Committee of Public Safety] whom I am accusing have made few mistakes of policy and they have no need to justify themselves on that account, except perhaps for the 18,000 [*sic*] men who were to be diverted from the Army of Sambre-et-Meuse.' In the spirit of the meeting of 23 July Saint-Just had intended to conclude by demanding that every act of the Committee of Public Safety be signed by at least six of its members. 'I make no accusation against those whom I have named. What I want is for them to justify themselves and for all of us to become more judicious.' His last sentence referred to 'institutions which will be drafted at once', which would set everything once more on an even keel.

Perhaps it would have made no difference if Saint-Just had been allowed to speak. There was a total lack of trust on all sides, and although he did not – quite – denounce Billaud, Collot and Carnot, he said enough to have made them feel threatened. No one could rely on his ability to restrain Robespierre. What he seemed to be recommending was a policy of business as usual under the two governing committees, from which his personal enemies, who were also those of Robespierre, would be excluded. Even if he had got his way, sooner or later – and probably sooner rather than later – the fears and jealousies of autocratic and anxious men, whose instinct for self-preservation meant that they dared not share power, would have set off another crisis.

What actually happened next was the revolt of Robespierre's Parisian clients in a desperate effort to save him by an insurrection. When the arrested deputies were persuaded with some difficulty to leave their prisons and make their way to the Hôtel de Ville, they put themselves outside the law. It was Saint-Just himself who had made it a capital offence to break arrest. Early in the evening the Convention outlawed all those who disobeyed the orders of the assembly or resisted the law, and Voulland had the five deputies identified by name. That meant that they could not pin their last hopes on trial by a revolutionary tribunal that Robespierre had packed with his own men. Once captured, all that was needed for their execution was their formal identification.

The historian Sainte-Claire Deville, in his admirable study of the Commune's revolt, brings out very well the contrast between the purposeful moves of the Convention in its own defence and the futile agitation at the Hôtel de Ville, but it is difficult to see what else the Commune could have done. This was no re-run of 2 June 1793. The Parisians were divided and intimidated by the threat of outlawry, and the defence of the assembly was in the hands of men as ruthless and desperate as their opponents. Robespierre and

Couthon occupied themselves with drafting meaningless appeals for support. Saint-Just appears to have done nothing. He was not the sort of person who easily resigned himself to the inevitable and he had practical experience of military operations, but, unlike Danton, he could not improvise a speech so as to carry a crowd.

When National Guards loyal to the Convention broke into the Hôtel de Ville between one and two in the morning on 28 July. Couthon apparently fell downstairs in his wheelchair, Augustin Robespierre tried to escape and injured himself badly when he jumped or fell into the street. Le Bas succeeded in shooting himself and Robespierre merely shattered his jaw in the attempt. Saint-Just did nothing. He had always been a man for the striking gesture, and his inaction was not lacking in classical dignity. Perhaps he was thinking of Socrates. His last recorded words, as he looked at a poster of the 1793 constitution, when he was awaiting the formality of identification, are said to have been 'After all, I am the one who made that.' Later in the day he and the other deputies were driven to their execution through a jeering and rejoicing crowd. That would not have surprised him, for the 'people' whom he idealized existed only in the abstract, and the savage faces of those who lined the streets belonged to men and women who were never going to be regenerated by his republican institutions.

Epilogue: The Voice from the Grave

Throughout the last year of his life Saint-Just had been increasingly preoccupied by the need to provide France with what he called 'republican institutions'. In April 1794 the Committee of Public Safety had commissioned one of its members – presumably him – to put these into legislative shape. The speech that he was not allowed to deliver on 9 *thermidor* would have included a plea to Providence 'to grant me a few more days to concentrate the attention of the French people and all its legislators on institutions'. He was not to have them but he left behind a good many notes which showed that he had already been working on what he saw as the culminating achievement of the Revolution.

These notes were first published in 1800, in a text that was often reproduced during the next 150 years. Soon after the Second World War the deposit of important collections of Saint-Just's papers in the Bibliothèque Nationale allowed the French historian, Albert Soboul, to produce a new edition, based on Saint-Just's own manuscript.[1] Soboul showed that the 1800 text had been

[1] Published in *Annales historiques de la révolution française*, 111 (1948). Saint-Just's handwriting is very difficult to read, and a slightly different version is to be found in A. Liénard, *Saint-Just, théorie politique* (Paris, 1976), pp. 247–311.

censored in several places. Two favourable references to Marat, for example, and some of his more radical proposals had been omitted. Other passages, which certainly read as though Saint-Just had written them, are to be found in the 1800 text but not in the Soboul edition. It is therefore necessary to consult both versions.[2]

It is impossible to date any of these notes, which seem to have been composed at different times and for different purposes. The earliest part was perhaps intended to be a revised version of *De la nature*, several paragraphs of which it reproduced either verbatim or with minor stylistic alterations. Elsewhere he incorporated ideas from *De l'esprit de la révolution*. At one point Saint-Just described what he was writing as *cet ouvrage*, which implies that he was thinking in terms of a published essay. Later on he called it a *discours*, which suggests that it was intended for delivery in the Convention and that it was probably composed during the spring or early summer of 1794. This is not of any great significance since the notes as a whole show the continuous development of his ideas as he worked out the implications of a vision of society that went back as far as *Organt*.

He had still not entirely shaken off the influence of Montesquieu. His emphasis on the social importance of moral censors and the respect due to the old, who were to have a monopoly of teaching, may have owed something to *De l'esprit des lois*, but they could have been part of the general baggage of a classical education. More striking was his bizarre proposal that once a year in each commune a rich and *vertueux* young man should marry a poor virgin 'in memory of human equality', which was presumably suggested by Montesquieu's praise for a somewhat similar custom amongst the Samnites.[3] Saint-Just, however, had travelled a long way since he wrote the *Esprit de la révolution*. He was no longer thinking in Montesquieu's terms of the protection of the liberty of the individual within a balanced polity, but of the creation of the ideal republic, something that Montesquieu had eventually rejected

[2] A reprint of the 1800 text may be found in J. Gratien, *Oeuvres de Saint-Just* (Paris, 1946), pp. 279–321.
[3] *De l'Esprit des Lois*, Book VII, ch. 16.

as incompatible with the freedom of the individual, as the eighteenth century understood it, and with the complexity of a modern state. Saint-Just preferred not to remember Montesquieu's observation that 'The laws of Minos, Lycurgus and Plato presuppose a remarkable attention to each other's lives on the part of the citizens. That is impracticable in the confusion, the negligence and the comprehensiveness of the affairs of an extensive society.'[4]

Saint-Just was still wrestling with his old problem of how to effect the transition from a political society that rested ultimately on force, to a civil or natural society of spontaneous harmony, neither willed nor enforced, but the automatic product of the concordant sentiments of its inhabitants, relegating the use of force to relations between different states. As he saw it, the problem of defending the French republic against its domestic and foreign enemies had been more or less resolved by the summer of 1794. After Fleurus there was no more risk of invasion. The internal challenge posed by the existence of political factions had been vigorously checked, if not entirely eliminated. These factions had been composed of men who had chosen to exclude themselves from the consensual whole that made up the republic. Like the king at an earlier period, they were aliens, with no rights in the society that they had threatened by their agitation. As aliens, they could be assimilated with the foreign enemy and there was no moral relationship between them and the republic, which could justifiably regard them, not as a political opposition but as a kind of moral pestilence.

So far so good, but Saint-Just could not deceive himself into confusing the society he saw around him with the heavenly city of his imagination. Even if one assumed that the whole nightmarish machinery of political repression applied only to outsiders, French society was still very much what it had been under the *ancien régime*: unequal, hierarchical, atomistic, an untidy agglomeration of discordant individual aspirations, where order rested ultimately on force. The Terror had produced an absence of opposition rather than any positive consensus and natural inclination towards

---

[4] Ibid., Book IV, ch. 7.

harmony and co-operation. As he put it, the Revolution was 'frozen'. It was not difficult, at least for someone like Saint-Just, to conceive of an alternative kind of society. The problem was how to bring it into being with the unsatisfactory human material at his disposal.

Saint-Just's answer, if one may judge by his republican institutions, was to elevate the concept of friendship into a form of social cement that would bind the various members of society together in ways that appeared to them to be natural and unconstrained.[5] Each year in the local 'temple' every man would be required to make a public declaration of who his friends were. Anyone who professed disbelief in friendship or could find no one to be his friend would be banished. Friends would be allowed to fight alongside each other in battle. This may have been suggested to him by an experience in Alsace when grenadiers from the Rhône, the Loire, the Mayenne and the Manche had requested to be allowed to serve together and Saint-Just had formed them into the *bataillon des amis*. The presence of a man's friends as witnesses was necessary to validate any contract. If a man was convicted of a crime his friends were to be banished. Anyone who wanted to separate himself from a former friend had to give a public explanation of his reasons for doing so. Friends who remained united throughout their lives were to be buried in the same grave.

It was an ingenious attempt to substitute the moral pressure that individuals might be induced to exert upon each other for traditional views on a man's allegiance to the community, founded on fear, self-interest, honour, religion or, as Robespierre believed, *vertu*. It was also wholly impracticable. At best it could only have been attempted in an extraordinarily primitive society, and one could scarcely see it operating between people like businessmen or sea captains. It implied the existence of separate clans of friends in isolation from each other, and this sort of clientage already existed in many French villages, where it was not exactly conducive to social harmony. If Saint-Just was thinking of

[5] See the excellent article by R. Rolland, 'La Signification politique de l'amitié chez Saint-Just', *Annales historiques de la révolution française*, 257 (1984).

his old days in Blérancourt and the Gellé faction, he ought to have had a better idea of the kind of mafias that he was calling into being. Friendship also left him with his initial problem unsolved, since it rested on sanctions that had to be enforced.

He made extensive use of banishment as the appropriate punishment for anti-social behaviour, as he had done in *De la nature*. It was the fate of the friendless, of those whose friends committed crimes, of anyone who refused to give an explanation of his quarrels, of those who committed offences whilst drunk, vandalized graves, censured the conduct of others, struck people so as to draw blood, became bankrupt for unacceptable reasons or revealed themselves to be 'ungrateful'. It was also the punishment for officials who acted arbitrarily or led scandalous private lives, and for priests of any religion who wore clerical dress outside the 'temples'. From Saint-Just's point of view it was no doubt misleading to think of banishment as a punishment. Those who had chosen to break the social code had excluded themselves from the community and banishment was merely the formal recognition by society of a state of affairs that they themselves had willed. That was all very well in theory but if one thought of it as deportation, Saint-Just's prescription would have made the eighteenth-century British penal code look comparatively humane.

Those who tried to defy their ostracism – murderers who failed to wear the black clothing prescribed for the rest of their lives, or deported civil servants who tried to slip back into the country – were to be put to death. Whatever logic there might have been in that scarcely applied to the imposition of the death penalty on anyone who struck a woman or hit someone in a 'temple', on soldiers who disobeyed orders, officers who struck their men, troops who looted in enemy territory or women who hung around army camps. This emphasis on death as the appropriate punishment for military offences brings out the Spartan aspect of Saint-Just's vision of the ideal society. This militarization of society was not something implicit in his initial assumptions, which it tended to contradict, but the product of other attitudes that had become more pronounced during his time in the Convention.

Education was obviously going to be called upon to play an essential part in inculcating the right social attitudes. This meant indoctrination, and Saint-Just was not the kind of man to resort to half-measures. Once again, the military bias that he imposed on his educational policy was quite gratuitous. His basic principle was very simple: 'Children belong to their mother, if she has breast-fed them, until they are five, and to the republic from then until their death.' Unlike Robespierre, he was thinking only of boys. Since women were not citizens and were not liable to military service they were consigned to a kind of respected civic limbo where public life was concerned, and their education was confined to the home. Boys were to be taken away from their parents at five and not allowed to see them again until they were twenty-one. From five until ten they learned to read, write and swim. They were to wear coarse cloth, sleep on straw and observe a strict vegetarian diet. It went without saying that 'children are subjected to a rigorous discipline'. From ten until sixteen education was 'military and agricultural', although those who wished could be apprenticed to a trade. The boys learned foreign languages and military manoeuvres, besides helping to bring in the harvest. They were organized in companies, battalions and legions, and every year they attended a camp at which they demonstrated military evolutions. All this is rather more reminiscent of the Hitler Youth than of the Boy Scouts. From twenty-one to twenty-five all young men did military service. This was something that he had already advocated in the *Esprit de la révolution*. It implied maintaining a standing army in the region of a million men, far in excess of the combined peacetime forces of all France's neighbours. The economic consequences of feeding and equipping an army of these dimensions did not seem to cause Saint-Just any concern.

Since the republican institutions survive only as a collection of notes it is impossible to say how far Saint-Just would have modified them before presenting them to the public, but his recent speeches suggested that when it came to thinking about the economy he was long on aphorisms and short on policy. 'All citizens must work and respect each other' did not get anyone very

233

far. 'We must have neither rich nor poor.' 'Opulence is infamous.' 'We must give some land to everyone.' These were sentiments rather than specifications, and they culminated in the fatuous assurance that 'If everyone works, abundance will return, we shall need less currency and there will be no more vice.'

Economic prescriptions were scattered through his notes without any attempt to combine them into a system. No one was to be allowed to invest capital abroad, but apart from that, everyone was free to enjoy his wealth in any way that did not harm others. His obligation to give an annual account of his fortune – in the 'temple', of course – was intended to deter the criminal rather than to impose any restraint upon legitimate private enterprise. No one was to be allowed to cultivate more than 300 *arpents* (about 175 hectares) himself, although he could apparently rent out the remainder of his land.[6] All landowners, whatever the nature of their soil and the local climate, were to keep one sheep (elsewhere he said four) for every *arpent*, one ox or cow for every ten and one horse for every fifteen. Since the entire adult population had to observe three meatless days in every ten, and boys were never to eat any, he looked like having a surplus of meat, but the horses would be useful for hauling guns. His usual denunciation of the *assignat* blamed inflation for corrupting working people by giving them too much ready money, so that people were inclined to leave the occupations of their fathers and to lead lives of idleness. Parish priests had been lamenting this kind of thing for a long time but one might have expected something rather more perceptive from Saint-Just, after his intelligent analysis of France's economic problems, in November 1792. Taxation, which was to be volunteered by the citizenry rather than assessed by the authorities, would consist of 10 per cent of one's income or one-fifteenth of one's industrial or commercial profit. This had the merit of simplicity. How the return would correspond to the commitments of the government he did not pause to investigate.

---

[6] This restriction on cultivation, which has been cited as evidence of Saint-Just's radicalism, was actually slightly more generous than that proposed in the Blérancourt *cahier* of 1789. See above, p. 23.

Saint-Just saw other men as part of the swarm rather than as individual bees, and he could be extraordinarily insensitive to the actual feelings of real people. He even suggested developing France's colonies by continuing to ship out African slaves, who were to be freed on arrival and given small plots of land. He did not seem to notice that the Convention had abolished slavery earlier in the year.

His admirers have tried to argue that the republican institutions were no classical fantasy but revealed Saint-Just as the champion of the peasant and the artisan. This is emphatically a case of the wish being father to the thought. By contemporary standards, 375 acres was a very considerable holding, and the obligation on the wealthy to rent out their surplus land might have done something to build up a yeomanry of substantial tenant farmers but would have offered precious little to impoverished peasants. He was always more concerned about yeomen than about the really poor and his proposal to banish those who did not own *enough* property was a somewhat draconian way of dealing with the problem of land shortage. If there was one thing that the mass of the rural population had detested above all others in pre-revolutionary France, it had been their obligation to serve in the militia. Saint-Just was now proposing to saddle them with four years of military service. Where the urban artisans were concerned, the high-water mark of the Revolution had been the imposition of price controls on necessities in the autumn of 1793, a policy that Saint-Just had enforced with some enthusiasm in Alsace. He now denounced the *maximum* as a plot to create shortages, invented by France's foreign enemies and foisted on the revolutionaries by 'the baron de Bats'. He may well have been correct in his rejection of price controls, but it was not what the sans-culottes wanted to hear. With the best will in the world, it is difficult to see Saint-Just's final views about the economy as adding up to anything more than de Gaulle's cheerful assurance that 'l'intendance suivra.' He was more interested in regulating the festivals that were to be celebrated in the 'temples' than in the creation or redistribution of wealth.

The republican institutions were the culminating point in his gradual retreat from reality into a world of myth and retribution.

Even in 1791 his concept of constitutional government and his praise for the work of the Constituent Assembly had been tempered by his desire to move France back towards what he saw as a primal natural society. When he was elected to the Convention and eventually to its Committee of Public Safety, this tendency became more pronounced as his own power to influence the course of events increased. In April 1793, in his speech on the constitution, he had still thought it necessary to assure his colleagues that he was thinking in terms of what was practicable and not of the ideal society. By the summer of 1794 the immediate construction of the New Jerusalem had become the only way to unfreeze the Revolution. In this he was following the logic of his own utopian thinking, which went back as far as *Organt*, rather than responding to the views of peasants and artisans, who were worthy citizens, no doubt, but scarcely *fellow*-citizens. At one time he had had quite penetrating views about the relationship between the principles of the government and the structure of the economy, but his preoccupation with the former had taken on an increasingly Spartan cast that made it more and more irrelevant to eighteenth-century France. When he told the Convention that the government was offering it 'the felicity of Sparta' he meant it literally, although it was more a matter of imposing than of offering.

From the beginning he had been convinced that he alone knew best. The ideal state might be one of consensus but he was the man who would draft the rules to which others would conform. He would make them worthy of the society that he had designed for their benefit. He was always an awkward member of any partnership that he did not dominate, and the 'modesty' that he urged on others never extended as far as a recognition of the possibility that he himself might be wrong. Circumstances had given him his political chance and helped to shape the direction of his thinking, but it was his own extraordinary will and sense of his own wisdom and rectitude that gave him the fanatical determination to translate the vision into political fact, whatever the human cost. If the sin of Lucifer was spiritual pride, which led him, almost incidentally, to the use of evil as the necessary means to a transcendental end, Saint-Just was Lucifer.

236

Bibliographical Note

An excellent and up-to-date bibliography of works on Saint-Just can be found in B. Vinot, *Saint-Just* (Paris, 1985), pp. 357–71. Rather than duplicate this, I have thought it more appropriate to conclude my own book with a brief essay on what seem to me the most imported sources of information about his writings, his life and the relevant aspects of French revolutionary politics which situate him in his political context.

COLLECTED WORKS

C. Vellay, *Oeuvres complètes de Saint-Just*, 2 vols (Paris, 1908), despite its minor errors and its omissions, contains most of his speeches, the text of his *Esprit de la révolution* and the decrees of the Committee of Public Safety that went out over his signature. It also includes the whole of *Organt*. The deposit of an important collection of Saint-Just's papers in the Bibliothèque Nationale in 1947 added new material: *De la nature*, a more comprehensive version of his orders and proclamations during part of his mission in Alsace and a manuscript of his 'republican institutions'. The last of these includes material omitted from the text published in 1800 that was reprinted by Vellay and others. The manuscript, however, does not include all of the material in the 1800 version, and it is therefore necessary to consult both. These manuscripts were edited by Albert Soboul and published in *Annales historiques de la révolution française*: 'Les institutions républicaines', no. 111 (1948), 'Un manuscrit oublié de Saint-Just' (*De la nature*), no. 124 (1951) and 'Sur la mission de Saint-Just à l'armée du Rhin', no. 136 (1954). The text of *De la nature* is very difficult to read, and a slightly different version may be found in A. Liénard, *Saint-Just, théorie politique* (Paris, 1976). See also *Saint-Just, oeuvres complètes*, ed. M. Duval (Paris, 1984).

BIOGRAPHIES

Of the older biographies, the most perceptive is perhaps that by the American historian E. N. Curtis, *Saint-Just, Colleague of Robespierre* (New York, 1935), and the most original, if not always the most convincing, A. Ollivier, *Saint-Just et la force des choses* (Paris, 1954). Two major works of research, which are indispensable reading, are J. P. Gross, *Saint-Just, sa politique et ses missions* (Paris, 1976) and B. Vinot, *Saint-Just* (Paris, 1985). The first of these deals mainly with Saint-Just's missions to the army but also includes some comment on his career in the Convention. Vinot's biography emerged from his research into Saint-Just's early life in Blérancourt, which takes up more than a third of the book. Each deals at length with important aspects of Saint-Just's life, but neither pays much attention to his political thought. This lies outside Gross's subject and receives comparatively little attention from Vinot. It is best explored in a number of articles. The *Actes du Colloque Saint-Just*, ed. A. Soboul (Paris, 1968)) contain several of these (some of them reprinted with relatively minor variations in the *Annales historiques de la révolution française*), a few additional documents and a bibliography by Gross. M. A. Abensour, 'La philosophie politique de Saint-Just', nos 183, 185 (1966), considerably extends his contribution to the *Colloque*. See also C. A.

Michalet, 'Economie et politique chez Saint-Just: l'exemple de l'inflation', no. 191 (1968) and F. Thuriot, 'Saint-Just, esprit et conscience publique' in the same volume. To these should be added P. Rolland, 'La signification politique de l'amitié chez Saint-Just', no. 257 (1984) which did not form part of the *Colloque*.

THE POLITICAL BACKGROUND TO SAINT-JUST'S CAREER IN THE CONVENTION

Despite all that has been published on the history of the Convention, its detailed political history remains very murky. Anyone bold enough to try to venture into the fog would do well to study the contemporary sources. All of these come from men who were themselves ignorant of much that was going on, prone to take their suspicions for facts and mainly concerned to vindicate their own judgement and motives. All have to be treated with considerable scepticism, but the actions of the men concerned were determined by their view of the situation, however erroneous this may have been. Their mistakes helped to decide what happened, and they have therefore a significance which the mistakes of historians do not. I have found the following illuminating in one way or another (BN references in parentheses give the Bibliothèque Nationale shelf-mark).

M. A. Baudot *Notes historiques sur la Convention nationale, le Directoire, l'Empire et l'exil des votants* (Paris, 1893)

J. N. Billaud-Varenne *Projet de Discours* in G. Walter, *La Conjuration du 9 thermidor* (Paris, 1974)

Réponse des membres des deux anciens comités (Paris, An III) (BN L^{c}38 1259)

Réponse de J. N. Billaud, représentant du peuple, à Laurent Lecointre (Paris, An III) (BN Lb^{41} 1444)

Seconde Mémoire des membres de l'ancien Comité de Salut Public, dénoncés par Laurent Lecointre (Paris, An III) (BN L^{c}38 1173)

(ed. C. Vellay) *Mémoire inédit de Billaud-Varenne sur les evénements du 9 thermidor* (Paris, 1910)

Bibliographical Note

L. Carnot *Opinion de Carnot, représentant du peuple, sur l'accusation
(BN L^{c}38 1305)
Mémoire sur Carnot par son fils (Paris, 1861)
J. M. Collot d'Herbois *Discours fait à la Convention nationale par
J. M. Collot* (Paris, An III) (BN L^{c}38 1309)
E. B. Courtois *Rapport fait au nom de la commission chargée de
l'examen des papiers de Robespierre et ses complices* (Paris, An III)
G. A. Couthon *Correspondance de Georges Couthon*, ed. F. Mège
(Paris, 1872)
V. Daubigny *Principaux Evénements pour et contre la révolution*
(Paris, An III)
L. Lecointre *Les Crimes des sept membres des anciens Comités de Salut
Public et de Sûreté Générale* (Paris, An III) (BN Lb^{41} 1441)
R. Levasseur *Mémoires*, 4 vols (Paris, 1831)
Prieur de la Côte d'Or *Discours de C. A. Prieur* (Paris, An III) (BN
L^{c}38 1309)
J. B. M. Saladin *Rapport au nom de la Commission des 21* (Paris, An
III) (BN L^{c}38 1259)
G. J. Sénart *Révélations puisées dans les cartons des Comités de Salut
Public et de Sûreté Générale* (Paris, 1824)
P. A. Taschereau-Fargues *A Maximilien Robespierre aux enfers*
(Paris, An III)
P. F. Tissot *Histoire de la révolution française*, 6 vols (Paris, 1839)
J. Vilate *Causes secrètes de la révolution du 9 au 10 thermidor* (Paris,
An III)
Anon. *Papiers inédits trouvés chez Robespierre, Saint-Just, Payan etc.*,
3 vols (Paris, 1828)

To list the works of historians dealing with the Convention
would be an interminable business and would not do much to
illuminate the career of Saint-Just. The following are some of the

G. Bouchard *Prieur de la Côte d'Or* (Paris, 1946)
R. Cobb 'Témoignage de Ruhl sur les divisions au sein des

comités à la veille du 9 thermidor', *Annales historiques de la révolution française*, 139 (1955)

P. Sainte-Claire Deville *La Commune de l'An II* (Paris, 1946)

N. Hampson *The Life and Opinions of Maximilien Robespierre* (1974)

'François Chabot and his plot', *Transactions of the Royal Historical Society*, 5th series, 26 (1976)

A. de Lestapis *La 'Conspiration de Batz'* (Paris, 1969)

A. Mathiez 'L'histoire secrète du Comité de Salut Public' and 'Un faux rapport de Saint-Just', both in *La Conspiration de l'étranger* (Paris, 1918)

'Les notes de Robespierre contre les Dantonistes' in *Robespierre terroriste* (Paris, 1921), reprinted in *Etudes sur Robespierre* (Paris, 1958)

'Les divisions dans les comités de gouvernement à la veille du 9 thermidor' in *Autour de Robespierre* (Paris, 1924)

'Les séances des 4 et 5 thermidor aux Comités de Salut Public et de Sûreté Générale' and 'Trois lettres inédits de Voulland sur la crise du 9 thermidor' both in *Girondins et Montagnards* (Paris, 1930)

A. Ording *Le Bureau de police du Comité de Salut Public* (Oslo, 1930)

R. R. Palmer *Twelve who Ruled* (Princeton, 1941), reprinted as *The Year of the Terror* (Oxford, 1989)

Stéphane-Pol pseudonym of E. J. P. Coutant) *Autour de Robespierre, le conventionnel Le Bas* (Paris, n.d.)

Index

Members of the Convention are indicated in bold type, and members of the Committee of Public Safety between September 1793 and July 1794 in small capitals.

Index